THE VIENNESE STUDENTS OF CIVILIZATION

This book argues that the work of the Austrian economists, including Carl Menger, Joseph Schumpeter, Ludwig von Mises and Friedrich Hayek has been too narrowly interpreted. Through a study of Viennese politics and culture, it demonstrates that the project they were engaged in was much broader: the study and defense of a liberal civilization. Erwin Dekker shows the importance of the concept of civilization in their work and how they conceptualized their own responsibilities toward that civilization, which was attacked from the political left and right during the interwar period. Dekker argues that what differentiates their position is that they thought of themselves primarily as students of civilization rather than as social scientists or engineers. This unique focus and approach is related to the Viennese setting of the circles, or 'Kreise,' scientific and artistic communities that constituted the heart of Viennese intellectual life in the interwar period.

Erwin Dekker is Assistant Professor in Cultural Economics at Erasmus University in Rotterdam, The Netherlands. He has published in the fields of cultural economics, economic methodology and intellectual history, and he is currently working on valuation and the qualitative measurement of quality.

HISTORICAL PERSPECTIVES ON MODERN ECONOMICS

Series Editor: Craufurd D. Goodwin, James B. Duke Professor Emeritus, Duke University

This series contains original works that challenge and enlighten historians of economics. For the profession as a whole, it promotes better understanding of the origin and content of modern economics

Other books in the series:

Steven G. Medema, Anthony M.C. Waterman (eds.), *Paul Samuelson on the History of Economic Analysis: Selected Essays* (2014)

Floris Heukelom, *Behavioral Economics: A History* (2014)

Roger E. Backhouse, Mauro Boianovsky, *Transforming Modern Macroeconomics: Exploring Disequilibrium Microfoundations, 1956–2003* (2013)

Susan Howson, *Lionel Robbins* (2012)

Robert Van Horn, Philip Mirowski, Thomas A. Stapleford (eds.), *Building Chicago Economics: New Perspectives on the History of America's Most Powerful Economics Program* (2012)

Arie Arnon, *Monetary Theory and Policy from Hume and Smith to Wicksell: Money, Credit, and the Economy* (2011)

Malcolm Rutherford, *The Institutionalist Movement in American Economics, 1918–1947: Science and Social Control* (2011)

Samuel Hollander, *Friedrich Engels and Marxian Political Economy* (2011)

Robert Leonard, *Von Neumann, Morgenstern, and the Creation of Game Theory: From Chess to Social Science, 1900–1960* (2010)

Simon J. Cook, *The Intellectual Foundations of Alfred Marshall's Economic Science: A Rounded Globe of Knowledge* (2009)

Samuel Hollander, *The Economics of Karl Marx: Analysis and Applications* (2008)

Donald Moggridge, *Harry Johnson: A Life in Economics* (2008)

Filippo Cesarano, *Monetary Theory and Bretton Woods: The Construction of an International Monetary Order* (2006)

Timothy Davis, *Ricardo's Macroeconomics: Money, Trade Cycles, and Growth* (2005)

Continued after the Index

The Viennese Students of Civilization

The Meaning and Context of Austrian Economics Reconsidered

ERWIN DEKKER

Erasmus University, Rotterdam, The Netherlands

CAMBRIDGE
UNIVERSITY PRESS

CAMBRIDGE
UNIVERSITY PRESS

University Printing House, Cambridge CB2 8BS, United Kingdom

One Liberty Plaza, 20th Floor, New York, NY 10006, USA

477 Williamstown Road, Port Melbourne, VIC 3207, Australia

314-321, 3rd Floor, Plot 3, Splendor Forum, Jasola District Centre, New Delhi - 110025, India

79 Anson Road, #06-04/06, Singapore 079906

Cambridge University Press is part of the University of Cambridge.

It furthers the University's mission by disseminating knowledge in the pursuit of education, learning and research at the highest international levels of excellence.

www.cambridge.org
Information on this title: www.cambridge.org/9781107565661

First published 2016
First paperback edition 2019

A catalogue record for this publication is available from the British Library

Library of Congress Cataloging in Publication data
Dekker, Erwin, 1984–author.
The Viennese students of civilization : the meaning and context of Austrian economics reconsidered / Erwin Dekker.
pages cm. – (Historical perspectives on modern economics)
Includes bibliographical references and index.
ISBN 978-1-107-12640-4 (Hardback : alk. paper)   1. Austrian school of economics.
2. Economics–Austria–History.   3. Economics–History.   I. Title.
HB98.D44 2016
330.15´7–dc23   2015030448

ISBN 978-1-107-12640-4 Hardback
ISBN 978-1-107-56566-1 Paperback

We felt that the civilization in which we had grown up had collapsed.
We were determined to build a better world.

Friedrich A. Hayek

Humans are—at best—in the process of becoming civilized.

Norbert Elias

Contents

Acknowledgments

This book is the outcome of a great number of conversations over many years. Most prominently, these conversations have taken place with my PhD supervisor Arjo Klamer, who taught me so many things that I frequently find myself wondering how much of the thoughts expressed here are his and how many are mine. More than anything, however, he has taught me – as he has so many people around him – the importance of conversations for academic work. Those conversations started a long time ago, but they especially took off during my study of economics at the University of Amsterdam, where I met Thomas de Haan, Pjotter Oudshoorn and Menno Broos who still willingly endure my conversations about economics every two weeks.

My encounter with the history of economic thought was made possible by the, unfortunately disbanded, History and Methodology group at the University of Amsterdam. Harro Maas, Marcel Boumans, John Davis and Geert Reuten showed me that economic thought was much more fascinating, deeper and especially broader, than any of the textbooks up until that point had suggested. I especially thank Harro for encouraging me to pursue the subject at the London School of Economics or LSE. At the LSE especially Mary Morgan showed me what serious academic work in the history of economic thought looks like. It was also the place where I first truly encountered the wonderful world of the arts under the friendly pressure of the many wonderful and generous fellow students and new friends I met.

Little did I know then that there was a field called cultural economics in which I would be teaching in less than two years. This dissertation although still firmly rooted in the history of economic thought has benefited greatly from the many cultural economists I met at Erasmus University of Rotterdam, and what they taught me about art, culture and economics. The conversations in the biweekly and later weekly Economics and Culture seminars are what have kept me going through the years. I would like to thank all the frequent participants to the seminar over those years: Hans Abbing, Renate Buijze, Aldo do Carmo, Thora Fjeldsted, Christian Handke, Lili Jiang, Priyateja Kotipalli, Cees Langeveld, Mariangela Lavanga, Slawek Magala, Anna Mignosa, Ad van Niekerk, Mark van Ostaijen, Sofia Patat, Lyudmilla Petrova, Diane Ragsdale, Claartje Rasterhoff, Ieva Rozentale, Bertan Selim, Liesbeth De Strooper, Joke Tacoma, Paul Teule, Marilena Vecco, Filip Vermeylen and Claudine de With.

My colleagues, P.W. Zuidhof and Peter Rodenburg, at the European Studies Department of the University of Amsterdam were a continuous stimulus for thinking broadly about economics and to never forget its political aspects. My colleagues Marleen Rensen, Carlos Reijnen and Marjet Brolsma were of great help in initiating me to the cultural studies of the interwar period. And I would like to thank Michael Wintle for his faith and honesty in me during my time at the European Studies Department. My fellow Ph.D. students at the Erasmus Institute for Philosophy and Economics were always willing to talk and discuss about the relevance and necessity of philosophy for the study of economics and the history of economic thought. I would like to thank especially Thomas Wells, Tyler DesRoches, François Claveau, Sine Bağatur, Luis Mireles-Flores and their academic director Jack Vromen.

After my graduation, Pete Boettke and Robert Leonard were very encouraging and of tremendous help in making the final steps that turned my dissertation into this book. I was also greatly helped by the anonymous reviewers who took the time and effort to read and comment on the manuscript. They pointed out many mistakes, so I take complete responsibility for any that remain.

When I started working on this book some six years ago, I also fell in love with Katinka, who would prove the most valuable support throughout the years. She proved what Arjo always tried to teach me, that our work is personal. I would like to thank her for enduring the lows and sharing the highs of the writing process with me. Finally, I would like to thank my parents and sister who have always supported me in my choices, even though they did not completely understand their direction or purpose.

Introduction

1 Late visitors to Pompeii

In 1931, Carel Willink a Dutch painter started working on one of his finest works: *Late Visitors to Pompeii* (see cover.)[1] He had been traveling with his brother Jan through Italy visiting Florence and Pisa. During his visit to Italy, he had been particularly impressed by the work of the surrealist De Chirico, whose influence can be seen in the use of light and shadow in his work of the period. But this is not the place to talk about his style of painting. I want to talk about what we see in this picture. We observe four well-dressed gentlemen standing with their backs toward one another. The figure closest to us seems rather stiff, but distinguished, while the gentleman in the back is contently puffing on his cigar with an air of contentment.[2] The gentleman on the left in his brown suit somewhat suspiciously looks over his shoulder toward us, while the gentleman in blue on the right is clearly facing away from us. It seems that they have stopped talking to one another quite some time ago.

In the background we see the ruins of Pompeii; they are still illuminated, or is it the other way around? Do the ruins still radiate some light? In any case, that light fails to reach the gentlemen. The formerly prestigious buildings have been in need of repair for a long time, and at certain places the bushes even overgrow the ruins. The forces of nature seem to be on the winning hand. To emphasize this even more, a volcano is emitting smoke in the background. This mountain of doom, the Vesuvius if these are the ruins of Pompeii, is about to erupt. It is clear that whatever these

---

[1] The picture *Late visitors to Pompeii* by Carel Willink is part of the collection of the Boijmans van Beuningen Museum in Rotterdam.
[2] The cigarsmoker has been confirmed as Oswald Spengeler in private correspondence with the painter's widow, see also Hupkes (1989).

gentlemen had in common, the civilization of which they were once part, is in serious danger. They seemed to have turned away from their common project; no longer are they willing to cooperate. And even though one of the four gentlemen is overlooking the ruins, he looks anything but alarmed.

Looking at the painting we cannot escape thinking of the period in which Willink was working on it. The early 1930s were indeed a time in which the various European countries turned inward and away from one another. It was a period during which international cooperation broke down, a period during which even more serious dangers in the form of fascism and Nazism were becoming clearly visible. The painting thus not only shows the ruins of an old civilization, but also the ruins of our own civilization. Willink presents a dark prophecy for Europe and its culture. The only beam of light is emitted from these ruins, as if Willink is saying there will only be hope if we somehow return to our common project, our shared goals and values. A first step in that direction would be for these gentlemen to turn around, and recommence a conversation which has long ceased.

Some commentators on the painting have pointed out that the gentle-man in the brown suit bears a close resemblance to the painter himself, Carel Willink[3]. If the light on the ruins symbolizes hope, than how should we interpret the role of the painter here? Is the painter also a source of hope; does he have a role, a responsibility, in the process? And how are we then to interpret his somewhat suspicious expression? Is the painter aware that we are observing him? Does he think we are expecting something from him, and is he unsure how to respond? What is the role of a painter when he feels that his civilization is in decline? Does he have a responsibility toward the other men, and the civilization behind him? Or even stronger, can he save that civilization? Or does the title *Late visitors to Pompeii* suggest that we have come to learn this lesson much too late, that all hope at this point is in vain?

You might wonder why a book on a group of scholars from Vienna starts with an analysis of Willink's picture. The reason is simple. This book will argue that the issues we just discussed and the questions raised by Willink's painting are at the heart of the work of the Viennes students of civilization. Of course this is only indirectly true, for this is a book about social scientists, philosophers and intellectuals from Vienna, rather than about Carel Willink or art. But the Viennese students of civilization who

---

[3] An observation easily confirmed by a comparison with some of his self-portraits from this period.

will be the main protagonists in this book are facing many of the same problems. During the 1930s, they felt that *their* civilization was in decline, or even about to be destroyed. When Ludwig von Mises, one of the Viennese students of civilization, walked along the grandiose Ringstrasse of Vienna with one of his students he gloomily predicted that grass would grow where they were walking now. But however depressed Mises and his fellow intellectuals might have felt at the time, they did feel that this civilization was worth preserving. Perhaps more importantly they asked themselves what their own role was in this process. Had they played a role in this decline? Were they to blame? Did they have a responsibility to defend their civilization, and even if they wanted to, was there anything they could still save?

It was not just a circle of scholars around Mises who were deeply worried. The intellectual mood in Vienna had been pessimistic since the period leading up to WWI. There were great concerns about the political developments within Vienna and the broader empire, most notably the populist anti-Semitism of Viennese Mayor Karl Lueger, and the various nationalistic uprisings in the Empire. When the Empire was broken up after WWI, many intellectuals felt that this was a great loss, one that broke up a natural unity. Only a small minority, mostly those on the left, believed that the dissolution of the Empire was the perfect opportunity for a new start. Liberal and conservative intellectuals on the other hand increasingly started worrying about the fate of their beloved Austro-Hungarian Empire and its culture.

Among them was a group of Viennese economists who are better known as the Austrian school (of economics). Before WWI the main figures in this school were Carl Menger, Friedrich von Wieser and Eugen von Böhm-Bawerk. In the interwar period its main representatives were Ludwig von Mises and Friedrich von Hayek. Joseph Schumpeter was trained within the tradition of the school, but moved away from it during the interwar years. The response of this group of scholars to the developments in Vienna, the Habsburg Empire and later Austria will be the topic of this book. More specifically I will examine how they conceptualized the importance of civilization for the study of the economy and of society, and secondly how they conceptualized their own relation, as scholars, vis-à-vis the economy and society. I will argue that these scholars from Vienna who are usually grouped as the Austrian economists are better understood if we consider them as Viennese students of civilization.

That is not just an issue of semantics, but an argument that our current understanding of them is flawed in at least three ways. The first of which is that the label 'Austrian' is misplaced. Traditional histories of this Austrian school start with a discussion of the founding father Carl Menger, who lived in the Habsburg (or Austro-Hungarian) Empire. The entire second generation, most notably Wieser and Böhm-Bawerk also identified themselves as inhabitants of the Empire rather than as Austrian. Even the younger members came of age in the Empire rather than Austria, so the Habsburg school of economics seems more appropriate. That is however not what I am after, for what is more troublesome is that the term 'Austrian' is primarily used to mark off a particular group of economists, not as a way to understand their work. I will argue that the Viennese context was of crucial importance to their work. All of these men including the scholars of the interwar period lived and worked in Vienna, and that is also where they very frequently interacted in intellectual circles. The city was the connection between them, socially as well as intellectually. As I will argue in Chapter 2 the Viennese conversations were the point of reference for their work. More importantly still, the political, cultural and economic developments in Central Europe prompted them to ask specific questions. So the quarrel is not merely over Austrian, Habsburg or Viennese, but also about the importance of this context.

The second way in which our understanding of them is flawed is that we tend to understand them as economic scientists in a rather narrow sense. Carl Menger's first book *Principles of Economics* is indeed relatively narrowly concerned with economics. But even he feels part of a broader group of social scientists and historians as is clear from his methodological writings. With the possible exception of perhaps Böhm-Bawerk all subsequent members of the school have published widely on methodology, economics, political philosophy and sociology. This is not surprising given the fact that the training at the university in Vienna and especially the intellectual conversations in Vienna were never restricted by disciplinary boundaries. Especially the scholars who are traditionally considered members of the school during the interwar period became increasingly concerned with the study of civilization as I will demonstrate in Chapters 3 and 4. Markets for them are an essential part of our civilization, they are cultural phenomena, just like language and law. This is of importance for two reasons, firstly because it is a different conception from markets than is common in economics. Secondly, it helps us to realize that markets are only a part of our civilization, and can thus only be understood within a wider cultural framework. So rather than being concerned with the economy, and how to study it, the Viennese were concerned with their civilization and how to study it.

This leads us to the third point, the emphasis I wish to place on *students*.[4] It is common among economists to think of themselves as policy advisors who can steer or even stronger engineer the economy. And even if some are somewhat critical of mechanistic metaphors they still think of themselves akin to doctors, who can diagnose the ills of society and are able to prescribe cures for the economy. The Viennese students of civilization on the other hand think of themselves as possessing very incomplete knowledge of their civilization. They do not fully understand the organically grown institutions which form an essential part of civilization. To emphasize this, Hayek repeatedly claims that we should 'marvel' at the workings of the market. The Viennese argue that economists cannot engineer or steer the economy, but are primarily students of markets or other cultural phenomena with an imperfect understanding of it. This does not mean that there is no positive role for economic knowledge. It does mean that economic knowledge does not easily lead to solutions or cures, but instead makes us aware of our limitations, both as human beings and as students. Economic knowledge shows us primarily what we cannot achieve. An insight which they hope will have a therapeutic effect on us. This puts them in a difficult predicament when they feel that the civilization they study and cherish is in danger. Only very reluctantly, and only some of them, attempt to stand up for their civilization, to act as its custodian or even to defend it; even though they remain skeptical of their own capacity to do so.

---

[4] For a long time I pondered over the right label, convinced that the label economist or economic scientist is unsatisfactory. The label of 'intellectual' springs quickly to mind. Intellectuals are not bound to any particular academic discipline, or form of writing. But both Schumpeter and Hayek wrote very derogatory essays about intellectuals ('those second hand dealers in ideas, who know a little bit about a lot'). So it would be rather odd to apply that label to them. I, of course, considered the term *political economists*, but that term only emphasizes the market-state dichotomy from which I want to get away. I also considered social scientists, but felt that it presented them as our contemporary interdisciplinary academics, rather than the scholars working in a field with little visible disciplinary borders. And these Viennese men, especially the younger generations, almost never held official university positions (at least not in Vienna). The final alternative term I considered was liberal, but that term although it captures much is also confusing. Firstly because liberal has very different meanings in Continental Europe and the United States, and secondly because the meaning of liberal is far from constant even within Central Europe during the period we study. But I think they do feel that they are contributing to a Western liberal project, broadly conceived.

I later found out, to my pleasant surprise that Boettke (2012) also uses the concept of student. There is also an instance when Hayek comes very close to this label, when he addresses a group of historians in Britain he writes: "What I want to talk about tonight is more specifically the role which the historians can play in this connexion – where by historians I mean really all students of society, past or present" (Hayek, 1944/1992: 203).

Willink's painting in other words really exemplifies the three major themes of this book. Firstly the meaning and the importance of civilization as represented by the ruins of Pompeii. Secondly the responsibility of the painter, or in our case the student of civilization, to his or her civilization. And thirdly the importance of the continued conversations to study this civilization, to cultivate it, and to move it forward. Even the fact that this conversation has ceased in Willink's painting will have a symbolic meaning as we will discover later.

2 Civilization?

Now I can imagine that at this point one becomes impatient with my frequent use of the word civilization, both in my analysis of Willink's painting and in my description of a group of Viennese students of this rather broad concept. As Norbert Elias observes in the opening paragraphs of his *The Civilizing Process*: "there is almost nothing which cannot be done in a 'civilized' or 'uncivilized' way" (Elias, 1939/2000: 5). On the other hand Elias' observation clearly points to the fact that civilization is always concerned with practices, how things are done: with greater or less foresight, with more or less specialization, with manners or without, with more or less technical sophistication. There is, however, also another connotation to the word civilization, when we for example speak of a certain level of civilization. We then use it to rank as it were certain practices or groups of people with more or less civilization.

Something which stands out in virtually all theories of civilization is the emphasis on the interaction between individuals; how they live together. The division of labor (and associated technologies) is invariably considered to be a central element of civilization. Another important element is the development of knowledge: practical, technological as well as scientific knowledge. As such it seems surprising that the concept has not been more central in economics, concerned as it is with the division of labor, the level of technology and human capital. This neglect of civilization is probably due to the cultural or moral connotation of the term. Civilization suggests not only various levels of division of labor but also various levels of culture or morality. This moral side is at odds with the subjective nature of modern economics which has been concerned with rationality and emphasized the purely personal nature of preferences. It is also, at first sight at least, at odds with the cultural relativism prominent in the humanities during the past decades.

In fact the concept of civilization has always been plagued by this problem of the combination of the economic, social and the moral. Elias shows in detail how in German the notions of 'Kultur' and 'Zivilisation' have become disconnected. The German term 'Zivilisation' refers to outer appearances, to technology, the division of labor and to manners. 'Kultur' on the other hand is used to refer to those accomplishments of which are really profound, and which make up the identity of a people, their art and their character. One could also say that 'Kultur' is the authentic of the two concepts, while 'Zivilisation' refers to the surface. Other people than the Germans could be civilized, but it was doubtful whether they could also acquire a true 'Kultur'. This distinction has been used to differentiate between the technical (civilization) and cultural, social and moral elements of civilization (culture), for example by Alfred Weber (Weber, 1921/1998: 196). As Elias observes, this distinction has also been used to stress national differences. This trend has continued more recently in Huntington's work to suggest a clash of mutually incompatible civilizations (Huntington, 1998). In this book I will not distinguish between culture and civilization in the German sense. I have purposely sought for a term which encompasses the moral, cultural, social and economic aspects of human interaction, which I believe the Viennese students study.

I have moreover found that among twentieth century authors on civilization (admittedly I only studied European authors) there is, contrary to my expectation, a surprising consensus on what the central element is of any type of civilization: restraint.[5] Hayek most extensively discusses the concept rather late in his life, in the postscript to *Law, Legislation and Liberty*. There he argues that civilization has become possible through restraint: the restraint of our natural inclinations, our instincts. But also, and that is especially important for Hayek, the restraint on our rationalism, the recognition of the limits of our rational faculties: our ability to know and design. Such restraints he argues have usually come about organically, they are: "a tradition of learnt rules of conduct which have never been 'invented' and whose functions the acting individuals usually do not understand" (Hayek, 1982: 155). Central in Norbert Elias' account of civilization are the interrelated effects of self-constraint and social constraint (constraint by others). And in yet another prominent account the anthropologist Malinowski argues that restraints are central to make civilization possible: "Culture (...) implies obedience and submission to

---

[5] Some references to non-European uses of Elias' civilizing process are collected in Mennell and Goudsblom, 1997.

certain restraints" (Malinowski, 1947: 33). And in Freud, too, civilization is considered to be made possible through restraints (Freud, 1930/1946). Authors from different fields share this central element in their analysis of civilization.

What they also share is that they tend to contrast civilization to barbarism, or a state of nature. What is however peculiar to the way we will use the word civilization here is that the escape from barbarism comes at a price. Popper describes this price as the 'strain of civilization'. Malinowski describes a similar phenomenon when he writes that:

> For all this there is a price to be paid in terms of obedience to tradition. Man must submit to a number of rules and determinants that do not come from his organism but from submission to his own artifact and machinery, to cooperation, and to the tyranny of words and other symbols.
>
> (Malinowski, 1941: 188)

This may sound strong, but Hayek and Popper reach similar conclusions. They also believe that civilization comes at a severe price, so much so that we must conclude that man is (at least initially) civilized against his wishes.[6] In this respect we should also mention Freud who agrees that civilization comes at a price, but concludes that this price might become unbearably high. And not only does he believe that the price is sometimes too high, but also that the submission to these norms and the repression of our instincts can lead to mental problems (Freud, 1930/1946).

This consequently means that freedom, for all these thinkers, is only possible through restraints: freedom is made possible by civilization. Civilization, the norms and institutions which regulate human interaction, enable us to be free. A good example of an institution which enables freedom is the division of labor. By the division of labor the possibilities for human flourishing multiply, but it does mean that we become dependent on others, and that we will only produce a small part of the wide array of goods we desire (although that part in abundance, so that we can trade). Freedom, in this perspective of the students of civilization, is made possible because the individual and his fellow individuals follow cultural norms. Our freedom is dependent on the fact that other people share our civilization, and do not permanently revolt against it.

Understood as such, freedoms are common goods, they come about because various individuals accept certain institutions and subject themselves to certain norms and rules. I like to illustrate this with the freedom

---

[6] Hayek also cites the anthropologist Geertz in support of his thesis.

of speech, which is increasingly interpreted as the *individual* right to say whatever is on one's mind. The perspective of the students of civilization on this freedom would be very different. They would, first of all, stress the common language which underlies communication, and which is essential to exercise speech meaningfully. Secondly they would emphasize the fact that freedom of speech can only exist if we restrain ourselves, that we provide others with the space to express their opinion. Freedom of speech in other words is a shared freedom which can only come about in a civilized conversation, in which certain norms regarding the art of conversation are observed. Freedom of speech does not entitle every individual to the unrestrained right to say everything he pleases, when he pleases. This might not mean a very significant difference legally, it makes all the difference in practice. It also highlights that this freedom is a common good, which can only come about if individuals comply with certain norms (although norm-following will never be complete). This view is illustrated by Elias with a conversation between Goethe and fellow German poet Eckermann. Eckermann once said to him: "I give open expression to my personal likes and dislikes", to which Goethe responded: "One must seek, even if unwillingly, to harmonize with others" (quoted in Elias, 1939/2000: 30). Goethe emphasizes the restraint, Eckermann the absence of these. Elias, sides, we now understand why, with Goethe.

A common complaint against the concept of civilization is that it suggests a process of natural development and especially of progress. For the authors we will analyze in this book that is not at all the case, they are very aware of the possibility or the danger of regress. Hayek speaks of a revolt against civilization and the often gloomy Mises repeatedly fears the destruction of the Western civilization altogether. The reason for Malinowski to write about freedom and civilization is because he too fears that our civilization is in danger. Such fears are clearly evident from the title of Popper's *The Open Society and its Enemies*. Norbert Elias has written extensively on the possibility and actual decivilizing process in Germany (Elias, 1996). In fact an important argument of this book will be that the Viennese students of civilization shifted from a belief in gradual (natural) progress in civilization, to a belief that their civilization was in danger, and that they had the duty to act as its custodian. This consequently means that for the Viennese students of civilization, as well as for Malinowski, Elias and the later Freud, the civilizing process was a positive process. Or as Popper would put it dramatically, civilization and the restraints on ourselves were the price humans had to pay, the 'cross we had to carry for being human' (Popper, 1945: 176).[7] That is obviously at odds with the modern idea of value-free social science, but it is precisely that contrast that we wish to make clear in this book.

3 Why civilization?

My purpose in this book reaches somewhat further than reinterpreting the Viennese students of civilization. At certain points I will attempt to show that the perspective of the Viennese students of civilization is a fruitful way of understanding the economy and more broadly our civilization. In those sections I will further explore the themes discussed in the preceding chapters and attempt to connect the Viennese tradition to contemporary authors on these subjects. So why, you might ask, should we be interested in studying civilization, reconsidering how we think about markets and the role of the scholar in relation to his object of study?

I have three reasons for believing so, or at least I will restrict myself to three reasons in this introduction. Reason 1: The market process has cultural effects, and it depends on a certain 'market culture' for its continued existence. To give but one example of the importance of this market culture, the arguments for (free) trade advanced in the seventeenth and eighteenth century were part of a moral discourse in favor of exchange and in opposition to conquering land and other resources through war.[8] Various progressive authors argued that a society in which war is not accepted as a means of appropriation will be more conducive to a market economy than one in which this is not the case. An idea which lives on to this day in the economic belief that market societies work better if property rights are respected *and* protected. That market societies function better if supported by a certain morality might not be very controversial. The former part of my claim, that markets have cultural effects, is perhaps less widely accepted. I believe, however, that a little reflection will make it clear to everyone that markets have cultural (including) moral effects. If we frequently engage in market processes, then this will shape our culture. It will, for example, influence our level of trust (for better or worse) and will change how we value other individuals. Market societies tend to foster

---

[7] A possible breakdown of civilization or a decivilizing process is further discussed in Chapter 10.

[8] The paper which paradoxically has made me most aware of this is Neurath's 'War Economy' paper, which takes very serious the economic benefits of war (Neurath, 1919/2004)

a culture in which effort is praised, instead of one in which, for example, descent is important. Embedding the economy in civilization I think allows us to take these interactions seriously, without resorting to speculative ethics. Economics is already about valuation of goods and the work of others, so to argue that such valuations are both an input and an output of economic processes should not come as a surprise, or be all that controversial.

Even though this broadens our domain of study it does not mean that economics is all of a sudden a part of ethics. I have struggled for a long time with the question of how these Viennese students of civilization could combine a claim of neutrality or at least impartiality with support for free markets. In fact this has puzzled me more widely when I studied economics, which claims to be value-free but at the same time seems to support market institutions. The solution to this riddle is not easy, I also do not think that I have developed a definite answer. But I think the tension can at least be better understood if we realize how central valuation is in economics. The argument that the Viennese students of civilization advance is all about valuation. The Viennese students of civilization argue that market processes collect (as it were) a variety of individual valuations; they allow valuation through resulting market prices to take place. Without such valuations we would have no basis to make decisions, we would not know how to weigh the options (rational choices would be impossible). So without valuation there would be nothing left of our basis for economics *and* ethics (see especially Hayek, 1962). Ethics is clearly more about how we *should* value than how we *do* value. But to engage in any ethical conversation we need the comparison between both: between how people *do* value and how they *should* value. The argument by the Viennese students of civilization is that the market is an essential part of our civilization or culture, because it is where such valuation process primarily takes place. Their argument is thus not (always) pro-market in the sense of pro-market and anti-state, but it is pro-market in the sense that it stresses the importance of the process of interactive valuation which takes place on markets. They do not necessarily argue for markets, but they argue that valuation is central to human interaction, and that markets are a very useful, perhaps uniquely useful, means to coordinate these valuations.

Reason 2: Social science is different from natural science to the extent that the social scientist is always part of what he is studying. Now this point is of course a commonplace in methodological writings on the social sciences, and even of some relevance in the natural sciences, especially in quantum physics. Already in the late 1920s the Viennese economist Oskar

Morgenstern argued that economic prediction was impossible because this prediction, if credible, would become part of the economy it was attempting to predict (Morgenstern, 1928). A well-respected economic prediction would defeat itself, Morgenstern argued, or on the contrary it would become a self-fulfilling prophecy. The argument I wish to make, which is very much inspired by the Viennese, goes somewhat further. It is an argument that we are part of the culture we are attempting to study, and that this implies limitations and possibly even responsibilities. Let us start with the limitations. Our perspective is always limited by the institutions we know and by which we were civilized. More generally the Viennese students of civilization argue that we cannot fully know or understand our civilization, and hence we should be very careful in trying to reconstruct it rationally. The organically grown institutions often contain a lot of knowledge, which is not always easily accessible to the student of civilization. To emphasize the limitations of the student, the Viennese place culture between the instincts which we call nature, and our rational faculties. Hayek argues that culture makes individual autonomy possible; cultural institutions such as language and markets 'make us intelligent'. Intelligence for him is a cultural product, and that implies limitations to what we can know about that culture. In other words we cannot step outside our own civilization to observe it from outside as it were, as is the ideal in natural science.

The Viennese students of civilization (with some variation between them) however also argue that we bear certain responsibilities to that civilization. In this book I will show how, when their civilization is under attack, these scholars attempt to defend their civilization, or at least to act as its custodians. They attempt to insulate it from the overconfident rationalism they associate with socialism and later against the threats of fascism and irrationalism. This defense in times of need is actually part of a longer tradition starting with Menger who already argued that it is the 'calling' of every social scientist to test the institutions of our civilization for suitability and to improve these institutions where possible. So, at least within the tradition of thought, we are discussing here, the social scientist (or student) is not just empowered and limited by his or her civilization, but also bears certain responsibilities toward it.

Reason 3 is perhaps somewhat more indirectly related to civilization, but it builds on this last point about responsibilities. Knowledge, scientific or of some other type, requires cultivation or it will like a civilization or heritage of any other kind crumble and ultimately disappear (remember the ruins in Willink's painting). I do not suspect that many will disagree with this rather general statement, but they might not draw the full implications from it. I think it has far-reaching implications for the way we practice our scholarship. It first of all raises questions about how to cultivate various types of knowledge. It raises questions about the institutional setting in which this is best achieved. The Viennese students of civilization for example worked outside of academia, in social circles with broad intellectual concerns.

It should also make us reflect on the increasing emphasis over the past decades on the progress of knowledge within economics and other social sciences. It in many ways reflects the reformist zeal of the rationalist of which the Viennese students of civilization are rather skeptical. Building on their arguments I think we quickly realize that traditionally the scholar's task is not only to improve our knowledge, but also to preserve it, to act as its custodian. In Michael Oakeshott famous words: "to acquire and enlarge will be less important than to keep, to cultivate and enjoy" (Oakeshott, 1962: 169). Perhaps we should be hesitant to throw entire traditions of economic knowledge out because they do not utilize our contemporary methods or current theoretical assumptions. The Viennese warn repeatedly during the interwar period, and earlier, against attempts for radical or revolutionary attempts to rationalize or overthrow traditions and norms. They argue that these institutions are only imperfectly understood, and that the knowledge contained in them, or produced by them is of great value. We could expand that argument to knowledge: we should warn against over-optimistic attempts to revolutionize fields and traditions of knowledge, and perhaps we also have a role as custodians of the knowledge which has been passed down to us. There should be room in any field of knowledge not only for those who improve, but also for those who reflect on that knowledge and, dare I say, protect it. To use Carl Menger's words again to test for suitability the knowledge that has been passed down to us.

I have tried to adopt this attitude when writing this book that there is more attention and space for reflection on existing traditions of economic knowledge than on progress. But I also hope that this book shows that the reflection on older traditions of economic knowledge is far from a passive process. Just as any other type of heritage conservation it is an active process, which poses acute questions about what to preserve, what to cultivate and inevitably what to neglect. This process of cultivation forces us to relate ourselves to the knowledge of the past, instead of conveniently ignoring or accepting it. I like to believe that our (economic) knowledge is like a city which consists of older buildings next to new architectural highlights, where the new buildings have sometimes replaced the old, and where they are sometimes extensions of older buildings. The city of modern economics, however, looks more like those cities which were run down by the modernist architects, in which the old had to make way for the new, and hardly a trace of the old constructions is left. Luckily most of that older economic knowledge is not yet completely lost, like some of these architectural highlights of the past. The older highlights of our economic knowledge, however, are too frequently neglected and in desperate need of restoration.

This is not to say that there has been no cultivation of the Viennese tradition. In comparison to some other traditions we might even say that the Austrian tradition has been particularly well treated in the past decades. The reflection on the Viennese economic tradition has tended to focus on its methodological individualism and even more prominently on its free-market conclusions. It has proved a great inspiration to American libertarians who felt closely related to the Viennese economic tradition. I have greatly profited from this renewed interest in the Viennese tradition, primarily through the enormous resources which are once again widely available online and in print. And I have benefited greatly from the emergence of an extensive body of secondary literature on the Austrian school that accompanied this renewed interest. Nonetheless my approach to the Viennese students, or Austrian economists if you will, is quite different. Rather than focusing directly on the individualism or free-market conclusions of the Austrian school, I focus on the different style of economics they practice, the way they envision economics as part of a wider study of civilization, and how they relate themselves as scholars to their object of study.

4 Interpreting the Viennese or the Austrians

So how does my account of the Viennese students of civilization precisely differ from other narratives about what is usually called the Austrian school of economics? To examine these differences I will first discuss the legacy of the Austrian school of economics. There are really two legacies of the Austrian school of economics. The first legacy is within economic theory, while the second legacy is closer to practical politics and political philosophy. A somewhat separate legacy is emerging around the work of Friedrich A. Hayek who, since he is so central in this book, will be discussed in Section 5.

Even within economic theory the legacy of the Austrian school can be divided into two strands. One strand believes that the contributions of the Austrian school are mainly of historical interest, while there is also a group of scholars who identify themselves as 'Austrian', and who attempt to keep this tradition alive and relevant. This latter group has been growing since the 1980s, but is still operating at the margins of the economics discipline.

The former group can perhaps be best summarized by looking at some standard histories of economics. In histories of economic thought the Austrian school of economics is primarily discussed because of their contributions to marginal analysis. Eric Roll's history is typical in dealing with the Austrian economists primarily as contributors to marginal utility analysis (Roll, 1973). He discusses a group of first generation marginal analysts, of which Carl Menger is a distinguished member along with other scholars such as Gossen, Jevons and father and son Walras. Carl Menger stands out from the other contributors of the first generation by being concerned with a general system and developing a fully subjective theory of value. Menger's disciples Böhm-Bawerk and Wieser are then treated together as solving some 'marginal' problems, which Menger had left open in his own work. Wieser's main contribution in this story is his development of a theory of costs on a subjective basis and the extension of Menger's marginal analysis of distribution. Böhm-Bawerk on the other hand is praised for extending marginal and subjective analysis to interest and capital, but as many other commentators agree he only partly succeeded in these efforts. The history by Ekelund and Hébert is one of the few which also considers the later generations with a special focus on competition and market processes (Ekelund and Hébert, 1983). Characteristic of this type of approach, as exemplified in the histories mentioned earlier, is that the focus is almost purely on the contributions to economic theory as an autonomous body of knowledge. The Austrians are understood as modern-day economists with some alternative views. A prime counter-example is the recent book by Robert Leonard who has constructed a wonderfully detailed and localized history of the mathematical economists from Vienna (Leonard, 2010). His book is not merely concerned with the contributions of the mathematical economists to the wider body of economic theory. He rather presents the mathematical economists as fascinating thinkers in their own right, embedded in the rich interwar and highly politicized context of Vienna, thinking simultaneously about parlor games, politics and economics.

The focus on the 'economic' aspects of the Austrian economists is also predominant among those who consider themselves to be part of the modern Austrian school or the Neo-Austrians. There are very good overviews of what they consider to be the Austrian legacy (Kirzner, 1987; Boettke, 1994; Boettke, 2010).[9] While these present-day Austrians are

---

[9] For a great collection of historical texts see Littlechild (1990, 3 volumes).

certainly more widely interested in the contributions to economics of the Viennese students of civilization, they too restrict themselves to economic issues. Especially subjectivism, methodological individualism, entrepreneurship, market processes, the role of uncertainty and information and the nature of competition receive ample attention within this neo-Austrian tradition. While there is sometimes a tendency toward political economy (concepts like capitalism and socialism, and more recently comparative institutional analysis are much more common in this tradition than elsewhere in the discipline of economics) they rarely attempt to include cultural or social aspects. For some this reflects the belief that economic principles are far more important, for others it means that they only attempt to explain a certain domain of society.[10] The emphasis in this 'Austrian revival' has been on the study of the economy, rather than the study of society or civilization.

This kind of uneasiness about the 'non-economic' is wonderfully demonstrated in Blaug's classic history of economic theory (Blaug, 1962). Blaug treats the marginal revolution mainly through Jevons and the only time that the Austrians take centre stage is when he discusses theories of interest. Then, however, hidden away in a technical discussion of marginal utility theory there is a discussion of the political significance of marginal utility theory and Blaug suddenly shifts gears. He argues that:

> It was the Austrian School that was markedly conservative and given over to attacks on socialism and the espousal of laissez-faire. The aversion to radical politics was a characteristic note in Vienna seminars, just as interventionism and a bored attitude to Marxism was characteristic of the Cambridge economist.
>
> (Blaug, 1962: 283)

Seemingly out of nowhere we are in the middle of a political economic debate, where marginal analysis was not only a contribution to pure economic theory, but also had political and social significance. What perhaps stands out most is Blaug's phrasing 'given over to', as if such non-economic views were merely subjective, part of an undesirable emotional involvement which was absent at Cambridge. Blaug for a moment considers whether politics were important in the development of modern economics, only to conclude that: "the idea that modern economics has no other *raison d'être* than to provide an apologetic for capitalism is too farfetched to be entertained" (Blaug, 1962: 283).

---

[10] There has been some interest in the context in which Austrian economics originates. Various authors have wondered about the 'Austrianness' of the Austrian school, but their conclusions are rather sketchy (Craver, 1986; Smith, 1990; Koppl, Horwitz and Desrochers, 2010).

Blaug's treatment is perhaps typical for the attempts of economists to keep matters political out of their work, and field.[11] Contrast that to what historian Tony Judt has recently argued, in his book *Ill Fares the Land* about the fate of social democracy:

We are the involuntary heirs to a debate with which most people are altogether unfamiliar. If we ask who exercised the greatest influence over contemporary Anglophone economic thought, we shall find that the greatest influence was exercised by a handful of foreigners, all of them immigrants from central Europe: Ludwig von Mises, Friedrich Hayek, Joseph Schumpeter, Karl Popper, and Peter Drucker.
(Judt, 2010: 97–98)[12]

Judt uses the term 'economic thought' but it becomes clear that he sees that influence as ranging much broader from philosophy of science, to political philosophy and from economics to management studies. What has been their influence? Judt believes that "the Austrian experience has been elevated to the status of economic theory [and had] come to inform not just the Chicago school of economics but all significant public conversation over policy choices in the contemporary United States" (Judt quoted in Homans, 2012).[13] Judt feels that the Austrians have unjustly reduced debates about social policy to a dichotomy between individual freedom and central state planning. This dichotomy, he argues, has over time killed all serious attempts at a social-democratic or 'third-way' alternative in the United States.

Another scholar critical of this legacy, Mirowski has recently argued that Hayek has shaped much of the post-war policy discussion through the Mont Pèlerin society; a society of scholars, intellectuals and journalists which, according to his account, influenced entire academic departments, and spawned various think-tanks. Mirowski argues that the Austrian school and Hayek more specifically has played a formative role in the establishment of what has come to be known as neo-liberalism (Mirowski, 2009). An ideology in which the belief that markets can be constructed is central according to Mirowski. These constructed markets can be

---

[11] Later editions of Blaug's *Economic Theory in Retrospect* consider some more extra-economic factors, but not many. Blaug's history is very much an internal history of economic thought.

[12] Peter Drucker is a scholar famous for his work in management, but we will also meet him in the chapter in which we examine the response of the Viennese to the rise of fascism.

[13] In these two quotes by Judt one is perhaps struck by a rather negative attitude toward these 'foreign immigrants from Central Europe'. Judt is certainly trying to maximize the distance between us and them, to make clear that we have little to learn from these men from a far and distant place.

employed to govern, and will replace alternative types of social relations and modes of governance. An ideology according to which the market even has the power to discipline states, although paradoxically enough the state is able to construct markets (Mirowski, 2009: 434–437). To give an example: the common market created in the European Union can be seen as both created by politicians to govern the European economy, and aimed at disciplining politicians. The underlying ideals of the creation of the common market and a common currency was not just to create one European market, but also discipline the industries and politicians of the (southern) European states.

That is one end of the political spectrum, where Hayek and other Austrians are heavily criticized for the role in the formation of modern (neo-) liberalism. They are also heralded by various libertarian groups in the United States. Those groups believe that the Austrians, including Menger but frequently excluding Wieser, are unique defenders of individual liberty, and staunch opponents of any kind of socialism. For them it is of importance that the Austrians were the staunchest opponents of socialism in any form or fashion. For them this political legacy, which includes Hayek's influence on Reagan, Thatcher – who proudly claimed that she always carried a copy of the *Road to Serfdom* in her handbag – and Pinochet in Chile is the most important legacy of the Austrians. A recent biography of Mises labeled him 'the last knight of liberalism' (Hülsmann, 2007)

Such political uses of the Austrian legacy are often quite far removed from the original intentions of the Viennese. In modern American libertarianism the Austrian legacy is often coupled with a strong belief in the capacities of the individual. As such it is at least as much American as it is Austrian, for the Viennese repeatedly warned against such optimistic individualism. But more generally one wonders if it has never struck these libertarians as odd that they have associated themselves with a group of scholars who were on the whole sympathetic to (and later nostalgic about) the Habsburg *Empire*. Even though Mises, and to a lesser extent Hayek, has been very critical of the state and state power, their vision was never one in which this state would be absent.

A similar problem plagues the critics of the political legacy of the Austrians. Mirowski's association of Hayek with the view of markets as constructs which can be designed completely ignores Hayek's criticism of precisely this view.[14] A more general issue with these political uses of the

---

[14]   When Mirowski writes that freedom can only be negative in the sense of Isaiah Berlin for the neoliberals he also misses a crucial points of the Viennese legacy (Mirowski, 2009: 437). As

Austrian legacy is that they tend to treat it as an ideology, an article of faith. And hence they ignore that the Viennese primarily sought to study markets and our wider civilization, rather than to formulate political ideals. Such interpretations are not wholly surprising; there are definitely elements of an ideology present in the work of the later Viennese. Hayek attempts to write a constitution of liberty, which clearly indicates that we are dealing with more than pure analysis. Mises increasingly emphasized the a-priori foundations of economic knowledge. This has led to vehement debates which are certainly suggestive of the fact that one was dealing with articles of faith, rather than arguments. That, however, should not obscure that their most important contribution was a scholarly one. It was a contribution to our scholarly knowledge, and the appropriate way to study the economy as a part of a civilization.

What is perhaps most striking is that these two legacies coexist, without many attempts to integrate the political analysis with the economic analysis. This brings us back to the matter at hand: how my interpretation of the Viennese students of civilization differs from that of other accounts. Firstly it differs in that it refuses to treat them as economists, or political philosophers. In fact they are neither, they study our civilization as a whole. They are neither scientists nor ideologues, but *interested* observers and interpreters. In the history of economics there is the famous Adam Smith problem: how is it possible that the same man who wrote a book about the wealth of nations, in which individuals (and states) pursue their self-interest, also wrote a book about the importance of our moral sentiments. A problem now considered irrelevant because the two books are best understood as an organic whole, the one supplementing the other. Let us not walk down the same path regarding the Austrians and attempt to isolate their economic theories from their political ideals and wider study of our civilization (including moral sentiments and the restraints on these), only to be forced to reconnect them later on.[15]

I will show in later chapters, and have already done briefly earlier, freedom according to the Viennese is always of a positive kind. It is civilization which enables freedom. And certainly 'free from external constraints' has no meaning in this tradition, for freedom is made possible precisely by accepting certain constraints.

[15] As such one might be tempted to think that my interpretation has elements in common with Heilbroner's notion of 'worldly philosophers'. Heilbroner, a student of Schumpeter, argues that the most interesting economists of the past also had a vision which allowed them to see further than others. And certainly I find many agreeable things in Heilbroner's work. But he tends to emphasize the fact that these worldly philosophers would be able to master our economies, and to fully understand both our contemporary society and its past: "Yet is was the faith of the great economists that just such seemingly unrelated

By emphasizing civilization as a unifying theme I hope to bring their ideas closer to their original context, and especially closer to their original intentions. That effort will occupy us in Chapters 3 and 4, and in Chapters 6 and 7. But, having reconsidered the meaning and intentions of the Viennese students, I will also explore what their vision might entail for modern economics, and how they are related to modern trends in economics. In this sense the book is a balancing act between two ideals. On the one hand the ideal to demonstrate the contemporary relevance of the insights about civilization and economics of the Viennese, to show that there are alternative ways of understanding the economy. And on the other hand the ideal of showing what they really meant, and how their work is part of a larger Viennese and Central-European cultural atmosphere.

5 The conversations about Hayek

The most famous Viennese of all the students of knowledge I will consider is Hayek. From recent scholarship there is starting to emerge a full picture of his body of work. By now there are three intellectual biographies about him by Hennecke, Caldwell and Ebenstein, as well as a book which contains the extensive interviews conducted with Hayek on his life and work (Hayek, 1994; Hennecke, 2000; Ebenstein, 2003; Caldwell, 2004). On the more political side of the spectrum Jeremy Shearmur has written an insightful book on Hayek's liberalism as a living research program (Shearmur, 1996).

As several reviewers have pointed out Ebenstein's intellectual biography unfortunately lacks a coherent narrative about the intellectual development of Hayek (Horwitz, 2005; Howson, 2006). It is rather a collection of fragments on various debates in which Hayek engaged, from which it is difficult to figure out how the various elements of Hayek's work fit together. It remains unclear how we can best understand his body of work as a whole. Hennecke in his German biography of Hayek explicitly states that he does not offer an overarching narrative, but only the stepping stones toward a comprehensive perspective. To some extent Hennecke is selling himself short; I certainly profited most from his biography. His

threads could be woven into a single tapestry, that at a sufficient distance the milling world could be seen as an orderly progression, and the tumult resolved into a chord (...) When the economists were done, what had been only a humdrum or a chaotic world became an ordered society with a meaningful life history of its own" (Heilbroner, 1953: 6–7). In his rather dramatic narrative the worldly philosophers are turned into masters of the economy, while the Viennese remained the students of it.

command and range of sources is impressive and his observations are often very insightful. More importantly I consider his idea of Hayek as maturing toward a liberal 'Sozialphilosoph' as an attempt to come to grips with his work as a whole, which is not too different from my own interpretation. Hennecke, like I am here, is looking for the appropriate concepts to capture Hayek and the Viennese tradition. He furthermore recognizes the importance of *traditions* within Hayek's work, a step up from many other authors who simply assume that Hayek is best understood as a modern social scientist.

A coherent narrative is present in Caldwell's intellectual biography.[16] Caldwell emphasizes the journey of Hayek from Vienna to London, to Chicago and later to Germany, but also his journey from business cycle theory and methodology to the role of knowledge in society and political philosophy, toward complex systems and emergent orders. More important-ly, I think Caldwell poses one of the central questions regarding Hayek. He asks how we make sense of Hayek's body of work as a whole: "These sorts of violent twists and turns in research interest cry out for explanation. Is it possible to make sense of Hayek's journey?" (Caldwell, 2004: 7). In the way that Caldwell poses the question, we also already find part of his answer. He thinks of Hayek as taking 'violent twists and turns', and later in the book he indeed argues that there is a particular point in time from which Hayek's intellectual interests seem to spring in many directions. Caldwell especially stresses the importance of Hayek's 1937 essay 'Eco-nomics and Knowledge', and the wider intellectual interests which it sparked in his work. What emerges from Caldwell's biography is an image of Hayek the economist pre-1937and Hayek the broad scientist post-1937, who was not only an economist but also a methodologist, an evolutionary psychologist, a complexity theorist and a political philosopher.[17]

---

[16] Caldwell has also published an earlier paper 'Hayek's Transformation', but from a comparison between the arguments in the book and the article it seemed clear to me that Caldwell's position in the later biography is more balanced (Caldwell, 1988), see also Foss (1995).

[17] Caldwell's explanation for this conclusion exemplifies his lack of emphasis on the Viennese context. He writes in a footnote: "When I say that Hayek turned away from economics, I do not mean that he would never again write about economics. I mean simply that, prior to 1936, all his published writings were on economics; afterward, his interests were broader" (Caldwell, 2004: 231). As I show in Chapter 2 the publications were only of secondary interest in the intellectual culture of Vienna, in which the circles and seminars were primary. Those conversations were renowned for their breadth, and we know enough about these conversations in Vienna to claim with confidence that Hayek's concerns had never been narrow in Vienna.

That thesis seems to me to be problematic for a number of reasons. Firstly the intellectual environment in London was much narrower, than it had been in Vienna. Hayek later commented that "I had become a little tired of a purely economics atmosphere like the London School of Economics" (Hayek, 1979). So even if the 1937 essay was a turning point it reflected concerns which had emerged much earlier in Hayek's mind, although not in his published work. Secondly it fails to explain Hayek's motivation for writing the *Road to Serfdom* which is not directly related to the 1937 article. It is one thing to develop broader scientific interests, but what sparked the political interest?[18] And thirdly it emphasizes, or rather assumes the existence of clear disciplinary boundaries that Hayek is crossing. Such firm boundaries, however, did not exist in the intellectual environment in which Hayek came of age: interwar Vienna. For Caldwell, Hayek remains a scientist to the end. Perhaps as a consequence of this Caldwell also sees Hayek as mainly solving theoretical puzzles: the role of money in the economy, how a monetary economy develops and adjusts through time, etc. I would, on the contrary, stress the importance of real-world problems to Hayek: the downfall of the Habsburg Empire and the culture associated with it, the rise of socialism and later fascism, the emergence of the welfare state and how entire generations of intellectuals and scientists were misled by mistaken ideas about what it means to do social science. Caldwell writes toward the end of the introduction to his intellectual biography: "[I]t would take nearly a lifetime of scholarly work before his particular vision of what it meant to do scientific economics would finally emerge" (Caldwell, 2004: 9). That might be part of the vision that emerged, but it certainly was not the whole of it.

Nonetheless I think that Caldwell's question is of great importance: how to understand Hayek's work as a whole? I have already stressed earlier how I think that conceptualizing him as a student of civilization helps us to put various elements of his work in place. Not all, I virtually ignore his work on psychology *The Sensory Order*.[19] I hope to demonstrate that the other parts can be coherently understood as an attempt to understand how our civilization functions, is maintained and how it develops. Underlying all these inquiries is a deep-rooted skepticism about the capabilities of the individual and the extent to which we can fully understand our own civilization.

---

[18] The clear distinction made here between the two should not obscure the fact that I believe there is no strong distinction between them.

[19] Caldwell (2004, chapter 12) offers an insightful analysis as to how this book relates to the wider body of Hayek's work.

This skepticism is given its due prominence by Jack Birner, who has also attempted to understand Hayek's work as a more or less unified project. Birner offers an alternative way to understand Hayek's work as a whole. He argues that Hayek set out a research program relatively early in his career (as early as the mid 1920s). Birner argues that Hayek stuck more or less to this program during his entire scientific career. Birner further argues that: "Research programmes are defined by *scientific problems* (or better: problem situations, as problems always arise against a particular scientific background) and *methodological principles*" (Birner, 1999: 54, emphasis in original). Often I found myself agreeing with Birner, for example the way in which he works out the tension between Hayek's individualism and his emphasis on evolution (although I believe that this tension emerges in the Viennese tradition even before Hayek).[20] I could not agree more when Birner writes that: "If we wanted to characterize the most general common motive in all of these fields, we could single out the idea of knowledge and its limitations" (Birner, 1999: 78). But the emphasis on methodological principles or a particular research program seems overdrawn to me. Birner, furthermore, seems to ignore, or unable to integrate the more political side of Hayek's work into his methodological framework.[21] Overall I think Birner is at his best when he looks for unifying themes in Hayek's work, more so than when he attempts to find a particular consistent research program. What remains stable in Hayek's work is an underlying perspective, a way of looking at the world, not the central problem, the way to solve these or the actual solutions. What remains central in his work is a concern about civilization and a desire to understand how our civilization can be maintained and improved combined with a highly developed awareness of the limits of human capabilities.

6 Economic knowledge and knowledge about civilization

The manner in which my account is perhaps most different from other narratives and interpretations of the Austrians is in how it understands economic knowledge. One will encounter novels, poems similar to how we started with a painting earlier. The references to art, or culture, are not common in books about economics. They might lighten up the cover or serve as an afterthought, but that is usually it. In my account they will do

---

[20] On this point see also Gray (1984: 54).
[21] For a more detailed criticism of the four methodological principles identified by Birner see appendix B in Caldwell (2004).

more, they are part of my interpretation, they contain knowledge as well. It took me some time to understand this. I think there were three sources of inspiration which convinced me that the real issue might lie in what we consider economic or social scientific knowledge. A real issue, not only because it has consequences for how we write as scholars, but also a real issue because it has consequences for how we understand the scholars of the past who do not neatly stick to scientific disciplines. Let me discuss these three first and then reflect on how my view of economic knowledge differs from more standard accounts.

The first source of inspiration was an anecdote told to me by Arjo Klamer about John Hicks. He remembered visiting John Hicks at his private home for an interview about his work. When idle for a moment Klamer noticed that Hicks' book collection consisted mainly of historical works. And when they came to discuss *Value and Capital* (1939), his magnum opus, Hicks made it clear that he was rather disappointed with the reception of his work. He felt that only the mathematical parts had had real influence on post-war economics, while Hicks had always believed that the real meat was in his understanding of the economy rather than in the equations. In an autobiographical account Hicks recounts how he visits the United States for the first time in 1946 where he is welcomed as a hero, the author of *Value and Capital,* by a new generation of economists: Paul Samuelson, Kenneth Arrow, Milton Friedman and Don Patinkin. With some humility Hicks then continues: "But I am afraid that I disappointed them; and have continued to disappoint them. (...) I have felt little sympathy with the theory for theory's sake" (Hicks, 1984: 287). What Hicks is experiencing is a shift in what is considered to be important economic knowledge. To him that knowledge is what he wrote, verbally, in *Value and Capital*; to a new generation it was contained in the equations at the end of the book.

The second source of inspiration was a more recent book by Thomas Sedlacek, *The Economics of Good and Evil* (2011). Rather than starting his history of economics book by going back to Adam Smith, François Quesnay or perhaps Aristotle he starts his story about the economics of good and evil with the epic of Gilgamesh. This epic is the first recorded story in human history. He analyzes the story for what it can tell us about the economy in general and about the views of the economy of the Sumerians. By modern standards this is clearly not scientific knowledge; the epic of Gilgamesh is just a story, a myth. Sedlacek, however, is able to extract valuable knowledge from it, about the relation between nature and civilization and the importance of cities for the economy and civilization more generally. In one of the other parts of his book he analyzes passages from the Old Testament. In Genesis 41 the Egyptian Pharaoh has a dream which Joseph interprets for him as an economic forecast of seven years of abundance followed by seven years of famine. Joseph in turn gives the following advice to the Pharaoh:

> And now let Pharaoh look for a discerning and wise man and put him in charge of the land of Egypt. Let Pharaoh appoint commissioners over the land to take a fifth of the harvest of Egypt during the seven years of abundance. They should collect all the food of these good years that are coming and store up the grain under the authority of Pharaoh, to be kept in the cities for food. This food should be held in reserve for the country, to be used during the seven years of famine that will come upon Egypt, so that the country may not be ruined by the famine.
>
> (Genesis 41:33–36 quoted in Sedlacek, 2011: 63)

This story from the Old Testament is economic knowledge or advice surely, but it has no place in the history of the academic discipline as we currently write and teach it. One could say that the behavior that Joseph advises here is prudent behavior, to use an old-fashioned term. It is using the things we have wisely, for prudent men: "can see what is good for themselves and what is good for men in general; we consider that those who can do this who are good at managing households or states" (Aristotle, Nicomachean Ethics: 1140b). In this sense we are reminded of the origins of the very word economy, which originally meant managing the household. That origin is not found in scientific knowledge, but practical knowledge of managing the family household and that of the state.

The third source of inspiration was the work of the Viennese students of civilization, especially Hayek. In his work he famously argues that next to theoretical knowledge there is another important type of knowledge: the knowledge of time and place (Hayek, 1937). He argues that the most important function of markets is to gather these varied bits of localized and dispersed knowledge in the hands of various individuals. It is clear that for Hayek scientific knowledge is not the only type of valid knowledge, and certainly not the only type of *valuable* knowledge. It was this insight which I saw confirmed time and again in my reading of the Viennese. What ultimately inspired me as much as it puzzled me was that I continuously was drawn to passages in the works of the Viennese which were hard to classify in traditional categories of economic knowledge. They were not empirical observations, not theoretical statements, nor explanations of these theories. Let me give a few examples:

> All provident activity directed to the satisfaction of human needs is based on knowledge of these two classes of quantities [the quantity of goods required and the quantity of goods at our disposal]. Lacking knowledge of the first, the activity of men would be conducted blindly, for they would be ignorant of their objective.

Lacking knowledge of the second, their activity would be planless, for they would have no conception of the available means.

(Menger, 1871/1950: 80)

The technical expert mocks the laymen who expect him to produce the miracle, of lifting a weight, for which he does not have the power; similarly the sociologist should mock the oft-repeated proposals, which will produce the greatest imaginable effects in society, before the necessary historical powers to bring these changes about are strong enough.

(Wieser, 1910: 144)[22]

If we are to understand how society works, we must attempt to define the general nature and range of our ignorance concerning it. Though we cannot see in the dark, we must be able to trace the limits of the dark areas.

(Hayek, 1960: 23)

Marxism sees the coming of socialism as an inescapable necessity. Even if one were willing to grant the correctness of this opinion, one still would by no means be bound to embrace socialism. It may be that despite everything we cannot escape socialism, yet whoever considers it an evil must not wish it onward for that reason and seek to hasten its arrival.

(Mises, 1919/1983: 217)

How are we to understand these statements? What type of knowledge do they represent? Some of them are phrased as imperatives, are they therefore moral? Or are they merely variations of a type of prudent advice, just like Joseph gave to the Pharaoh? They certainly emphasize the importance of interpretation of the world, and our own relation, as students of society, to the world. They also seem to represent a type of wisdom reminiscent of the philosophical or Buddhist aphorisms one occasionally comes across. There is also a methodological element to them, about how scholarship ought to be conducted, but they are certainly not statements of methodological principle.

Later I will suggest that understanding them is central to understand the contribution of the Viennese students of civilization. I will argue that these statements are perhaps best understood as therapeutic statements. They are therapeutic in the sense that they help us deal with the world, instead of helping us to understand or change that world. It is knowledge that makes us aware of our place in the world, aware of who we are, and what our role in the world is.

---

[22] My translation, in German: Der technischen Fachmann spottet über den Laien, der von ihm das Wunder verlangt, eine Last zu heben, ohne die nötige Kraft parat zu haben; so muss der Soziolog über die immer wiederholten Vorschläge spotten, welche die größten gesellschaftlichen Wirkungen hervorbringen wollen, ohne geschichtlich vorbereitete Mächte von genügender Stärke zur Verfügung zu haben.

2

Cultivating economic knowledge

The student of civilization in Paradies

Manchmal denkt man sich, hat denn einen Sinn
Diese ganze Problemspalterei?
Draußen fließt derweil froh das Leben hin
Und selbst ist man so wenig dabei.
Wars nicht kliiger, im Strom zu schwimmen,
Als die Wasserkraft zu bestimmen?
Ließ man nicht besser alles Denken sein,
Lebte einfach froh in den Tag hinein
Und genosse des Augenblicks Rausch?
Doch man weiß ja, hier gibts keinen Tausch.

Oh the time, it comes, when we must question why,
Is such questioning really that smart?
Life goes on and on, it just keeps flowing by,
And we all play a very small part.
We could swim along, take no notice
Of the tide's direction, the world's focus.
Should we not, perhaps, keep these thoughts at bay,
Push our cares aside, and relish what's today.
And yet there's no tradeoff at hand,
Somehow we must take a stand.

Felix Kaufmann, Final verse of the Mises-Kreis Song

Before we concern ourselves with the ideas of the Viennese students of civilization, we will first look at their practices. This will familiarize us with the most important figures as well as introduce the Viennese context that is so important to understand them. An important element of that context was the social space in which scholarly, intellectual and artistic work took place: the Viennese circles. Those circles, which existed next to the university, were the heart of the Viennese cultural and intellectual life, and membership to one or several of them constituted the intellectual identity of economists and other intellectuals in Vienna. These circles, the most famous of which is appropriately known as the Wiener Kreis or Vienna Circle, have attracted attention in part because both fin-de-siècle and Inter-war Vienna were incredibly creative places. Perhaps the special structure of intellectual life in Vienna might help explain that extraordinary creativity.[1]

The desire to explain some of that creativity is heightened if we just for a moment consider the breadth of fields to which important contributions have been made in fin-de-siècle Vienna: in physics Ernst Mach and Ludwig Boltzmann, in psychology Sigmund Freud and Alfred Adler, in economics Carl Menger, Eugen von Böhm-Bawerk and Friedrich von Wieser, in the visual arts Gustav Klimt, Oskar Kokoschka and Egon Schiele in music Gustav Mahler, Arnold Schönberg and Albarn Berg, in architecture Otto Wagner and Adolf Loos, in literature Hugo von Hoffmanstahl, Arthur Schnitzler and Robert Musil and in cultural criticism Karl Kraus. In some of the sciences, however the more important period was the interwar period that has attracted less attention. In philosophy, the Wiener Kreis and Karl Popper shaped the interwar scene. In economics, Othmar Spann, a German romantic, competed with at least three alternative approaches to economics: Austro-Marxism, Austro-liberalism and the emerging math-ematical economis. Hans Kelsen developed his pure theory of law, Hermann Broch, Stefan Zweig and Joseph Roth wrote their most import-ant works and some of the artists mentioned earlier continued to contrib-ute (Leser, 1981). Even though the Habsburg Empire had collapsed during World War I (WWI) Vienna continued to flourish intellectually. An obvious question that emerges from that fact is whether there was some-thing special about Vienna during that period.

Schorske's explanation of the outburst of the fin-de-siècle period has attracted most attention, although his complex argument is not easily summarized. Schorske argues that political liberalism never gained a strong foothold in Vienna, and therefore the bourgeoisie turned to culture as an alternative outlet. He furthermore suggests that the collapse of the moral order and the failure of political liberalism generated a tension that allowed the Viennese intellectuals to foresee, as it were, the twentieth century (Schorske, 1980). Other commentators have emphasized the Jewish

---

[1] Some of the more notable cultural histories of the period are Johnston 1972; Janik and Toulmin 1973; Schorske 1980. There is a complete bibliography on the Habsburg Empire and its culture on my website: www.denktankvizier.org/wp-content/uploads/2015/02/Dekker-Bibliography-The-Habsburg-Empire-1700–1956-General-Surveys-and-Historiographies-2003.pdf.

background of many of the contributors to this Viennese culture (Wistrich, 1996). Additionally we should not neglect the fact that the Viennese society, especially during the Habsburg period, was extremely unequal. The cultural (and political) elite was formed by a couple of hundred families who were often related by blood or through more recent marriages. To give just one example, economists Böhm-Bawerk and Wieser were life-long friends, who attended the same prestigious gymnasium, later they both served in various political functions. Böhm-Bawerk later became minister of finance, and Wieser was appointed minister of commerce. Böhm-Bawerk also married Wieser's sister. Or take Hayek's description of the personal relations in Vienna:

> I began to go through the list [of famous people from Vienna], and I found I knew almost every one of them personally. And with most of them I was somehow connected by friendship or family relations and so on. I think the discussion began, 'Did you know Schrödinger?' 'Oh, yes, of course; Schrödinger was the son of a colleague of my father's and came as a young man in our house'. Or, '[Karl von] Frisch, the bee Frisch?' 'Oh yes, he was the youngest of a group of friends of my father's; so we knew the family quite well. 'Or, Lorenz?' 'Oh, yes, I know the whole family. I've seen Lorenz watching ducks when he was three years old'. And so it went on.
>
> (Hayek, 1979: 7–8)

And then Hayek is not even mentioning his family relations to the Wittgenstein family. We are familiar with Ludwig the philosopher, but Maurice Ravel wrote his famous 'Piano Concerto for Left Hand' for his Ludwig's brother Paul, an accomplished pianist, who lost his right hand during the war. The cultural world of pre–WWI Vienna in other words, is ill-described as cosmopolitan, it was a small village.

The situation, however, was different during the interwar period. Far from turned inward many intellectuals were politically motivated and active. Economic as well as social differences were diminishing and many migrants arrived, especially from the east following the break-up of the Habsburg Empire. During that period, the most important Viennese economic circles were formed (although they sometimes had pre–WWI predecessors). To understand the outburst of the interwar period, it is essential to study the Viennese circles ('Kreise'). In a recent article, Timms has produced a visual representation of these scientific and artistic circles in Vienna in which he suggests that there were as many as fifty (Timms, 2009: 25). Perhaps even more striking than the sheer number of these circles is their overlap. Earlier, we have already emphasized the importance of personal relationships, but these were further cultivated through the participation in a number of partly overlapping circles. If one did not know someone directly, he was never more than one or two circles away. The historian Friedrich Engel-Janosi, for example, belonged to four of such circles (Engel-Janosi, 1974: 108–128). It should hence come as no surprise that gossip was pervasive in Viennese society; social bonds were thick.

A proper understanding of these circles is crucial to understand the contribution of the economists from Vienna for three reasons. First, because their work was the outcome of the debates between 'members' of these circles, the circles are the most important intellectual context (on the appropriate term to describe the members/participants of these circles, see n.3). Secondly the character of the knowledge that emerged from these circles differed from that produced in strictly academic settings. While in many other European countries modern universities were coming to dominate the intellectual atmosphere, Viennese intellectual life took place within the social sphere. While knowledge production became organized along disciplinary lines in many other European countries (and the United States), intellectual life in Vienna remained both broad and relatively informal. While in many other countries theoretical concerns came to dominate scholarly discussions, in Vienna such discussions were invariably tied to social and cultural concerns as, for example, has been shown by Janik and Toulmin for the work of Wittgenstein (Janik and Toulmin, 1973). Third, the strong identities formed in these circles influenced the identity and prospective careers of these economists in significant ways when they migrated to the New World. The biweekly seminar was one such ritual that was identity-forming, but we will explore many more of them in Section III.

The analysis, in this chapter, of a number of intellectual communities ties in with a shift away from the study of individual scholars to creative communities. This shift occurred slowly when in physics, historians of science realized that many of the great breakthroughs including quantum mechanics were achieved in small communities of about a dozen scholars (Heims, 1991; Cushing, 1994). A milestone was Collins' monumental study *The Sociology of Philosophies*, which showed that nearly every major philosopher had been part of a face-to-face community (Collins, 1998). As Collins puts it in a later book: "the major thinkers are those most tightly connected to other important intellectuals (. . .). Successful intellectuals are the most socially penetrated of introverts" (Collins, 2004: 358).

This trend is also reflected by a recent issue of the journal 'History of Political Economy' (Spring 2011) devoted to intellectual communities. Robert Leonard contributed an article on Vienna to this issue. He describes in great detail how Morgenstern established a community of mathematical economists during the early 1930s, and how this community was broken up by the rise of fascism and the consequent migration. Leonard mentions all the important factors that will be taken up in this article: "a pervasive feeling of anxiety; the close geographical confinement; the lack of anonymity; the presence of a cultivated elite; and the existence of a lively public sphere in which politics, science, and culture were objects of serious attention" (Leonard, 2011: 84). He, however, does not develop any of these themes to explain the Viennese circles; instead they are the background to the story of Oskar Morgenstern. Consequently, Leonard does not reflect upon the nature of intellectual life in Vienna, and how practices in such circles differed from those in academia. This chapter will, to the contrary, focus explicitly on the practices in such circles, and how they were situated more generally in Viennese cultural life.

In that sense the analysis is in line with the efforts of Edward Timms, who has sought to examine the practices and institutions that have stimulated and hampered intellectual life in interwar Vienna. For him, the overlap between circles is especially important, to which, what he calls, the erotic subculture contributed further (Timms, 1993; Timms, 2009). Timms, the biographer of Karl Kraus, does not pay much attention to economists, however. He instead studies more literary and artistic circles. He does observe that political factors play an increasingly important role during the interwar period, which is true for economists as well as I demonstrate below. So, more than either Leonard or Timms, we will study the alternative strategies pursued by Viennese intellectuals to establish legitimacy for their contributions and the rituals that sustained Viennese intellectual life, and that consequently shaped the character and style of their work.

1 Wiener Kreise, in plural

The most important circle (or Kreis in German) for the Viennese students of civilization was undoubtedly the Mises Kreis. It was centered round, as the name suggests, Ludwig von Mises and was held biweekly from October to May.[2] The summer season was spent away from Vienna in the

---

[2] The song of the Mises-Kreis, which frequent participants knew by heart, contained the lines: "Und dort geh ich hin, auch wenn ein Maitag ist / Süß und duftend wie keiner noch war" or in English: "I'll be there for sure, even if it's May/ And the day is the sweetest thus far". For the songs, including the verse in the epigraph, I have used the translation of Arlene Oost-Zinner available at mises.org.

mountains by most of the affluent Viennese. The subject matter would range from philosophy and problems of phenomenology, to social sciences, economics and history. Mises liked to describe himself as 'primus inter pares' of this seminar, but he was probably quite clearly its leader. Or as he describes it, the participants: "came as pupils, but over the years became my friends" (Mises, 1942/1978: 97). The circle was initially a kind of continuation of the famous seminar Böhm-Bawerk had held before the war for his advanced students such as Schumpeter, Rudolf Hilferding and Otto Bauer. The seminar evolved into an intellectual community in which he truly was 'primus inter pares', but this was also when several of its participants decided to start their own (complementary or rival) seminars.

In Figure 1, I have collected circles that are most relevant to the group of scholars that we will analyze.[3] In the middle, we see the Mises Kreis.[4] The second prominent circle for us is the Geistkreis.[5] This circle was formed by a group of advanced students around 1921 led by Herbert Fürth and Hayek. The regular participants of this group overlapped to a large extent with that of the Mises Kreis, but its focus was quite different. Members were asked to lecture on a field that was not their specialty and hence the focus was broader than in the Mises Kreis. Rather than just science the Geistkreis also discussed contemporary developments in literature, music

[3] In the notes that follow, I will present lists of members or rather regular participants to these circles. Membership to most of them was not a formal but an informal affair; nonetheless there was a degree of adherence to the shared perspective from some participants that others did speak of members. Such a distinction is nicely illustrated by what Alfred Schütz recounts about the involvement of his friend Felix Kaufmann with the Wiener Kreis: "Kaufmann was never a member and refused to be considered as such, yet attended their meetings regularly" (Schütz quoted in Helling, 1984: 144). In the following lists you will find regular participants.

[4] An alphabetical complete list of regular participants: Ludwig Bettelheim-Gabillon, Viktor Bloch, Karl Bode, Martha Stephanie Braun (later Steffy Browne), Walter Fröhlich (later Froehlich), Herbert Fürth, Gottfried von Haberler, Friedrich von Hayek, Marianne von Herzfeld, Felix Kaufmann, Fritz Kaufmann, Rudolf Klein, Helene Lieser-Berger, Rudolf Löbl, Getrud Lovasy, Fritz Machlup, Karl Menger, Ilse Mintz-Schüller, Ludwig von Mises, Oskar Morgenstern, Elly Offenheimer-Spiro, Paul N. Rosenstein-Rodan, Ewald Schams, Erich Schiff, Karol Schlesinger, Fritz Schreier, Alfred Schütz, Alfred Stonier, Richard von Strigl, Gerhard Tintner, Erich Vögelin (later Voegelin), Robert Wälder, Emmanuel Winternitz (list compiled from Kurrild-Klitgaard, 2003 and Craver, 1986).

[5] An alphabetical complete list of regular participants: Otto Benesch, Friedrich Engel von Janosi (later Engel-Janosi), Walter Fröhlich (later Froehlich), Herbert Fürth, Franz Gluck, Gottfried von Haberler, Friedrich von Hayek, Felix Kaufmann, Fritz Machlup, Karl Menger, Max Mintz, Oskar Morgenstern, Georg Schiff, Alfred Schütz, Erich Vögelin (later Voegelin), Robert Wälder, Johannes Wilde, Emmanuel Winternitz (list compiled from Craver, 1986).

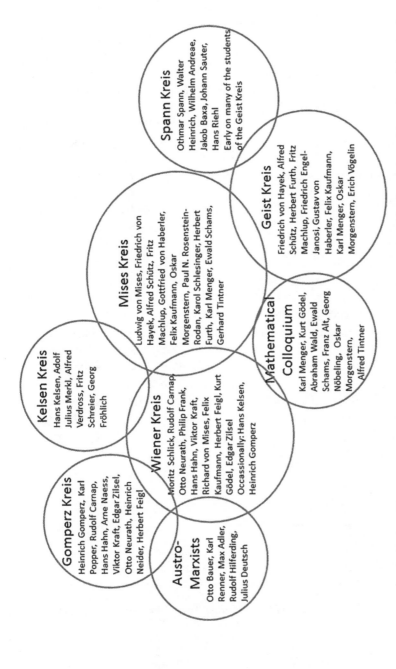

Figure 1: The Wiener Kreise most directly surrounding the Mises Kreis around 1928. For the sake of clarity I have limited the visual overlap between the circles, which in reality is often greater.

and art (for a list of subjects discussed see Engel-Janosi, 1974: 225–228). Some of its members graduated in law and later became well-established art historians. Since all members were roughly from the same generation there was less hierarchy than in the Mises Kreis. The Geistkreis did not meet in a fixed place, but circulated from one member's home to the next. Its focus was not only more cultural but they also frequently discussed the political situation in Vienna and when the time came, the possibilities of migration (Craver, 1986: 16–17).

Later in the 1920s the third important community for (future) economists was founded by Karl Menger (Carl's son), the Mathematical Colloquium.[6] He and some of his friends became increasingly dissatisfied with the antimathematical atmosphere in the Mises Kreis. Discussions in the mathematical colloquium instead focused almost completely on mathematical subjects, and were in fact frequented more by mathematicians than social scientists. Like Mises emphasized the unity of the social sciences under the banner of human action, so the members of the mathematical colloquium felt that mathematics could be applied across a whole range of fields. Karl Menger himself would end up writing a mathematical book about moral beliefs and ethics, and the colloquium was the place where the existence problem of the economic general equilibrium model was first discussed. It was also where Kurt Gödel first presented his famous impossibility theorems about logical systems. While there was some overlap between this circle, the Geistkreis and the Mises Kreis, this community increasingly distanced itself from the other two circles, a process that Leonard documents in detail. Hayek and Mises increasingly wrote in defense of a civilization they believed was quickly disappearing, Morgenstern and Menger were increasingly attempting to purify their economics, increasingly emptying it of any 'political' content (see Leonard, 1998; Leonard, 2010; Leonard, 2011).

To do so, the participants of the Colloquium could draw inspiration from the discussions in what has become the most famous of the Wiener Kreise, *the* Wiener Kreis (or Vienna Circle).[7] The Vienna circle was not a

---

[6] An alphabetical (but perhaps slightly incomplete) list of regular participants: Franz Alt, Gustav Beer, Gustav Bergmann, Kurt Gödel, Hans Hahn, Bronisław Knaster, Karl Menger, Oskar Morgenstern, John von Neumann, Georg Nöbeling, Ewald Schams, Karl Schlesinger, Otto Schreier, Alfred Tarski, Olga Taussky-Todd, Alfred Tintner, Abraham Wald (compiled based on Ingrao and Israel, 1990 and Leonard, 2011).

[7] A more or less complete list of regular participants: Gustav Bergmann, Rudolf Carnap, Herbert Feigl, Philip Frank, Kurt Gödel, Heinrich Gomperz, Hans Hahn, Olga Hahn-Neurath, Béla Juhos, Felix Kaufmann, Hans Kelsen, Viktor Kraft, Karl Menger, Richard

homogenous whole, as it has been portrayed in the past. There was at least an important division between the left wing of the circle, consisting of Neurath, Carnap, Feigl and Waismann, and a more conservative wing. In especially the work of Otto Neurath, but also in the pamphlet published by the circle *Wissenschaftliche Weltauffassung* (Scientific World Conception), there was a clear link between socialist and emancipatory ideals and scientific knowledge (Hahn, Neurath and Carnap, 1929/1979). The conservative wing of the circle headed by professor Schlick was more interested in pure science, free of values and metaphysics, the philosophical program for which the Wiener Kreis has become famous post– WWII (see also Reisch, 2005 and Dekker, 2014). At the same time there were links with the Mises Kreis via the phenomenologist Felix Kaufmann. One might expect the same via the Mises brothers Ludwig and Richard, but both brothers hardly talked to one another and pursued very different intellectual goals. Karl Menger, at various points in time, frequented all four circles we have discussed so far and was thus well informed on a very broad spectrum of intellectual discussions, and consequently was socially very well connected.

The left wing of the Wiener Kreis was closely connected with the Austro-Marxists who governed Vienna during the 1920s via the social-democratic party. The community of Austro-Marxists however is not really a circle, since many of the people associated with it held official political positions, and many of their organizations were far more institutionalized. There were, however, also links with the Mises Kreis, because many of the intellectual leaders of this movement had met Mises before the war at Böhm-Bawerk's seminar and at other occasions in the Viennese coffeehouses (Mises, 1942/1978: 88–90). Closely associated with the left side of the Wiener Kreis was Heinrich Gomperz, who, for several years also organized a circle.[8] Gomperz was for a couple of years the most important teacher of Karl Popper and his seminar was frequently attended by many of the younger members of the Wiener Kreis.

Two other circles deserve to be mentioned. The first circle was formed around Hans Kelsen,[9] a prominent law scholar who developed 'A Pure

---

von Mises, Otto Neurath, Rose Rand, Josef Schächter, Moritz Schlick, Olga Taussky-Todd, Friedrich Waismann, Edgar Zilsel (Stadler, 2003: n. 5).

[8] I compiled a somewhat tentative list of its frequent visitors: Rudolf Carnap, Herbert Feigl, Heinrich Gomperz, Hans Hahn, Arne Naess, Olga Hahn-Neurath, Viktor Kraft, Heinrich Neider, Otto Neurath, Karl Popper, Robert Reininger, Edgar Zilsel (Heyt, 1999 and Stadler, 1994).

[9] I compiled a somewhat tentative list of frequent participants: Josef Dobretsberger, Georg Fröhlich, Walter Henrich, Felix Kaufmann, Hans Kelsen, Josef L. Kunz, Adolf Julius Merkl,

Theory of Law' along positivist lines. He was widely known because he drafted the Austrian Constitution on behest of the Austro-Marxist chancellor Karl Renner. Kelsen was a good friend of Ludwig von Mises, although not a political ally – a combination of relationships with Mises not many could sustain (Hülsmann, 2007: 41). The other circle worthy of mention is that of Othmar Spann,[10] who developed a universalist philosophy, and was a supporter of German nationalism (and consequently of the Anschluss). His romantic political-economic philosophies initially attracted many of the young students of civilization we have been analyzing, but they soon left Spann's circle. Spann was able to exert this influence over these young students because he held one of the professorships in economics at the University of Vienna. The other heir of the chairs once occupied by Wieser and Böhm-Bawerk, the two giants of Austrian economics, was Hans Mayer who failed to attract a circle of like-minded scholars (for more details see Craver, 1986).

These Kreise were not only important for the overlap between them and the mutual inspiration, but also for their mutual rivalry. The interwar work of Mises, Hayek and Morgenstern can only be understood as part of the ongoing conversations and discussions between these circles. The famous socialist-calculation debate was waged between Otto Neurath and Ludwig von Mises, and Morgenstern increasingly objected to the 'political' nature of the work of both the Austro-Marxists and the work of Mises. On a deeper level these communities were identity forming, one's membership to a Kreis or various Kreise formed one's intellectual identity, frequently well into the postwar years when many of the scholars had migrated.

2 Between coffeehouse and university

To describe the intellectual scenery in Vienna we need more than a description of the intellectual breadth of its circles, especially since we

---

Leonid Pitamic, Fritz Sander, Fritz-Schreier, Alfred Verdroß, Erich Voegelin (for an introduction to this circle see Jabloner, 1998 and the website of the Hans Kelsen Institute: www.univie.ac.at/staatsrecht-kelsen/kreis.php).

[10] I compiled a somewhat tentative list of frequent participants: Wilhelm Andreae, Jakob Baxa, Walter Brand, Walter Heinrich, Hans Riehl, Johann Sauter, Othmar Spann, Friedrich Westphalen and early on many of the students of the Geistkreis (Haag, 1976; Wasserman, 2014; Craver, 1986). The most comprehensive work on the Spann-Kreis is the recent monograph by Wasserman, he argues: "Conservatively, the Spannkreis included several hundred active members in Vienna, most of whom were university-educated, often with advanced degrees" (Wasserman, 2014: 92). The Kreis, as we discuss it here, is smaller and consists of the active participants in the most advanced conversations. But at public lectures audiences were far greater, both for Othmar Spann as well as for members of other Viennese circles, see also the remarks by Karl Menger below.

started the chapter with the purpose to partially explain why cultural and scholarly life was so vibrant in Vienna. The cliché about cultural life in Vienna is that it took place in the famous coffeehouses, where one could sit and chat all day while paying for only one cup of coffee. As with all clichés, there is some truth to this. In fact, for many Viennese these coffeehouses were much more than just a pub, it was closer to a living room. It was where they read the newspapers, met their friends, and regularly had their mail and washed clothes delivered. Like any living room, there were very specific rules to be observed by its visitors. In certain cafés, for example, tables or even specific chairs belonged to some of the intellectual hotshots, and in some of the literary coffeehouses, each group of authors had their own table. Quarrels over such tables and the rights to it would not infrequently lead to physical disputes. As an homage to this tradition, one can find a life-size figure of the author Peter Altenberg who still sits in his regular chair in Café Central. To many it was a semipublic space where one could be together alone. The entire Mises-Kreis, to take one example, set off on their regular Fridays toward Café Kunstler. But contrary to the cliché, one might expect that they sometimes had more than one drink.

On a more serious level, the coffeehouse cliché is also in need of some correction; private spaces were at least as important for the circles (Fuchs, 1949: 5–16). None of the Kreise we discussed earlier actually met for their discussions in one of these coffeehouses, they all met in private homes or offices. The availability of such private spaces depended on private wealth and professional positions. We should not forget that the various 'von's' we have been talking about were (inherited) titles of nobility. Some circles depended on more recently acquired wealth, the prime example was the Wittgenstein family who had acquired its wealth through iron and steel, and was estimated to be the wealthiest family of Vienna (after the Habsburgs presumably). On the other hand, social stratification did become less during the 1920s in Red Vienna.

Such processes of social integration did not always go smoothly. Take the Wiener Kreis where Moritz Schlick was the most prominent individual; not only was he the only one holding a professorship but he was also much wealthier than most other members. Schlick had always refused Otto Neurath into his house. Neurath had grown up in a working-class environment and he cultivated this background to some extent, frequently wearing a characteristic working man's cap and refusing to adjust his language and accent. This led Schlick to exclaim: "I cannot invite this man; I cannot bear his loud voice" (Schlick quoted in Neider, 1973: 48). Neurath was undoubtedly somewhat offended that Schlick refused to receive him at his house, but at the same time he made fun of the 'aristocratzic' accent of Schlick. Such social inequalities had further consequences. Schlick could arrange certain jobs for his students, Feigl for example, became librarian at the philosophy faculty, but this also meant that Feigl was merely his assistant.

Mises too was quite good at arranging jobs for his students. In 1927 he even managed to set up a new institute under the umbrella of the Chamber of Commerce where he was secretary: the 'Institut for Konjunktur-forschung' (Institute for business-cycle research). The first director of this institute was Hayek who could hire Morgenstern as his assistant. And Morgenstern was able to take over this position when Hayek left for a position as professor in London, first as managing director and later as director (Klausinger, 2006: 622). On the one hand, this can be interpreted as evidence that there were various opportunities for the Viennese scholars to get a job. One the other hand, it exemplifies the uncertainty in which they operated. The University of Vienna did not hire Jews and more generally offered very few opportunities for young (liberal) scholars (Klausinger, 2006; Klausinger, 2014). This made young intellectuals highly dependent on a few wealthy and powerful individuals. No wonder that the topic of migration frequently came up in the discussions of the Geistkreis. Even Mises was subject to these uncertainties and dependencies.

Around WWI all chairs in economics, then occupied by Eugen von Böhm-Bawerk, Friedrich von Wieser and Eugen von Philippovich, opened up. Böhm-Bawerk passed away and was succeeded Carl Grünberg, an economic historian (Craver, 1986: 2). Othmar Spann filled the vacancy that opened up when Philippovich retired. Hans Mayer, who had already been considered for the position of Philippovich, ultimately succeeded Wieser in 1922 (Klausinger, 2014: 2–3). Perhaps more important, however, than individual factors – why Mayer and not Mises? and why not Schumpeter? – was a general trend at the University of Vienna. It failed to hire and/ or attract the most talented individuals, and hence became increasingly marginalized in Viennese intellectual life. The effects for this was different for the various circles. Students of Spann had many opportunities within the University, but gained little international recognition. While members of the Wiener Kreis as well as those of Mises Kreis and the Mathematical Colloquium gained international recognition, but failed to acquire positions in Austria (Wasserman, 2014: 91). This was further reinforced by a growing anti-Semitism in Vienna generally and at the university in particular. Janik and Toulmin in their cultural history of Vienna even speak of an 'authority gap', by which they mean the absence of any legitimating institutions in Viennese society and for intellectuals especially (Janik and Toulmin, 1973: 248, see also Fleck, 1996).

This authority gap was not complete, as Janik and Toulmin also recognize. For the left-leaning Viennese intellectuals, there was the opportunity to associate themselves with the social-democrats. During the 1920s Vienna was ruled by the social-democratic party, hence its nickname 'Red Vienna'. The social-democrats set up extensive social programs most famously to improve the housing conditions in Vienna. This development did not improve matters for the liberal-conservative students of civilization. For them, the changing political wind meant that political positions that many Viennese economists had occupied before WWI had become unavailable. Schumpeter, as an exception did obtain such a position. His position as liberal economist, but officially neutral expert, in a socialist government however was bound to cause insurmountable problems, which it quickly did, greatly damaging his reputation (McCraw, 2007: 96–103).

Another institution that was still standing strong was the gymnasium system, which provided a solid basic intellectual knowledge for many in the Viennese elite. Gymnasiums such as the Schottengymnasium that Böhm-Bawerk, Wieser and no less than three twentieth-century Nobel Prize winners attended were of a high quality. This gymnasium system, however, was also a reflection of the highly stratified society of Vienna. In his reminisces Karl Menger points to yet another factor that contributed to Viennese intellectual life:

The unusually large proportion of professional and business people interested in intellectual achievement. Many members of the legal, financial, and business world; publishers and journalists, physicians and engineers took intense interest in the work of scholars of various kinds. They created an intellectual atmosphere which, I have always felt, few cities enjoyed.

(Menger, 1994: 9)

This interested group of professionals regularly participated in the Kreise. To give some examples from the participants of the Mises Kreis: Mises combined it with his work at the Chamber of Commerce, and established the business cycle institute. Karl Schlesinger was also a banker, Machlup worked in his parents' cardboard factory, and Schiff was a newspaper editor (Schulak and Unterköfler, 2011: 133–135). It was also from this professional class that a more general audience could be drawn, for example, for the public lecture series that various members of the Wiener Kreis organized.

Intellectual life, as a consequence, became separated from the official institutions. Famous is the artistic Viennese 'Sezession' movement (literally: separation), which sought independence from the existing artistic styles and institutions. It is not unhelpful to think of Viennese intellectual life as also separating itself from the official institutions. This is in line with Schorske analysis of the failure of political liberalism in Vienna. For the scholar, however, it meant that, like the artists of the Sezession, he or she was in need of alternative institutions, alternative sources of finance, alternative sources of legitimacy, even an alternative identity.

3 The rituals of the Kreise

Academic life is so full of rituals, that we sometimes hardly notice them: extensive rituals when (PhD) students graduate, or when a professor accepts a chair or retires and smaller rituals such as the celebration of centenaries of famous predecessors, or the opening of our academic year. Such rituals have a double function: they honor the people involved, the renowned scholar or the graduate, but they also legitimize the institutions that organize such rituals. A conference about economics is an opportunity for individuals to present themselves and their scholarship, but it also legitimizes the discipline of economics, and its particular subdisciplines. Not least importantly, such rituals keep a discipline alive, if they are successful at least. They ensure the continued scholarly conversation about a particular subject. Such legitimization was not self-evident in Viennese intellectual life. A position at the University of Vienna was the exception rather than the rule, and the continued conversation often depended on particular individuals within the Kreise, rather than on more formalized and official institutions. It should thus perhaps come as no surprise that Viennese intellectual life was full of rituals, and alternative strategies to establish legitimacy. These rituals could also help to establish a scholarly identity for the intellectuals in Vienna, so that they could give an answer to those piercing questions: who are you and what do you do?

Although no one has, to my best knowledge, ever paid very particular attention to the function of such rituals in the Wiener Kreise, we are fortunate to know quite a bit about the rituals themselves. Kurrild-Klitgaard for example, describes a whole series of them. The meetings of the Mises Kreis always started punctually at seven on a Friday evening. Mises would be sitting at his desk and usually he had a large box of chocolates that he passed around. The meeting would last until half past nine or ten, after which the participants would have dinner at the Italian restaurant 'Anchora Verde'. Those who wanted to continue the discussion would then head to Café Künstler (Kurrild-Klitgaard, 2003: 47). But undoubtedly the most striking ritual of the Mises Kreis has to be the songs that Felix Kaufmann wrote in honor of the seminars. The songs deal with the critical spirit of the circle ('Geschliffener Geist in Mises-Kreis'), particular debates within the circle, the Austrian tradition ('Der letzte Grenadier der Grenznutzenschule'). Other songs were written for special occasions; there is a song of celebration for the opening of the statistical institute, a goodbye song to Mises when he departed for his position in Geneva in 1933 and a song lamenting this departure. One of the most striking of these songs is called 'Der Nationalökonom im Paradies' (The economist in Paradise). So no, that is not a typo in the subtitle of this chapter in case you were wondering.

Now it is easy to think of these songs as a kind of curiosity, but that would be too easy. Many years later, Haberler was still able to sing these songs word for word, and he emphasizes that all regular participants could recite these songs (Haberler in Kaufmann, 1992: 9–10). The songs were written to well-known melodies and Haberler stresses that these songs were meant to be sung, not to be read (although even reading them is a delight). Such rituals established a certain rhythm to the meetings of the Mises Kreis, and provided a sense of belonging where the university could not do so. The songs legitimized the discussion taking place in the Mises Kreis. Take for example, the following fragment: "An economist moved to Germany/ A learned position to pursue / This should have been a certainty /For in Wien he'd learned a thing or two / But the good man learned the tragic tale / Marginal Utility was deceased" (Kaufmann, 1992: 21–22).[11] In the official Mises-Kreis song, all the rituals discussed, including the delicious chocolates, are celebrated. In the final verse of the song – the epigraph to this chapter – Kaufmann wonders whether all these intellectual discussions lead anywhere, while life outside goes on as usual. Was it not easier to follow the stream, instead of attempting to change its course? Only to conclude affirmatively: "And yet there's no tradeoff at hand/ Somehow we must take a stand" (Kaufmann, 1992: 28).[12]

Such rituals established internal coherence and legitimacy, the overlap between the circles meant that a strong internal identity would also become known in other circles. In fact, there was a curious interdependence

---

[11] In German:"Nach Deutschland zog Jüngst ein Volkswirt hin/ Der wollte sich unterfangen / Auf Grund einer venia legendi in Wien / 'ne Professur zu erlangen / Da hörte der Brave die traurige Mär / Die Grenznutzenschul' sei gestorben".

[12] Once again I have used the translation by Arlene Oost-Zinner. In German Kaufmann concludes:"Doch weiss man ja, hier gibts keinen Tausch".

between all these Kreise. The identity of such circles was often defined in opposition to other circles. The Mises Kreis was opposed to the positivism of the Wiener Kreis and the romantic universalism of the Spann Kreis. The Geistkreis was more informal and more cultural than the Mises Kreis. It was also only open to men and restricted to twelve members. A degree of secrecy was not alien to these circles, Mises in his recollections written around 1940 explains: "Outsiders knew nothing of our meetings; they merely saw the works published by the participants" (Mises, 1942/1978: 98). But who in the intellectual elite of Vienna was really an outsider? The Mises Kreis was well known in intellectual circles in Vienna and far abroad, and regularly foreign visitors joined the seminar. The most prominent foreign visitor was perhaps Lionel Robbins, who would later offer Hayek a professorship at the LSE. That who was, and who was not, invited to the meetings was, however, sometimes a sensitive issue becomes instantly clear from the following passage from Popper's autobiography:

The Circle [Wiener Kreis] was so I understood, Schlick's private seminar, meeting on Thursday evenings. Members were simply those whom Schlick invited to join. I was never invited, and I never fished for an invitation. But there were many other groups, meeting in Victor Kraft's or Edgar Zilsel's apartments, and in other places; and there was also Karl Menger's famous 'Mathematische Colloquium'. Several of these groups, of whose existence I had not even heard, invited me to present my criticisms of the central doctrines of the Vienna Circle.

(Popper, 1976: 84)

The reliability of Popper's autobiography has been questioned by some, but it is beyond doubt that the tension between him and the Wiener Kreis was as much social as intellectual. Popper's biographer Hacohen writes about the issue: "his personality made collaboration difficult. Even Popper's defenders [within the Wiener Kreis], Carnap and Kraft, admitted that he was a social problem" (Hacohen, 2000: 209). So we should perhaps also read Popper's claim that he did not know 'these groups' with some suspicion. Perhaps he did know them, but was upset for not being invited to join.[13] His recollections at least make the extent to which rivalry was part of this intellectual environment somewhat clearer.

---

[13] The insider-outsider discussion is also interesting with respect to the very negative essays that both Schumpeter and Hayek have written about intellectuals (Schumpeter, 1943/1976: 145–155; Hayek, 1949). One is tempted to think of the Viennese scholars of the interwar period as (public) intellectuals but in their search for legitimacy they had to distance themselves from outsiders. Their repeated arguments against intellectuals or men of science are perhaps best understood as an attempt to create a professional identity outside academia, they are testimonies of a certain existential angst.

The Wiener Kreis is also interesting to study for its search for legitimacy. Its most famous publication is a manifesto *Wissenschaftliche Weltauffassung*, which is usually translated somewhat awkwardly into 'Scientific World-Conception'. Let us pause for a moment, to realize what is happening here. A group of philosophers (!) who seek to purify science from metaphysics and values publish a manifesto. The pamphlet or manifesto was, and is, a rather revolutionary form: Marx and Engels published a manifesto, and the Italian Futurists published one to declare a revolution in art. It is, however, not the form one would expect from a group of philosophers. In fact, the most traditional of them, Moritz Schlick, was seriously taken aback by the publication (Mulder, 1968). The pamphlet as a scientific form is of course still far from accepted, but understood as an alternative strategy to seek legitimacy it makes sense. It succeeded in providing the Wiener Kreis with a clear identity, and the movement soon attracted followers in other countries (McGill, 1936; Gruen, 1939). It also provided the stimulus for cooperation between members of the Wiener Kreis and the cultural avant-garde in Europe. Especially Otto Neurath and those around him set up connections with the Bauhaus in Weimar and later with the CIAM (Congrès International d'Architecture Moderne). Neurath had also founded a museum for the education of the public through visual statistics, where he and others found employment. If not through the University these communities could build a strong reputation through associations with other social institutions and movements.

Even though there were, thus, clear alternative strategies to establish legitimacy, looking back on the interwar situation in Vienna, it becomes clear that the situation was ultimately unstable. The uncertainty and the lack of official positions made it tempting to migrate. The more senior and successful scholars and artists were the first to migrate, not uncommonly before the political situation in Vienna became critical. Hayek for example, already migrated in 1931, when the circles were still operating as usual. The domestic situation did become more problematic in 1934 when the Dollfuss government came into power. Between 1934 and 1938, the year of the Anschluss, Austria was ruled by the Austrofascists and public life was increasingly restricted. Mises, who expected the worst for the future, left for Geneva in 1933, only to move to New York in 1940. The Wiener Kreis was particularly disturbed by the shooting of Moritz Schlick, by a former student. Although the murder was not motivated by anti-Semitic sentiments, the press did justify the murder in such terms (Stadler, 2003: xvi). Migration was not easy for everyone. Those with little international visibility depended on friends from Vienna who migrated earlier. Karl Popper for example, had to migrate to New Zealand in 1937 where he held a low-prestige job at the university. The adaptation to these foreign *and* academic cultures would require a separate chapter, but it is safe to say that this process was not always easy. Individuals with considerable prestige in the Kreise of Vienna sometimes ended up at the bottom of the ladder at rather marginal universities.

It is tempting to argue that first Austro-fascism and later the Anschluss with Nazi-Germany caused the migration, but that might also be too easy. The social situation for many of the intellectual talents was uncertain even apart from the political situation. On the one hand, the Viennese intellectuals were, as Fürth wrote years later to Hayek, 'spoiled' by the intellectual stimulation around them (Fürth quoted in Hennecke, 2000: 25). On the other hand, they could not obtain an official academic position, they were dependent on not more than a handful of powerful and wealthy individuals, and there were few signs of future improvement. So when Hayek was offered a position at the LSE, he knew what he left behind, but also what he stood to gain. What also helped in his particular case was that he was offered a full professorship. Overall it is doubtful how long Vienna would have been able to retain its greatest talents, even if the political situation would have remained stable.

4 Conversation as scholarly practice

Another central aspect of the Viennese tradition is emerging from our analysis of the Kreise: the importance of the conversation. They were opportunities to meet *face-to-face,* to share ideas, to spar, to argue, to stimulate one another and to interact. The conversation, or the seminar was the center of Viennese intellectual life, it was the scholarly *practice* par excellence for Viennese intellectuals. Not experiments, not armchair observations, not statistical methods, not modeling, but talking. One of the downsides for the historian is that little remains of such conversations. All we have left are some lists of topics discussed during the seminars. In fact if one looks back on the interwar period one notices a peculiar absence of written work. Hayek hardly published anything during the 1920s, and was hired at the LSE based on the *lectures* he delivered there. Mises *wrote* his most important books before and after the flourishing period of his seminar. I certainly do not want to claim that there was no output, but it seems that the conversations were indeed more important than the written word. On the other hand, I do believe that many of the participants of the Viennese Kreise were able to draw on these conversations for the rest of their careers. As such, much of the visible output only came much later, when they migrated to an academic culture in which the written word, and academia itself was far more important than it was in interwar Vienna.

If they did write, it was just as often a contribution to some contemporary political debate as it was an academic paper. In fact, a recent volume that collects the writings of Mises during the interwar period shows that his reflections on political and economic developments far outweigh the more traditional academic-economic issues (Mises, 2002). Additional in-depth research is needed to definitively answer the causal question of whether this different character of their work was caused by the specific intellectual culture of interwar Vienna, I certainly do get that impression from my study of the Wiener Kreise. This impression is further strengthened by the image that Reisch paints of the Wiener Kreis in Vienna. He portrays them as a practical, a political *and* philosophical movement. He shows to what extent this practical and political side of their work was misunderstood and ultimately smothered by the American academic culture and Cold War political pressure (Reisch, 2005).

This, as we will discuss in more detail in Chapter 9, is also evident in Hayek's nostalgia for the Viennese circles and his desire to recreate them when the opportunity presented itself. He realized that to some extent they had been 'in Paradies'. Kaufmann's song with that title emphasizes the negligible role of the economist in a world without scarcity, the Viennese students of civilization, however, thrived in this world of abundance: the abundance of intellectual conversations. It has also become clear that while the intellectual culture might have been ideal, the situation was far from ideal in other respects. The Viennese intellectuals longed for more security, both politically and careerwise. Nonetheless, I think it should make us pause for a moment that some of the major contributions in economics, philosophy, political philosophy and so many other fields originated in an intellectual environment that was free from disciplinary boundaries and other academic constraints. These contributions originated from an environment in which interaction was absolutely central, and in which scholars mainly practiced the art of conversation. In these conversations there were no clear borders between science, society, culture and politics (they were all part of the conversation about civilization). The goals that these scholars consequently pursued were often as much social, cultural and political (civilizational, if you pardon the neologism) as they were academic. But enough for now, about the practice of conversations, let us turn to what they were about.

3

Trapped between ignorance, customs and social forces

The individual in the tradition of the Viennese students of civilization

Wer seine Schranken kennt, der ist der Freie, wer frei sich wähnt, ist seines Wahnes Knecht

Who knows his limits, he is free, who believes he is free, is a slave to delusion
—Franz Grillparzer, *Libussa*, 1848

The individual is the cornerstone of any kind of liberalism. It is the individual who is endowed with agency, a will, preferences, rationality, sometimes with rights, and somewhat less often with duties. In economics, the individual is similarly the central agent; it is he who steers the economy through his decisions on the market. In economics taking the individual as the starting point of an analysis has come to be called methodological individualism. Traditionally this methodological individualism has especially been strong in Austrian economics, whose adherents have put much emphasis on it. It is for example, the first methodological principle discussed in the *Elgar Companion to Austrian Economics* (1994). More broadly in economics the principle gained renewed interest when macro-economics was criticized for its lack of microfoundations during the seventies and eighties of the twentieth century. In the context of my thesis, that the Viennese are best understood as students of civilization, it becomes a pressing issue how the emphasis on the individual is to be reconciled with the civilization of which he or she is part.

It might seem at first sight that methodological individualism is incom-patible with the emphasis on culture, and the limits of the individual. We, however, do know that the Viennese students of civilization have always been critical of the mathematical approach associated with individualist micro and macroeconomics. They have especially been critical of the assumption of rationality and the assumption of full information associ-ated with it. Instead the Viennese have stressed the ignorance, lack of willpower and uncertainty that individuals have to deal with. What has received less attention is the extent to which the Viennese students of civilization have emphasized the limited autonomy of the individual. His or her actions are constrained by his or her own knowledge (or lack thereof) by social forces (such as competition and conformity) and by traditions, customs and morals (summed up in the German word Sitte). What has received even less attention than this limited autonomy, is that the Viennese students of civilization do not merely think of these 'constraints', as, well, constraints. They reject the idea that cultural, social and economic forces merely constrain an already free, rational and autonomous individual. Instead they argue that such social and cultural ties enable the individual to be free, rational and autonomous. What emerges from their work are interacting people who at the same time constrain and enable one another. This puts into question the extent to which methodological individualism helps us to understand the contribution of the Viennese students of civilization. If the explanation of individual behavior is as much dependent on the analysis of these interpersonal norms, beliefs, traditions and institutions (social, cultural and economic) as it is on the decision-making of the individual, we might question to what extent we can truly explain social and economic phenomena starting with the individual.

This insight is not completely new. Madison has put into question the methodological individualism of Hayek and he points out that Hayek was reluctant to use the term (Madison, 1990). Madison also shows the importance of interpersonal processes for the individual. Caldwell in his biography of Hayek notes that Hayek over time emphasized the evolution of norms and traditions more than individual behavior (Caldwell, 2004: 261–288). Hayek himself attempted to distinguish his type of individualism from other types of individualism in his essay 'Individualism: True and False' (1948). The reluctance about individual rationality and reason is, however, an older trait of the Viennese tradition. The importance of the lack of knowledge is an important feature in the work of Menger and the emphasis on cultural and social constraints is especially strong in the work of Wieser. In the work of Mises we can find a somewhat stronger individualism, especially in his attempts to deduce the science of praxeology from some postulates about individual human behavior.

In this chapter, I will show the development in Viennese thought about the individual and his economic, social and cultural ties. I will do so in relation to the (political) context in Vienna, the Habsburg Empire and later Central Europe. The Viennese students of civilization were initially, that is during the 1860s and 70s, quite optimistic about the role of the individual and the extension of human knowledge. That optimism was soon tamed by subsequent political developments in the Habsburg Empire and other European countries, especially by the rise of mass parties and the failure of Austrian political liberalism. Friedrich von Wieser extensively reflected on these developments and he stresses the importance of moral and social forces that constrain and enable the individual. He also argues that certain social elites will be able to break from these constraints. Hayek is more critical of the role of such elites and emphasizes the importance of cultural constraints that ultimately enable the individual to flourish.

1 Emancipating the individual

To reach the starting point of Viennese thinking about the individual we will take a rather strange detour that will take us to the University of Chicago in 1924. There Albion W. Small, today a little-known sociologist, is working hard to establish sociology as a scientific discipline. To prove the importance of the field of sociology, he is writing a history of it, with special attention to its early European beginnings. Albion Small finds an ally who, some sixty years earlier had also struggled to establish economics as a scientific field in Vienna, freed from a priori assumptions and freed from the historians who had claimed that economics was within 'their field'.

Any student of Austrian economics will now expect that Albion Small is writing about Carl Menger. But according to Small, it was not Menger, but Schäffle who was the first to shift the emphasis of economics from things to people. Goods for Schäffle are not ends, but means (Small, 1924).[1] In his first major book Schäffle indeed distinguishes himself from many of his contemporaries, by arguing that neither the optimization of monetary nor that of material wealth is the ultimate goal of economic actors or states. Instead, Schäffle argues, the individual aims to fulfill his complete psychological and physical needs via the goods and people around him. This places the individual and his interaction with fellow men at the center of economic analysis. His or her goals determine what economics is all about, Menger would follow suit. As German economists had grasped before

---

[1] This historical claim that Schäffle was the first to do so is hard to verify, broad as it is. An alternative strategy is to study the shifts in the set-up of economic (text)books. For Smith wealth comes first, Ricardo focuses on the production of goods, while many German midcentury (19th) textbooks start with goods as human needs. Menger and Schäffle on the other hand, start with the goals of the individual.

Schäffle this meant that economics as a science was no longer just serving the state, and advising the state how to maximize the national wealth.[2] The dedication on the title page of Schäffle's main book "For Educated Men of All Classes" makes clear that this is not economics for state officials but for interested laymen (Schäffle, 1861).

Schäffle's economics, however, did not merely start from the individual it also ended with the individual, and this was perhaps a more novel contribution than his starting point:

Economics originates in the inner-lives of people and leads as means for human development back to its origin; therefore its task is not, to produce goods for their own sake, but to bring people the external goods for their worldly development.

(Schäffle, 1861:4)[3]

Menger concludes similarly that: "Man with his needs and his command of the means to satisfy them, is himself the point at which human economic life both begins and ends" (Menger, 1871/1950: 108). This was quite a break with many of their German contemporaries who stressed the development of the Volk and civilization as a whole. That does not mean that the notion of civilization was absent or unimportant for Menger and Schäffle. In fact even for Menger, who is further removed from this German tradition than Schäffle, civilization remains a central concern. In his most important work *Grundsätze der Volkswirtschaftslehre* (1871) the concept of 'Cultur', appropriately translated as civilization by the English translators, is one of the central concepts. This is often obscured because many later economists have mostly been interested in Menger's theory of value, exchange and prices.

Menger discusses in various places the importance of civilization, which he mainly employs to distinguish between different levels of development. In his analysis of the origins of money he, for example, shows how different types of money are appropriate at different levels of civilization. At other instances, he uses the idea of levels of civilization to distinguish those with a more advanced division of labor and especially more knowledge from those who are closer to a primitive state. He writes for example, about the causes

---

[2] An early proponent of this view is Hermann in 'Staatswirthschaftliche Untersuchungen' (1832).

[3] My translation, in German: "In Wahrheit aber geht überall die wirkliche Wirtschaft aus dem inneren Leben der Persönlichkeit hervor und führt als Mittel menschlicher Entwicklung auf dieselbe zurück; denn ihre Aufgabe ist es nicht, Güter um ihrer selbst willen anzuhäufen, sondern dem Menschen die äußeren Mittel seiner irdischen Entfaltung zu bringen."

that have elevated: "mankind from barbarism and misery to civilization and wealth" (Menger, 1871/1950: 73). The most important place, however, in which Menger uses the notion of civilization is his theory of goods. Menger distinguishes between higher- and lower-order goods. Goods of the first order are those that can be directly consumed, such as bread. Goods of the second however cannot be directly consumed, but can be used to produce goods of the first order, flour to bake bread for example. Goods of the third order can be used to produce goods of the second order, and so on. This might sound rather straightforward and of little importance, but for Menger producing goods of higher orders is a prime mark of civilization.

He argues that in the most primitive states men are confined to gathering goods of the first order. As their knowledge progresses they are able to produce these goods instead of gathering them. This enables them to bring the supply of them, to some degree, under their control. The extent to which they are able and willing to produce goods of higher orders is thus dependent on the state of their knowledge. As Menger argues:

Increasing understanding of the causal connections between things and human welfare, and increasing control of the less proximate conditions responsible for human welfare, have led mankind, therefore, from a state of barbarism and the deepest misery to its present stage of civilization and well-being.

(Menger, 1871/1950: 74)

Both Schäffle and Menger emphasize that the division of labor stressed by Smith is *not* the main driving force of economic development. The true cause of progress is the advancement of our knowledge and consequently our ability to produce goods of a higher order and control the production of lower order goods

Menger's argument extends even further; he does not only want to show that the advancement of knowledge is more important than the division of labor. His discussion of the various orders of goods leads straight into the heart of his theory of the economy and economic goods. Menger argues that since the production of these higher order goods takes time it becomes necessary to plan for our needs in advance. This planning for our needs in advance is according to him another mark of civilization: "Wherever we turn among civilized peoples we find a system of large-scale advance provision for the satisfaction of human needs" (Menger, 1871/1950: 79). To do so, all civilized men must become aware and deliberate about their (future) requirements, and the quantity of these goods they will need: "Lacking knowledge of the first, the activity of men would be conducted blindly (...) lacking knowledge of the second their activity would be planless" (Menger, 1871/1950: 80). Or, consider what Schäffle says about the matter: "If human beings, without planning, without calculation, without insight, without foresight, without precautions would act economically, their successes would be limited, without lasting value" (Schäffle, 1861: 22).[4] The process of civilization is thus not only aimed at producing higher order goods through the advancement of scientific knowledge, but it is a cultural and moral process as well. It requires foresight, calculation, planning, or to use an older word, it requires prudence.[5]

Civilization advances when we plan further ahead, when we produce goods of an ever higher order according to Menger. This also leads to an increased division of labor, and not the other way around as Smith had argued: "The further mankind progresses in this direction, the more varied the kinds of goods become, the more varied consequently the occupations, and the more necessary and economic also the progressive division of labor" (Menger, 1871/1950: 73). Most importantly, for Menger, this shows the crucial role of knowledge for a society or community. The community is emancipated from barbarity through this process of the extension of human knowledge about causal processes that allows them to plan for and produce goods of a higher order. The welfare of the individual, the fulfillment of his needs becomes possible through the awareness of and deliberation about future needs.

Menger sketches an optimistic picture of the individual and his community; the community becomes more knowledgeable and is able to plan further ahead. This process does not occur without hiccups. Contrary to those two other marginal thinkers with whom he is often associated, Jevons and Walras, Menger devotes much attention to errors of judgment and planning. He argues, however, that at least some of the uncertainty in human decision-making can be overcome through the extension of knowledge. That optimism is shared by his brother Max Menger.

2 Liberal hopes

Where Carl is most concerned with theory, his brother Max is more practically oriented. Max was actively trying to formulate a solution to

---

[4] My translation, in German: "Wenn der Mensch ohne Ordnung des Planes, ohne Berechnung, ohne Einsicht, ohne Vorsicht, ohne Fürsorge für dauernde Befriedigung wirtschaftlich sich bethätigte, dann wären seine Erfolge gering, ohne Nachhaltigkeit."

[5] See also Elias, who argues that increasing interdependence requires more: 'foresight, more complex self-discipline' (Elias, 1939/2000: 387).

what in the nineteenth century euphemistically had come to be called the 'social question'. This social question was pressing in Vienna mostly because of the recent expansion of the city. The new districts were slums: full of abominable homes with poor hygienic circumstances. Poverty and contagious diseases spread through the city. This social problem had been primarily recognized by socialists and progressive liberals. Intellectually, the socialists had found their eloquent spokesmen in Ferdinand Lasalle, who was very popular in the German-speaking world.[6] He expounded a popular version of Marxism in which one of the central elements was that workers were entitled to their share of the profits. While Carl Menger was active as journalist and economic theorist, his brother Max Menger went directly to the laborers and independent shop-owners to explain to them why socialism was not the way forward (Yagi, 1991). To do so, he needed an alternative solution to the social question. This answer came from Lasalle's main opponent in Germany, the progressive liberal politician Hermann-Schulze Delitschz. He had founded the first 'Genossenschaft' in 1849, a cooperative that was based on the principle of self-help. These ideas formed the basis for Max Menger's lectures for the society of printers in Vienna in 1866.

In his lectures to the society of printers Menger sketches a dreadful picture of everyday life for the workers. Their labor depletes all their energy and stumps their minds. They are in constant danger of being fired, in which case they would be condemned to stealing and begging. On top of that, the work is often dangerous and the workers constantly run the risk of being injured and being unable to continue working (Menger, 1866: 3). Rather than drawing the conclusion from these circumstances, that socialism is the way forward, he attempts to show that there is something fundamentally wrong with socialist programs for the future. These programs deny the basic laws (Gesetze) of the economy. Most importantly they ignore the importance of competition and personal responsibility.[7]

The alternative he offers are 'cooperatives'. Such cooperatives could take on many forms; they could provide insurance against illness or unemployment, they could organize forums for worker-education, and they could

---

[6] Lassalle would later also be influential in founding the German social-democratic movement.

[7] These lectures can also be studied as an early instance of the emerging Austrian school of economics, for one of the crucial objections against the plans of the socialists by Max Menger is that they deny the basic laws of the economy. He then argues that under the socialist plans the right incentives would not be in place to stimulate competition and its associated virtues.

publish newspapers, brochures and magazines. The co-operatives would operate based on small weekly or monthly contributions from the workers or shop owners. Aside from such measures that would support the weak and unfortunate among the workers, Menger argued such cooperatives could also improve the position of the independent workmen as a group. They could do so by setting up 'Volksbanken' that could provide loans to members for mortgages, or to set up small businesses. These 'Volksbanken' would provide an early form of microfinance. Another possibility would be to set up consumer cooperatives, to buy in large quantities and thus save on costs. Through such institutions the people with little capital could compete with big capital. Finally, but certainly not least importantly, Max Menger suggests that these cooperatives could become property developers and thus improve the housing conditions for the workers, and lower middle classes.

These initiatives were based on the concept of 'Selbsthilfe', self-help. It was neither the state nor the generosity of the higher classes that was called upon, but the workers would help themselves and each other. The liberals had a special reason why such a scheme was not based on outside help of any kind. Such cooperatives would stimulate the right virtues, to create 'independent free men' (Menger, 1866:10). The virtues one needed as independent free man were above all those of thrift and self-control (Sparsamkeit und Selbstbeherssschung). Such cooperatives would teach these men first to save from their somewhat meager income and the long-term goals of housing or starting an own business would teach them self-control. Max Menger believed that such cooperatives could even have additional positive effects. Since they would be democratically governed, the members would learn to express their own interests, and more importantly individuals would learn to subordinate their personal interest to the general interest.

These latter concerns fed right into that other central concern of the late nineteenth century, the extension of the right to vote. It was, for the optimistic Max, important that workers would develop into responsible Bürger, liberal individuals with the right virtues. These individuals would no longer be oppressed by church, state or moral weakness. It was this ideal that Max Menger held up to the workers he was lecturing. He claimed that with self-help it would become possible for the workers and the lower middle-class to climb the social ladder and to strengthen the middle-class. "There is no better political school than these cooperatives. Such societies are the proper schools for liberal autonomy" (Menger, 1866:53). Max Menger was aware that such processes would take time and patience, as someone close to him wrote about the housing problem:

A nation [like ours] that has hardly emerged from the primitive conditions of a natural economy cannot be transformed overnight into a nation of shopkeepers. This nation must be educated to thrift, it must learn the value of its own work and the true value of money (...) it must learn how to delay gratification for a safer future.

(Friedmann, quoted in Judson, 1996: 138)

Where Carl Menger was arguing that higher-order goods would lead to higher levels of civilization, on a more practical level the Viennese liberals were promoting liberal autonomy and virtues such as thrift, prudence and self-control.

Carl Menger was never far removed from some of the more practical political issues. In a series of two newspaper articles published in 1890 he explains the compatibility of the idea of self-help with classical political economy.[8] Earlier in his career he had been active as an economic journalist for various Viennese newspapers. Based on his excellent reputation as journalist and economist, he became a full professor at the age of 33, the Emperor asked him to tutor Rudolf, the crown prince (Hamann, 1979; Streissler and Streissler, 1994). It was well-known within the Empire that while Emperor Franz Josef was conservative, his heir Rudolf was more progressive. Rudolf looked with great admiration at France, and especially the ideals of the French revolution. In Menger, he found a mentor who could nourish these liberal sympathies but also dampen them somewhat. Menger attempted to instill in the crown prince the ideals of the Scottish Enlightenment, more than those of the French. He even took Rudolf on a study trip to Glasgow and Edinburgh to show him where Hume and Smith had worked.

The tutorship of Menger developed into a relationship of mutual trust, and Menger became the personal confidant of the crown prince. Through

---

[8] He explains in those articles the relation between self-help and classical political economy: "What distinguishes classical political economy from the school of modern Sozial-Politiker in the social question is by no means its intention. Both recognize the unfavorable economic position of a large part of the workers, both desire a change in favor of the workers, neither rejects state-support on principle. Their opposition is that the Smithian school expects the improvement of the economic position of the workers to come from the elimination of all state and social factors which negatively influence the competitive position and the income of the workers, while it only deems advisable positive interventions of the state in the economy, when the self-help of the workers and their free associations are not sufficient. The Social-Politiker on the other hand – I mean those, who are seriously concerned with the fate of the workers – place more emphasis on positive interventions of the state, all the more since they believe that the majority of the legislation of earlier ages that favored the propertied classes over the poor and weak has already been eliminated" (Menger 1891/1935: 234, my translation).

Menger, Rudolf also came into contact with the founder and editor of the popular liberal newspaper *Neuen Wiener Tagblatts*, Moritz Szeps. The daughter of Moritz Szeps, Bertha has written about this first meeting in her diary (28th of October, 1880):

Today, while we were sitting in Father's Library after lunch, the butler announced Professor Carl Menger. He has often been to the house before, and has spoken to my father about Crown Prince Rudolf, whose tutor and friend he is.

(Szeps, 1938: 25)

Moritz Szeps would provide the outlet for various anonymously published articles throughout the 1880s by the crown prince. The most influential of these articles was 'Der Österreichse Adel und sein konstitutioneller Beruf' (The Austrian nobility and its constitutional vocation). In this article, which was most likely coauthored by Carl Menger, Rudolf was critical about the life-style of the nobility in his time. He believed them to be lazy, unproductive and concerned with obscurities. He argued that they instead should strive to be industrious, curious for knowledge and productive. Rudolf argued that the nobility had the obligation, the social duty, to lead by example: to be the moral leader to the working classes, to promote cultural progress and to support the 'Bildung' of its own sons and daughters and that of other classes. One could say that Rudolf argued for an enlightened leadership by the nobility that would help emancipate the masses. With regard to the virtues to be promoted he agreed largely with Max Menger: autonomy, self-control, industry and thrift (Hamann, 1979: 19).

Both Menger brothers, Carl and Max were promoting a process of emancipation and civilization for the people of the Habsburg Empire. Max believed that this could best be done bottom-up, or at least he was doing so, while the crown prince, under the tutorship of Carl Menger, emphasized the importance of moral leadership by the upper strata of society. Both realized that this would be a slow process, and that suffrage could only be extended slowly (M. Menger, 1873; Streissler, 1994). They hoped that the emancipated and civilized individuals would come to support the new (liberal) constitution of 1861. This constitution was of great political and symbolic value, especially since it limited the influence of the Emperor and increased the power of parliament. Carl and Rudolf had written about the 'constitutional' role of the nobility. Max Menger had written enthusiastically about 'Verfassungsleben', which can be translated as a kind of 'constitutional life', which he hoped would characterize the lifestyle of those individuals with the right to vote in the Empire.

Such dreams would soon shatter. Rudolf, who committed suicide under mysterious circumstances in 1889, would never succeed his father, whose conservative rule would last until 1916. The liberals failed to secure a prolonged majority in parliament. The stock market crash of 1873 practically meant the end of their political influence and the Empire came under control of Christian-conservative coalitions. In fact, such optimistic liberal dreams had always been somewhat tainted.

3 Liberal frustrations

The new constitution of 1861 was liberal in spirit, but the 'Ausgleich' of 1867 did not only reverse some of these developments, it had also split the Empire into two parts. Hungary dominated by the Magyars was granted a large degree of autonomy. Except for the Emperor who still reigned over the entire Empire, the political unity between Austria and Hungary was lost. More importantly, many of the other peoples of the Empire – there were more than a dozen significant ethnic minorities – demanded similar privileges and at the very minimum a more federalist state. The German liberals in Austria, however, favored a centralist system in which their universal principles could dominate and in which parties were not based around regional or national issues, but around universal issues, such as the social and economic order.[9] As Mises summed up just after WWI the German liberals had been mistaken in their hopes for emancipation:

They [the Germans] were far from wanting to Germanize all non-Germans compulsorily, but they thought that this would take place on its own. They believed that every Czech and South Slav would try, even in his own interest, to adopt German culture. That these peoples also could develop independent cultures and independent literatures, that from their midst they could also bring forth independent national characters— they did not think of that at all.

(Mises, 1919/1983: 44–45)

This meant that to secure the constitutional life effectively came to mean to secure a German majority in the parliament. It was difficult however to defend this on purely liberal grounds. Nonetheless Max Menger tried to do so. He argued that for stability and order a German majority was needed. The Germans would be able to prevent the Empire from falling apart. The German peoples had played an important historical role in Austria and

---

[9] Historian of economics Henry W. Spiegel even suggests that Carl Menger was aiming for an economic theory that stressed the common element to all humanity to overcome the nationalistic sentiments in the Empire: "The Austrian School did not start out to rebut Marx, as some students of doctrinal history have surmised, but to fortify the multinational empire of the Habsburgs" (Spiegel, 1983: 532).

they surpassed all the other peoples of Austria in 'number, Bildung, wealth and entrepreneurial spirit' (M. Menger, 1873: 39).[10] This advantage gave them a natural prominent role in the government of Austria according to Max. He also argued that the other peoples had not progressed far enough in terms of civilization and they could only be given an equal place in parliament if: "the Czechs, the Poles and the Slovenes would found a political party, which does not completely ignore the current situation in the world and the political ideas which rule this modern world" (M. Menger, 1873: 41). A cynic might say that Max Menger was willing to grant these peoples political rights if they would become more liberal and centralist. But it is more helpful to think of Max Menger's proposals as a way to retain the unity of the Empire given the nationalist and democratic impulses of the time.

To illustrate this tension, one could also point toward the most liberal and respectable paper in Vienna the *Neue Freie Presse*. This newspaper remained, even during this period of liberal dominance, rather conservative. On democracy, it commented in 1866 (so after the liberal constitution came into place):

Parliamentarianism, which twenty years ago still called to rule the world in the spirit of the educated (Gebildeten), has cleared the field for universal suffrage. The result is that like violence deforms the law, so the raw instincts of the masses terrorize intelligence.

(quoted in Franz, 1955: 387–388)[11]

Even one of the most prominent liberal politicians of the age Ernst von Plener had doubts about liberal democracy. In his 'Erinnerungen' he argues that John Stuart Mill in his *On Liberty* should have been more aware that the masses were trapped in ignorance and lacked an independent will (Plener, 1911: 380–381). A series of articles in the *Neue Freie Presse* gives us another unique insight into the way in which liberals around 1910 looked back on the developments since the revolutionary years of 1848 and 1861. Friedrich von Wieser reflects in a series of articles on these developments. It is safe to say he did so with much frustration, and this frustration ultimately led him and fellow intellectuals to rethink the role of the individual.

For Wieser the 'golden age' of liberalism in Austria was the period between 1861, when the first liberal constitution had come into place,

---

[10] My translation, in German: 'An Volkszal, Bildung, Wolstand und Unternemungsgeist'.

[11] My translation, in German: "Der Parlamentarismus, vor zwanzig Jahren noch berufen, die Welt durch Geist der Gebildeten zu beherrschen, hat den allgemeinen Stimmrecht das Feld geräumt, und wie die Gewalt das Recht gebeugt, so terrorisiert der roh Instinkt der Masse die Intelligenz."

and 1867 when the Ausgleich broke the Empire in half – only seven years, hardly an age indeed. He argues that afterward, social and nationalistic questions had come to dominate politics and those led to both confusion and partisanship, while the unity within the Empire and within the liberal movement was lost (Wieser, 1907a; Wieser, 1907b). During this golden era, there was a progressive unity among the liberals. In parliament, the different powers in society were rightfully represented. This meant in practice that the German minority and the aristocracy were overrepresented relative to their shares of the total population. The landowners still had great power in parliament, but they were willing to support the lead of the liberals in their moderate reform proposals and there seemed to be a consensus about the national interest of Austria. Moreover, this golden age of liberalism was the only moment in which parliament had the full power to form the cabinet, which traditionally had been the Emperor's right; a privilege that the Emperor regained after the Ausgleich in 1867.

Wieser is aware that this golden age had to come to an end, for it rested on outdated foundations, especially since an increasing amount of taxpayers were not represented in parliament at all. An electoral reform that extended voting rights to a larger share of taxpayers had to take place eventually. This also meant that the number of seats in parliament would be increased. The new situation turned out unfavorable for the German liberals, as well as for the country according to Wieser. It led to the formation of many factions and new mass parties such as the Christian socialists and various parties along ethnic or nationalistic lines. This was the first great liberal dilemma in the Empire: while the liberals sought to extend the 'political nation' gradually and broaden the civilized and enlightened middle class, they came to realize that the majority of these to-be enfranchised people would not vote for the liberals.

This however was not the only problem. The new parties that entered parliament, refused to do so on the terms the liberals were expecting of them. They did not primarily seek to promote the general interest, but formed factions around particular class or group interests. It became consequently harder to form stable majorities within parliament. Wieser argues that these new parties were 'regierungsunfähig', unready for and incapable of governing. They did not support the unity of the Empire, in a time when this was much needed. The liberals in Austria found it very hard to deal with these 'interest groups', who flat out denied the liberal rhetoric and belief that politicians should attempt to pursue the general interest of the country. Wieser concludes that the Austrian liberal constitution has failed. It had not succeeded in gradually emancipating the middle classes and shaping them into stable supporters of the liberal constitution and the general interest. Instead, it had caused the country to become fragmented and to lose its sense of direction, a sense of progress. The Empire and its society had not been ready for the liberal constitution and the extension of franchise. Moreover the newly enfranchised groups had lacked the moral leaders who could guide and shape them into good liberal citizens.

Where the Menger brothers had hoped that individuals could be emancipated by the right moral examples, by acquiring the right virtues, and the extension of knowledge, Wieser is more skeptical. He argues that the masses (not individuals) will always need leaders to direct and empower them. Wieser gives up the hope that the masses will be emancipated any time soon, and he emphasizes that only patience, a lot of patience and gradual development can bring these important changes about. Beneath Wieser's analysis lays a conception of liberalism and the constitution that needs to be affirmed time and time again, rather than laying the groundwork once and for all. Just as Max Menger had spoken of a 'constitutional life', Wieser argues that the constitution is a process, which has to be constantly affirmed and organically improved during this process.[12] The constitution is not a procedural prescription; it is a living and continued moral commitment to certain norms and values. Upholding it, cultivating it, therefore requires continued active support by the members of society.

4 Social forces and elites

In Wieser's next work, six lectures on freedom, the law and power, those themes are further developed (Wieser, 1910). In the first lecture on external and internal powers, he argues that contrary to popular belief it is not the external powers (punishment and armed force) that are the most powerful, but that internal forces are much more important. Wieser argues that customs, traditions and the governing morality (Sitte in German) are the most powerful forces in society. These anonymous forces are at the heart of our culture. This moral constitution, if appropriate, is what really upholds our written constitution (Wieser, 1910: 8). The limits set by the law only become important if they are shared in a certain morality, and in traditions. This is also how Wieser praises the economic theorists of the eighteenth century. They started from individuals who maximized their utility, as far as they were "not constrained by the law or customs and

---

[12] For a very similar analysis written by a nonliberal see Fuchs (1949: 5–39).

morality" (Wieser, 1910: 17).[13] At the same time Wieser feels that there is a tension between the idea of an individual constrained by an inner morality, and the freely acting autonomous individual at the heart of modern economic theory.

At some point Wieser wonders: "Isn't it anachronistic that in the age of the psychological novel economic science still presents a caricature?" (Wieser, 1910: 18). Every single individual in the classical theory is able to break habits, to act against the dominant morality and most of all to invent better ways to produce things. These characteristics Wieser argues are only true for a very select few, the leaders in society. Only the leaders are able to pave new ways, to experiment, to act against moral standards and to invent new things and modes of productions. These leaders set an example to the masses. Economic and social processes are thus not characterized by freely moving individuals but rather by elites, followed by the masses.

That these considerations contained a fundamental dilemma about freedom and liberalism was perfectly clear to Wieser. His last lecture, which is devoted to freedom, ends with a personal confession in which the dilemma he and his fellow liberals face at the start of the twentieth century is central. The inner, moral problem is best expressed by the most important writers of the age such as Tolstoy, Nietzsche and Ibsen, argues Wieser. Just as the liberal hero Schiller had written about the dreams of freedom of classical liberalism, these three authors are seeking what it means to be free around 1900, argues Wieser. Their theme is no longer that of external political freedom that the old liberals were fighting for; these modern authors are seeking an inner freedom. They are analyzing what freedom means when most individuals have become absorbed in groups, associations or parties. The opposite of their freedom is no longer political oppression or power as Wieser calls it; the opposite of freedom for these modern authors is the social, the group. The classic liberals had fought against political oppression, but these modern authors are fighting against social and moral oppression.

In his analysis of Nietzsche's work, Wieser concludes that Zarathustra represents individuality, the Übermensch who does not care about the opinions of others but seeks his own individual way. Nietzsche, according to Wieser, understands perfectly well that this path can only be trodden by the few, a small elite endowed with the mental capacities and courage to

---

[13] In German 'soweit er nicht durch Recht und Sitte beschränkt ist'.

live such a life. Tolstoy praises the simple, agrarian life; he worships the common people and their physical life, which contrasts so sharply with his psychic life. This intellectual life, however, is what distinguishes Tolstoy from the people, according to Wieser; it elevates him above the common people, and he becomes their natural leader (Wieser, 1910: 152). Even in the most progressive of these authors, Ibsen, Wieser finds evidence that ultimately Ibsen does not truly believe in the power of the common people. The true belief in the power of morality, the power of Bildung and thus the belief in freedom for all is lost, he concludes melancholically (Wieser, 1910: 153).

The Viennese liberals whom Wieser represents are deeply disappointed about politics and their old ideals. They had truly believed that the masses could be elevated out of their poverty and mental backwardness, that they could learn to be responsible and autonomous individuals. This project failed, and Wieser has little suggestions where to go. His final hope is that the leaders will not turn away from the masses and they will not give up completely. "He, who feels like an Übermensch, does not need to turn away from the masses. He could perform a superhuman task, when he raises the masses, like the prophets have always done" (Wieser, 1910: 154).[14]

This is also the context from which we should understand the theory of economic development of Wieser's pupil Joseph Schumpeter. Schumpeter argues that change in the economy is similarly brought about by an elite of industrial leaders, the captains of industry, who dare to go where no one had gone before. These entrepreneurs would be the economic counterpart to the strong leaders whom Wieser believed to be so necessary in the political domain. This is not the usual way we understand Schumpeter, but if one reads the first German edition *Theorie der wirtschaftlichen Entwicklung* (1911) the links with Wieser's analysis of the political domain are clear. Schumpeter argues that only the elite are able to set the economy in motion, to change it. The majority of people lack the mental strength and energy to change their ways, they: "practice what they have learned, carry on inherited ways, in short they do what everybody else does" (Schumpeter, 1912: 125).[15] Or later: "The effort to stay upright takes up all their energy and eliminates any desire to look further. (. . .) They lack

---

[14] My translation, in German: "Wer sich als Übermensch fühlt, braucht sich nicht von der Masse abzuwenden. Er kann ein übermenschliches Werk tun, indem er die Masse erhebt, wie es die Propheten immer getan haben. "

[15] My translation, in German: "Das Anwenden dessen, was man gelernt hat, das Arbeiten auf den überkommen Grundlagen, das Tun dessen, was alle tun."

any inclination to try something new" (Schumpeter, 1912: 162).[16] The entrepreneur or the 'Mann der Tat' as Schumpeter calls him in the first edition of his *Theory of Economic Development* is completely different:

In the economic sphere also Der Mann der Tat acts on foreign ground with the same determination and the same vigor as on well-known ground. The fact, that something is not yet done, is no reason for him to hesitate. He does not feel those impediments, which otherwise determine the behavior of economic subjects.

(Schumpeter, 1912: 132)[17]

Schumpeter makes it clear that this special class of individuals should lead the economy and wider society: "Not just economically, socially as well the entrepreneur should be at the top of the social pyramid" (Schumpeter, 1912: 525).[18]

At this point, it is crucial to realize how far we have strayed from the widely accepted image of the Austrian school of economics, as an individualist school of thought. The social analysis of Wieser is no longer about individuals, but about a small group of individuals, the elites who empower the masses, and who are responsible for change in society. This development does not so much reflect methodological considerations – although both Wieser and Schumpeter are aware of these – but they are influenced by social developments within the Empire. It reflects a belief that many humans are not accurately described as autonomous, freely moving individuals, even if these are the individuals described by Menger, prone to make mistakes due to a lack of knowledge or uncertainty about the future.

One can, and should, wonder whether Wieser and Schumpeter perhaps represent a deviating current within Viennese economic thought, and whether things will be set back 'in order' by others. Within the Austrian school, there is indeed a tendency to place Schumpeter and the later work by Wieser outside the school, but I believe wrongly so. Instead of rejecting

---

[16] My translation, in German: "Das Bestreben sich aufrechtzuhalten nimmt ihre Kraft in Anspruch und erstickt alle Lust nach weitern Ausblicken (...) Mit neuen zu experimentieren haben sie keine Neigung."

[17] My translation, in German: "Der Mann der Tat handelt auch auf wirtschaftlichen Gebiete außerhalb der gegebenen Bahn mit derselben Entschlossenheit und demselben Nachdruck wie innerhalb des erfahrungsgemäß Gegebenen. Die Tatsache, daß etwas noch nicht getan wurde, wird von ihm nicht als Gegengrund empfunden. Jene Hemmungen, die für die Wirtschaftssubjekte sonst fest Schranken ihres Verhaltens bilden, fühlt er nicht."

[18] My translation, in German: "Nicht nur wirtschaftlich, auch sozial muß der Unternehmer an der Spitze der gesellschaftlichen Pyramide stehen."

this current, both Mises and Hayek build on it and develop it further (I will postpone a discussion of Mises until Chapter 4). What they do not follow, and neither will I, is Wieser's development of these theories in an increasingly nationalistic German direction.

The critical response to Wieser's theories, however, follows quite quickly. In 'Macht oder ökonomisches Gesetz' Böhm-Bawerk poses the question whether social powers could change the course of the economy (Böhm-Bawerk, 1914/1924). He contrasts the idea that economic laws – which he compares to natural laws – with the idea that trade unions, capitalists and government control the economy. Böhm-Bawerk concludes that while such powers could temporarily alter economic outcomes – he especially focuses on the power of trade unions to alter wages – they cannot permanently do so. In the long run, the economic laws, especially the force of competition, would be too strong. Böhm-Bawerk too, however, is forced to recognize that external powers can have all sorts of influences on the economy, especially when they manage to alter the structure of property rights.

What however stands out most in the response of Böhm-Bawerk to those who claim that social powers can alter economic laws and outcomes, is that he resorts to a dichotomy between nature and conscious human interventions. Where in Wieser's work we find a strong emphasis on social norms and customs, Böhm-Bawerk merely contrasts economic laws (eternal and ever-present) with human attempts to overcome these. One could say that Hayek, inspired by the Scottish enlightenment, combines these two elements. On the one hand, he recognizes the strength of economic forces, but on the other hand, he recognizes that they are shaped by cultural norms and that they can only function when they are supported by a morality conducive to a society in which the market is prominent. Wieser claims that the constitution, and political leadership, can only be effective if it is supported by the values of the people, and Hayek extends that theory to the market.

5 Civilization and restraint

Hayek's great achievement in the rethinking of the individual within the Austrian tradition is to show the importance of civilization as a check on the individual. While he shares much of the analysis of Wieser on the importance of morality and traditions, he is more skeptical of the desire, and even the desirability, of some individuals to break free from such constraints. Where Wieser's analysis exhibits a longing for change, for an

ability to break free from certain traditions,[19] Hayek's analysis is characterized by renewed appreciation for these traditions. But before we delve
into the differences, let us focus on how much they share.

Like Wieser, Hayek refutes the idea of 'economic man'. He argues that it
rests on a false rationalistic psychology and that it is a misconception that
Adam Smith believed in such a simplistic notion of 'economic man':

It would be nearer the truth to say that in their view man was by nature lazy and
indolent, improvident and wasteful, and that it was only by the force of circumstances that he could be made to behave economically or carefully to adjust his
means to his ends.

(Hayek, 1948: 11)[20]

In the same essay on individualism he credits Adam Smith for focusing not
on what man might achieve when at his best, but with finding the circumstances under which he could do least harm. It was this interplay between
institutions, norms and individual behavior that is at the heart of the
concerns of Hayek. While Menger was still optimistic about the extension
of human knowledge and the consequent spread of prudent behavior, Hayek
is more concerned with the limits of individual autonomy. In contrast to
Menger's hope for more extensive knowledge, Hayek emphasizes the limits
of human knowledge. Instead of assuming rationality to show the efficiency
of the market, Hayek believes things to be the other way around. He argues
that man is limited in both his concerns and his knowledge:

This is the constitutional limitation of man's knowledge and interests, the fact that
he cannot know more than a tiny part of the whole of society and that therefore all
that can enter into his motives are the immediate effects which his actions will have
in the sphere he knows.

(Hayek, 1948: 14)

These limitations are overcome by social institutions that enable the
individual to do more than he would be able to do alone. They enable
him to communicate, to choose, to learn about the value of various means
and ends and to pursue his own goals within a somewhat broader domain.
Institutions such as social norms, laws, language, the law and markets
enable the individual to act, to act reasonably. Or as Hayek put it later in
life: "Man did not adopt new rules of conduct because he was intelligent.
He became intelligent by submitting to new rules of conduct" (Hayek,

[19] This longing for change is also very strong among the entrepreneurs who are at the heart
of Schumpeter's theory of economic development (Schumpeter, 1912).

[20] Hayek first gave his lecture 'Individualism: True and False' in 1945, it was soon thereafter
reprinted in *Individualism and the Economic Order* (Hayek, 1948).

1982: 163). Market processes are not made possible because man is rational or possesses all the relevant knowledge, but markets make rational behavior possible and knowledge available. Human agency is made possible through these cultural institutions.

If we think back to our first section in which we argued that Menger and Schäffle changed the start and end point of economics, we recognize that in Hayek the individual is not the starting point anymore. What is perhaps even more surprising, he or she is also not the end point. Hayek argues that the submission to constraints is the only way that the individual can contribute to something that is 'greater than himself' (Hayek, 1948: 8); that, which is bigger than himself is the civilization of which he is a part. Hayek argues that civilization makes individual autonomy possible, and that individual actions contribute to that civilization. In no straightforward way can this be called methodological individualism anymore. It also means that Hayek thus responds critically to Böhm-Bawerk. Böhm-Bawerk sketched a dichotomy between power and economic laws, or economic laws and interventions, whether they are social or governmental. Hayek argues that the most important processes happen in between: they are cultural processes. Economic laws are no longer natural; they are cultural or civilizational processes. They are the (unintended) outcomes of human interaction on markets.

Freedom for the Viennese students of civilization, and especially for Hayek, is not the absence of constraints. Freedom for them is enabled by traditions, morality and institutions to which the individual must submit so that he can be free. This view is already present in Menger, although he is much more optimistic about the amount of individual freedom that the development of civilization will allow to everyone. Wieser makes a distinction between elites and masses. The elites are able to move freely, free from constraints, and are able to lead the masses. Hayek on the other hand, is very skeptical about the role of (especially political) elites who attempt to shape society. He has experienced during the interwar period that this might lead to the destruction of the very foundation on which civilization is built, a theme that will occupy us in Chapter 4. He argues on the one hand – following Böhm-Bawerk – that human freedom is necessarily limited by economic, cultural and social forces outside our control. He recognizes on the other hand – following Wieser – that such norms are highly dependent on the support of important parts of society: "we shall never build up a successful free society without that pressure of praise and blame" (Hayek, 1962: 48). What remains constant is the idea that for markets, or laws (the constitution) to function continued support and submission to these institutions is needed. Max Menger's phrase 'constitutional life' captures this continued affirmation and cultivation beautifully.

* * *

Development, civilization and progress, which had seemed to go hand in hand in the nineteenth century, did not do so any longer after the turn of the century and in the following decades. Both intellectual elites and the masses were turning against traditions, including the liberal political tradition. That 'revolt against civilization' will be at the heart of Chapter 4. I believe that this revolt, first analyzed by Wieser, drives the research of both Mises and Hayek, well beyond the interwar years. They sought to understand how the ideals that they, and their predecessors, cherished so much could have become so unpopular. When Mises' wrote in the 1930s about economic theory, he no longer wrote about what it claimed, but rather about why there was some much resistance against it (Mises, 1931). When Hayek gave his inaugural lecture at the London school of Economics, he was concerned with the trend of economic thinking, rather than with problems of economic theory (Hayek, 1933). This he would expand into a project about the use and abuse of reason, which sought to understand how the intellectual currents had turned against the institutions that had enabled cultural and intellectual life to foster in the first place. It is to those themes that we will now turn.

4

The market: civilizing or disciplinary force?

On the role of markets in the civilizing process

Man is not born free. He is born to a new freedom
which he can only achieve by taking up the chains of
tradition and using them, for paradoxically,
these very chains are the instruments of freedom
—Bronislaw Malinowski, *Freedom and Civilization*, 1947

We usually think of the market as a sphere where buyers and sellers come together to trade goods and services. It is, however, well known that within the Viennese tradition the market has also been conceptualized as a sphere where knowledge that is dispersed in society becomes available to other market participants. There is however a third way of thinking about the market, within the Viennese tradition, that has received far less attention. The Viennese students of civilization also think of the market in cultural and moral terms. In Chapter 3, we have seen that the Menger brothers believed that the market could stimulate certain virtues, and in this chapter, we will see how Böhm-Bawerk believes that the existence of interest promotes not only thrift, but more generally temperance. The idea that the market has moral effects is also prominent in the work of Hayek. While certainly not a widely studied phenomenon, the moral effects of markets are occasionally studied by economists, two notable examples are the work of Hirschman (1982) and McCloskey (2006). The question is consequently not whether the market has moral and cultural effects, but what effects these are. In this chapter, it will become clear that during the interwar period the idea that the market has civilizing effects loses ground to the idea that the market disciplines individuals. This transformation takes place in the context of growing dissatisfaction and resistance against the market from the right and the left. Those on the left frequently complain about the irrationality of market processes, and they wish to replace them by more rational economic planning. Those on the romantic right criticize the market process for its unheroic nature, for lacking a soul and promoting the superficial.

The Viennese students of civilization, however, do not seek to put all the blame on these alternative ideologies. They also critically look at their own tradition and the failure of this tradition both intellectually and politically. They argue that the Viennese liberal tradition had lost intellectual (and political) leadership due to its own passivity and a lack of political ideals to strive for once the constitution of 1861 had come into place. Looking back on the period Hayek concludes: "liberal thinkers turned to problems of detail and tended to neglect the development of the general philosophy of liberalism, which in consequence ceased to be a live issue offering scope for general speculation" (Hayek, 1949: 428). But more importantly they come to realize that freedom and markets come at a price, what Popper would call 'the strain of civilization'.

Another Central-European analyst, Karl Polanyi, famously drew the conclusion that society had come to revolt against the free market and that society should once again take control of this market (Polanyi, 1945). The analysis of the Viennese students of civilization of the crisis is not very different; they also observe a social revolt against the market society. But they differ from Polanyi in their response. They seek to resist this revolt; they argue that the market is a fundamental cultural institution of our modern society, an institution that is indispensable for informed decision making and indispensable because of the moral and cultural effects it has. So, through this interwar crisis, they come to a better understanding of the cultural role of markets. The first step in that transformation is their analysis of the failure of socialism and fascism that we will analyze in the next two sections.

1 Socialism and the social engineers

The Viennese students of civilization operated in a hostile environment during the interwar period. The intellectual atmosphere at the university was dominated by the German-Romanticist Othmar Spann, because Wieser's successor Hans Mayer was unable to be a serious counterweight (see also Craver, 1986). More importantly, the intellectual and political sphere breathed socialism. The Viennese students of civilization, sympathetic to liberalism, started to wonder how the tables had turned on liberalism, and why socialism had been so successful in capturing the minds of the people.

Both Mises and Hayek argue that socialism has been successful mainly because it provides a utopian alternative to the real world, full of suffering. The promise to relieve this worldly suffering has attracted many to socialism. That in itself is not a new phenomenon. Menger had already argued that the classical economists were just as concerned with the welfare of the common man as the 'Sozial-Politiker' of his day (see n. 8 of chap. 3). And Hayek argues that putting an end to worldly suffering was often the motivation for economic inquiry in the first place. Hayek approvingly quotes Pigou to that extent: "It is not wonder, but the social enthusiasm which revolts from the sordidness of mean streets and the joylessness of withered lives that is the beginning of economic science" (Pigou, quoted in Hayek, 1933: 123). To continue somewhat exaggerated perhaps: "It is probably no exaggeration to say that economics developed mainly as the outcome of the investigation and refutation of successive Utopian proposals" (Hayek, 1933: 123).

What is interesting for our present concerns is that Hayek starts to develop a more general critique of the mindset represented by these Utopian proposals. In the work of Wieser, we already find caution about what is to be expected of the social scientist. He argues that the powers of the social scientist to bring about social change are limited by the customs, traditions and morality of the period (Wieser, 1910).[1] Along these lines Hayek starts to develop a criticism of what he calls 'scientism': "the mechanical and uncritical application of habits of thought to fields different from those in which they have been formed" (Hayek, 1952: 16).[2] This 'scientistic' mindset is the mindset of the engineer who wishes to construct markets or other types of social order, in the same way that the engineer would construct a bridge.[3] In Vienna, this type of scientism was best exemplified by Otto Neurath, member of the 'Wiener Kreis'. During the 1920s he developed various large-scale projects to improve the housing conditions and the education of the working class. In his scholarly work, he argues that progress in the social science could be used for social engineering. His idea was that the extension and spread of social knowledge would lead to an increasing rationalization of society and the spread of 'scientific' view of the world (Hahn, Neurath and Carnap, 1929).

---

[1] This is discussed in more detail in Chapter 6.

[2] Hayek publishes these views in a series of articles during the 1940s, but they are published in book form in 1952.

[3] That Hayek opposes the idea of constructing markets marks a clear difference between him and later neoliberals, on constructing markets see also Zuidhof (2011).

The belief that social orders can be planned and constructed in a similar manner to technology rests according to Hayek on two fundamentally flawed assumptions. The first of these assumptions is that knowledge about society is of the same type as knowledge about the natural world. From this false assumption it is often concluded that the methods of natural science can be applied to the study of society. Hayek argues on the contrary that since social behavior is purposeful behavior, and human beings act upon their own subjective knowledge (rather than objective knowledge), this subjective knowledge is the primary material of the social scientist. The other assumption is that every type of order in society must be the result of some form of organization. Or as Hayek states, following the formulation by Mises: "we refuse to recognize that society is an organism and not an organization [and that this organism or system], without our knowledge, and long before we tried to understand it, solved problems the existence of which we did not even recognize" (Hayek, 1933: 130).

It is this type of spontaneous organization that Hayek will redefine as civilization in his later work. The essential building blocks for this theory are already in place during his work on the 'Counter-Revolution of Science', during the late 1930s and early 40s. It is during this period that Hayek increasingly starts to emphasize that many economic institutions and the very order existent in the economy is *not* planned, *not* constructed, and *not* willed by any single mind (Hayek, 1933: 130). His argument, and that is more important here, also contains grounds for believing that such spontaneous or unorganized order is much harder to understand and hence to control than other types of order (he will later call such orders complex orders). This means consequently that economic knowledge does not infrequently lead to the conclusion that nothing can be done about the evil in the world, or that we do not yet know how socials ills can be cured or prevented. Hayek argues that this quickly frustrates the laymen, who expect practical solutions from the economist. The sincere economist therefore faces the difficult task of demonstrating: "inconsistencies in a kind of ordinary reasoning which everybody employs and the validity of which no one would ever doubt" (Hayek, 1933: 128). The economist will have good reason to disagree with almost every proposal: "which spring most readily and regularly to the lay mind" (Hayek, 1933: 133). Mises had already shown this with a practical example about the dangers of capital consumption:

To see the weakness of a policy which raises the consumption of the masses at the cost of existing capital wealth, and thus sacrifices the future to the present, and to recognize the nature of this policy, requires deeper insight than that vouchsafed to statesmen and politicians or to the masses who have put them into power.

(Mises, 1922/1951: 458)[4]

This means that laymen and political movements alike are prone to revolt against economic knowledge. And this is precisely what was happening in Vienna during the interwar years according to Hayek and Mises.[5] It is not just that socialism offers a utopian vision, but also that liberalism and economics emphasize the complexity of understanding and improving the world.

Schumpeter, in his *Capitalism, Socialism, and Democracy* also examines the growing hostility toward capitalism. In Schumpeter's analysis there is a sharp distinction between the masses and the elite:

the mass of the people never develops definite opinions on its own initiative (...) [the] case [in favor of capitalism] could never be made simple. People at large would have to be possessed of an insight and power of analysis which are altogether beyond them.

(Schumpeter, 1943/1976: 144)

Schumpeter argues that the root of the problem does not lie with the masses (passive as they are). To foster the growing resentments there has to be a social group with an active interest to work up and organize these masses. This group according to Schumpeter is the intellectual class. Mises and Hayek would similarly write derogatory essays about the influence of intellectuals – those 'second-hand dealers in ideas' – which have helped to promote socialist ideas. This elitism, the resentment against the masses and their 'intellectual' leaders, should be understood in its Viennese context, in which it already emerged in Wieser's work in response to developments around the turn of the century. The social and political developments in Vienna during the interwar years led to further distrust.

Hayek would transform this criticism of lay understanding, to a larger argument about a general tendency to overestimate the powers of the human mind. This belief in the rationalism of the individual or the expert, and his capability to improve the world around him would lead to proposals to plan the economy and to improve our morality. Such a belief is

---

[4] Mises' esteem of the masses, like that of Wieser and Schumpeter, is rather low: "It is true that the masses do not think. But just for this reason they follow those who do think. The intellectual guidance of humanity belongs to the very few who think for themselves" (Mises, 1922/1951: 508).

[5] See also Michael Polanyi's essays collected in *Contempt of Freedom*, a fellow Viennese with interests closer to the natural sciences.

for Hayek nothing short of hubris. It overestimates how much the human mind could do, and underestimates how much we rely on norms and interpersonal interaction. In short, it underestimated the importance of cultural institutions, such as the market.

2 The return of natural instincts

The political scene of the interwar period was not just dominated by socialism and the belief in scientific social programs of these social engineers, although they were definitely the dominant force during the 1920s. During WWI and the 1930s – the period before and after the twenties – the force of romantic and nationalistic politics was at least as strong. This other intellectual and political current would provide a kind of opposite pole to socialism in Hayek's theory of civilization and markets.

The irrational nature of war and its strong nationalistic sentiments were hard to grasp for the liberals, who had promoted a measured outlook on life. The total war waged between what appeared to be civilized nations were beyond their understanding. Did countries and individuals not have much more to gain from cooperation and trade with one another? To make matters worse, there were some German intellectuals who glorified the experience at the front, the 'Fronterlebnis'. Famous in the German-speaking world are the accounts of Ernst Jünger that glorified the values of war: the bravery, the courage and the sacrifice. The war for Jünger had shown what had been lost during the rise of a soulless capitalism, and he preached a politics that would seek a return to these values.[6]

Finding a response to these sentiments proved very difficult for the liberals in Vienna. Ludwig von Mises, who had served as an officer in the Habsburg army, attempts to reflect on WWI in 1919. But in the preface of 'Nation, Staat und Wirtschaft' he cautions the reader that: "it exceeds human capacity to treat vital questions of one's time without anger and

---

[6] The socialists interpreted the war rather as a late stage of capitalism. Some of them already noted tendencies toward the order of the future. The true violent nature of capitalism had been exposed by the War they argued, just as the war had shown the inevitable rise of planning. During the war, central planning had been brought to a new level by Walther Rathenau in Germany, who was not only the president of the prestigious AEG company, but who had also planned the German raw materials and labor supplies during the war, when both became increasingly scarce because of a naval blockade. He was a hero to many after the war and he would inspire the Viennese economist Otto Neurath to develop a similar type of planning for the Habsburg army. Neurath, among many others, was convinced that war-time planning would provide a kind of bridge from capitalism to a fully planned peace-time economy (Neurath, 1916/2004; Neurath, 1917/2004).

partiality" (Mises, 1919/1983: vii).[7] Much of his book can be read as an attempt to come to grips with nationalist sentiments within a more or less rationalistic framework. At times, Mises is quite perceptive of previous flaws in liberal beliefs, but overall he struggles to make sense of irrational, nationalistic and militaristic tendencies of so many people all over Europe. The explanation that Mises offers is that the romantic longing central to imperialist and aggressive war politics might have been caused by the fact that the liberal age had increased material welfare, but it had not enriched inner life; it might have even impoverished it. This might explain some of the romantic sentiments, but they would not satisfy those same sentiments: "The romantic longing for wild adventures, for quarreling and freedom from external restraint, is itself only a sign of inner emptiness; it clings to the superficial and does not strive for depth" (Mises, 1919/1983: 248–249). Only to observe a little later that: "Warlike activity assures a man of that deep satisfaction aroused by the highest straining of all forces in resistance to external dangers (...) in his feelings man is always an imperialist" (Mises, 1919/1983: 249–250).

That ambiguity, if not confusion, about the outburst of imperialistic sentiments is characteristic of Mises' account. Should we acknowledge such urges as a fundamental part of human beings? And if so should they be canalized, or repressed? Just after the admission that they might give some satisfaction, he immediately claims that: "Reason forbids giving free rein to feelings. To want to beat the world to ruins to let a romantic longing exhaust itself contradicts the simplest deliberation so much that no word need be wasted on it" (Mises, 1919/1983: 248–249).

Schumpeter's analysis of the war is strikingly similar, although arguably much clearer. He argues that imperialism and its associated instincts of conquest and domination have been carried over from previous times. They are atavistic sentiments, cultural remnants of earlier levels of civilization, which have lost their utility (Schumpeter, 1919/1951: 82–83).[8] These sentiments were kept alive by certain ruling classes and groups in society who stood to gain from war. Schumpeter is much more optimistic than Mises that such sentiments will disappear over time: "It [imperialism] tends to disappear as an element of habitual emotional reaction, because of progressive rationalization of life and mind" (Schumpeter, 1919/1951: 85). This allows Schumpeter to show that imperialism is not an essential

---

[7] The 1983 translation of this book by Leland B. Yeager is used.
[8] Schumpeter's essay from this period have been collected and translated by Heinz Norden and Paul M. Sweezy, I use their translation from 1951 here.

part, or as the socialists claimed a (final) phase of capitalism, but rather an atavistic element of European culture.

For Schumpeter the emerging nationalism is also a late manifestation of such sentiments: "In conservatives, nationalism in general is understandable as an inherited orientation, as a mutation of the battle instincts of the medieval knights, and finally as a political stalking horse on the domestic scene" (Schumpeter, 1919/1951: 125). Such progressive optimism is more in line with nineteenth century liberalism, or the optimism of the socialists about the rationalization of our life. During the first half of the twentieth century, it seems strangely out of place. Schumpeter's analysis is unable to account for the enormous scale of WWI. Moreover, the outburst of imperialism in Germany was often considered the outcome of a period of progress and the very successful second industrial revolution, rather than a counter-reaction to it. His analysis surely has little predictive power for the aggressive nationalism that would dominate the politics of the 1930s. Mises clearly disagrees with Schumpeter on this point; he does not want to write off these sentiments as mere cultural atavisms. He writes in seemingly direct response to Schumpeter, whose very wording he adopts:

[Warlike activity] is no mere atavistic reawakening of impulses and instincts that have lost their utility in changed circumstances. The inner feeling of happiness aroused not by victory and revenge but rather by struggle and danger originates in the vivid perception that exigency compels the person to the highest deployment of forces of which he is capable and that it makes everything that lies within him become effective.

(Mises, 1919/1983: 249)

This deep satisfaction is created by the 'enrapturing experience of the deed', according to Mises.[9] We will see that Hayek agrees with Mises and refuses to write off such sentiments or urges as cultural atavisms.

Hayek himself never wrote extensively on imperialism and the sentiments underlying it. Nonetheless he was sensitive to the importance of

---

[9] If one examines Schumpeter's theory of the entrepreneur in its original German version one cannot but conclude that Schumpeter is aware of the continued presence of such sentiments. The motivation of the entrepreneur in his theory of economic development seems also to lie in the will to create and dominate. Schumpeter's praises the will-power of the entrepreneurial spirits and claims that: "[T]he joy of creation, of giving new forms to the economic things rests on the same basis as the creative acts of the artist" (Schumpeter, 1919/2006: 142). My translation, in German: "Die Freude am Neugestalten, am Schaffen neuer Formen der wirtschaftlichen Dinge ruht auf ganz denselben Grundlagen wie das schöpferische Tun des Künstlers". And later: "What such individuals want are more and more deeds, ever more victories" (Schumpeter, 1919/2006: 146). My translation, in German: "Was solche Individualitäten wollen, sind weitere und immer weitere Taten, immer neue Siege."

instincts and their importance in politics. He discusses such sentiments mainly in relation to his discussions with Freudians in Vienna during the 1920s. According to Hayek, Freud argued that we should get rid of most of the existing morality since it merely repressed our instincts and would eventually give rise to psychological problems. Or in Hayek's much more forceful words: "his [Freud's] basic aim of undoing the culturally acquired repressions and freeing the natural drives, has opened the most fatal attack on the basis of all civilization" (Hayek, 1982: 174). His experience is that Freud's students claimed that we should get rid of the artificial cultural constraints, which repressed the individual. The main problem with this analysis is that, as Hayek sometimes reluctantly acknowledges, it runs contrary to Freud most important work on the subject 'Civilization and its Discontents'. Consider for example, this fragment from one of the interviews Hayek gave late in his life:

HAYEK: Man was civilized very much against his wishes. It's reallythe innate
               instincts which are coming out. (laughter)
LEO ROSTEN: That's a very Freudian statement.
HAYEK: In a way. Well, it's Freudian and anti-Freudian, because Freud, of
               course, wanted to relieve us of these repressions, and my argument
               is that by these repressions we became civilized.
ROSTEN: His whole point is that civilization is the repression of guilt, and that
               without that you can't have–
HAYEK: In his old age, of course.
ROSTEN: – and the repression of aggression, of the hostility.
HAYEK: When he wrote 'Civilization and Its Discontents', he was already
               getting upset by what his pupils were making of his original ideas.
                                                            (Hayek, 1979: 75–76)

In the 'Civilization and its Discontents' – as Rosten attempts to point out to Hayek – Freud argues that civilization means constraining ourselves. Freud argues that morality works through a sense of guilt, and that restraint and hence civilization is created and upheld by this sense of guilt. As civilization progresses, this sense of guilt has to be intensified or heightened. This is in line with Hayek's ideas, as we will see later, but Hayek refuses to acknowledge this. This is partly due to the fact that Hayek's ideas of Freud's position are inspired by his discussion with students of Freud during the 1920s rather than with the later Freud (Hayek, 1979: 74). More importantly the cultural significance of Freudian theory has indeed been more in the direction that Hayek suggests. The influential idea that we should rid ourselves of the (bourgeois) morality of previous generations had other origins than just Freud. One could think of

Nietzsche who wrote extensively on the paradoxes and repression caused by civilization and more generally about the revolt against the modern world.[10] In *On the Genealogy of Morality* he argues that civilization has made the individual sick and alienated from his true nature (Nietzsche, 1887/2006: 70–71). So even though Hayek might be attributing some views to Freud, which Freud perhaps did not hold at the time, the intellectual currents that he was opposing were real.

3 Markets and the civilizing process

It is so important to sketch out these competing poles because Hayek would develop his theory of the market and its moral effects in response to these two positions. Between the position that was based on a strong rationalism from which it was argued that society and markets should be designed and the position that argued that modern civilization put too many constraints on the individual from which it was argued that individuals should be free to follow their urges and instincts.[11] Between these two opposing poles Hayek places culture. And he argues that cultural constraints, such as those that originate from the market, are neither natural, nor artificial, but they emerge as the unintended consequence of human interaction.[12] But he

---

[10] See also the essays collected by Sternhell (1996), especially the essay by Wistrich in that volume.

[11] In his later work Hayek would come to call these poles physis (natural) and nomos (man-made) (Hayek, 1988: 145), between which he sought to position the cultural (see also Gray, 1984: 29).

[12] It is an interesting side issue when this view developed in Hayek's intellectual journey. It would be too much of a digression into Hayek scholarship to consider now completely how early these ideas formed. The place where Hayek most extensively discusses them is in the lecture 'Three Sources of Value', reprinted in the third volume of 'Law, Legislation and Liberty' (1982). But a combined reading of 'The Trend of Economic Thinking' (1933) and his work on the *Counterrevolution in Science* (1952), the essay 'Individualism: True and False' (1948) and certain passages in *The Road to Serfdom* (1944) (the last three were originally conceived as a project called 'The Use and Abuse of Reason') have convinced me that Hayek must already have been quite close to the position expounded in this lecture relatively early in his career. Although not all elements might have had their definite place yet, he was clearly already thinking along the lines developed in the values essay. Hennecke, in his German biography of Hayek, observes that Hayek starts connecting his economic work to themes of the constitution and civilization in writing as early as 1931 (Hennecke, 2000: 85–91).

Another piece of evidence that convinces me that Hayek must already have been quite close to this position around say 1945 is that his position is congruent with the Austrian tradition of thought in which he grew up. The central claim of his lecture is that: "We owe our freedom to restraints of freedom" (Hayek, 1982: 163). An idea that is captured in the poem by the Austrian poet Grillparzer in the epigraph of the previous chapter. But the

comes to realize that these constraints, are real constraints that individuals would like to throw off. It is this view that is on his mind in the lecture 'Three Sources of Human Values' that is reprinted as postscript to *Law, Legislation and Liberty*, but Hayek developed his theory in the 1930s and 1940s. Let us examine in more detail the steps he takes.

The first two steps we have seen earlier, the analysis of the success of socialism and fascism and secondly the analysis of the resistance against economics – this resistance against economics is further developed in *The Road to Serfdom* and 'Individualism: True and False' into an analysis of the resistance against any cultural institution that is not rationally planned or justified. In the chapter 'Material Conditions and Ideal Ends' that can be considered the final chapter of *The Road to Serfdom*, Hayek takes the next steps. He argues that people of his time are decidedly unwilling to sacrifice any of their demands for economic considerations and that they are particularly intolerant of any restraint upon their immediate ambitions. They are: "unwilling to bow to economic necessities" (Hayek, 1944: 203). It is this unwillingness to accept restraint and to accept some of the ills of the market that has caused men to flock to utopian ideologies such as socialism and fascism. As he writes some years earlier: "If free competition from time to time inevitably endangers the livelihood of some, and if security to all could be attained only be restricting the freedom of economic activity, then that price did not appear too high" (Hayek, 1939: 1). Hayek realizes very well that markets have negative consequences for some, and that they frustrate some of the ambitions that individuals hold, but it is only by accepting these restrictions, these restraints, that in the long run we can fulfill those ambitions. That is however not how his generation feels: "Man has come to hate, and to revolt against, the impersonal forces of the market to which in the past he submitted" (Hayek, 1944: 203).

That line of thought is continued in the 'Individualism: True and False', originally delivered as a lecture in December 1945. There he analyzes the conflict between our personal sense of justice and the impersonal decisions

---

analysis as mentioned before has much in common with the analysis of Freud in *Civilization and its Discontents* (1930), although the conclusions differ somewhat. The similarity with another work from that same intellectual environment, *Civilization and Freedom* (1947) by anthropologist Bronisław Malinowski, both in purpose and in actual analysis is striking. And one could also point to the similarity of both Hayek's purpose and analysis with fellow Viennese thinker Karl Popper especially with his work in *The Open Society and its Enemies* (1945). These similarities further pursued later in this chapter and in Chapter 6.

of the market. Individuals frequently feel that on the market not everyone is rewarded based on merit, but argues Hayek: "we must face the fact that the preservation of individual freedom is incompatible with a full satisfaction of our views of distributive justice" (Hayek, 1948: 22). But it is not just our sense of justice that is violated on markets:

The individual, in participating in social processes, must be ready and willing to adjust himself to changes and to submit to conventions which are not the result of intelligent design, whose justification in the particular instance may not be recognizable, and which to him will often appear unintelligible and irrational.

(Hayek, 1948: 22)

As if to drive the point home Hayek puts it even more forcefully a little later in that same essay:

The necessity (. . .) of the individual submitting to the anonymous and seemingly irrational forces of society—a submission which must include not only the acceptance of rules of behavior as valid without examining what depends in the particular instance on their being observed but also a readiness to adjust himself to changes which may profoundly affect his fortunes and opportunities and the causes of which may be altogether unintelligible to him.

(Hayek, 1948: 24)

Although Hayek is never generous with examples in his work, it becomes clear from the essay that the impersonal forces of the market are certainly part of these 'forces of society'. But it is clear that he also refers to the norms and social customs that are so prominent in the work of Wieser. The language has changed though, it is no longer a theory of masses and elites, but a theory about the relation of the individual to his culture.[13]

---

[13] Mises is far less prone to use the language of submission and discipline when he talks about market processes. Aside from occasional references there is one notable instance in which Mises emphasizes the discipline of the market. In a section on work and wages he writes: "Wage rate fluctuations are the device by means of which the sovereignty of the consumers manifests itself on the labor market. They are the measure adopted for the allocation of labor to the various branches of production. They penalize disobedience by cutting wage rates in the comparatively overmanned branches and recompense obedience by raising wage rates in the comparatively undermanned branches. They thus submit the individual to a harsh social pressure. It is obvious that they indirectly limit the individual's freedom to choose his occupation. But this coercion is not rigid. It leaves to the individual a margin in the limits of which he can choose between what suits him better and what less. Within this orbit he is free to act of his own accord. This amount of freedom is the maximum of freedom that an individual can enjoy in the framework of the social division of labor, and this amount of coercion is the minimum of coercion that is indispensable for the preservation of the system of social cooperation" (Mises, 1949/2007: 599–600).

Hayek makes that very clear when he argues that through the acceptance of these conventions and impersonal forces that: "by thus submitting we are every day helping to build something that is greater than anyone of us can fully comprehend" (Hayek, 1944: 204). That greater thing is the culture that we share, our civilization of which markets are an important part. Such an analysis is also present in the work of Mises:

Men who create peace and standards of conduct are only concerned to provide for the needs of the coming hours, days, years; that they are, at the same time, working to build a great structure like human society, escapes their notice.

(Mises, 1922/1951: 513)[14]

But would individuals be willing to restrain themselves and submit to norms and traditions for this greater goal?

It is that willingness that is quickly disappearing in the modern age, argues Hayek. It is not just disappearing in the economic sphere, but it is also evident in the efforts to create and artificial language, to do away with moral conventions and the efforts to rationalize the process of the growth of knowledge. All these processes are cultural processes that benefit from the contributions of individuals that help to create something that is greater than themselves: a language, a market, morality, a body of knowledge, or indeed a society (Hayek, 1948: 25). The effort to replace these with engineered or constructed systems are all part of an unjustified belief in Reason and a false individualism argues Hayek. But that 'false' individualism has been able to gain ground not just for intellectual reasons, but also because traditional sources for the support of these traditions and conventions have gradually disappeared.

The support of these norms and conventions, and even the acceptance of seemingly irrational forces was previously sustained by institutions such as the church, the family and civil society. Civil society has in particular suffered from the rise of the modern nation-state with its centralizing tendencies and the replacement of regional conventions, norms and traditions by national standards. Religion no longer had the status it once had, traditional hierarchies were no longer respected, and the older liberal philosophy of responsibility was clearly losing ground, family life was no longer as prominent as it had been.

---

[14] Hayek has at other times criticized Mises for his rationalism, and indeed in the same book 'Socialism' one can find statements that suggest that cultural norms were designed by human beings: "Human society is an issue of the mind. Social co-operation must first be conceived, then willed, then realized in action" (Mises, 1922/51: 509). See also the foreword by Hayek to the Liberty Fund re-issue of Mises's *Socialism* (Hayek, 1981).

Hayek's analysis of these matters focuses on the role of the church and religion. He argues that "the declining influence of religion is undoubtedly one major cause of our present lack of intellectual and moral orientation" (Hayek, 1948: 2). In the interesting interviews with Hayek late in his life, he was repeatedly asked whether his call for the acceptance of a moral framework necessary for a free society had any connection to religion. In his answers, an interesting tension emerges. He says, on the one hand, that he is not a Christian, and was brought up in a more or less nonreligious family. On the other hand, he realizes that his call for an uncritical belief in moral principles can be thought of as a religious belief (Hayek, 1979: 240). He furthermore argues that religion might be crucial to instill certain values in people: "I've never publicly argued against religion because I agree that probably most people need it. It is probably the only way in which certain things, certain traditions, can be maintained which are essential" (Hayek, 1979: 487). Even though religion lost much of legitimacy in the modern world, it does promote the right values to sustain civilization.

Schumpeter pays more attention to the morals of the bourgeois family and how these are changing:

Family life and parenthood mean less than they meant before and hence are less powerful molders of behavior; the rebellious son or daughter who professes contempt for 'Victorian' standards is, however incorrectly, expressing an undeniable truth.

(Schumpeter, 1943/1976: 157)

The analysis of Schumpeter follows closely the development of the 'Buddenbrooks' family, Thomas Mann's novel about the family of industrial entrepreneurs with the same name. That novel describes how values such as prudence, temperance, industriousness erode over three generations. Not surprisingly, the novel was often read as a story about modern society, rather than just a family history. This novel was also discussed in the meeting of the Geistkreis of which Hayek was a prominent member (Engel-Janosi, 1974: 126).

Mises, too, examines the origins of the resentments against the market process. On the one hand, he traces anticapitalist sentiments back to ancient times (Mises, 1931: 288). On the other hand, he realizes that it is a particularly modern problem that a rational justification for every norm is necessary. When he discusses the norm of private property this becomes clear. In the metaphysical natural law tradition, property was always believed to be sacred. Liberalism has destroyed this belief, it has: "debased property into a utilitarian worldly matter". The respect for property once a sacred issue has been shattered, and property has become a means toward other goals. "What was once certain becomes uncertain; right and wrong, good and evil," traditional distinctions become uncertain (Mises, 1922/51: 513). For Mises it was now up the liberals to show the importance of the respect of property and other conventions, norms and laws.

Hayek was less certain that justifications that would satisfy modern individuals could be provided in every instance. That comes out clearly in his discussion of the gold standard: "Government has always destroyed the monetary systems. It was tolerable so long as government was under the discipline of the gold standard, which prevented it from doing too much harm; but now the gold standard has irrevocably been destroyed, because, in part, I admit, it depended on certain superstitions which you cannot restore" (Hayek, 1982: 156). The gold standard, part of the international monetary markets in the nineteenth century, secured discipline. This discipline restricted governments in their spending and artificial creation of money. The problem with the gold standard was that on purely rational grounds it did not hold up. It was based on the arbitrary choice of gold, as a privileged metal. Like other widely shared beliefs in the nineteenth century it collapsed when it came under rational scrutiny. The only solution to restore discipline is through the market, and thus Hayek continues: "I don't think there's any chance of getting good money again unless we take the monopoly of issuing money from government and hand it over to competitive private industry" (Hayek, 1982: 156-7). Competition is supposed to instill the values previously taught, shared and cultivated. Competition will discipline individuals and governments, where this was previously done by widely shared fictitious beliefs. An interesting analogy is that the Viennese students of civilization believed that something similar was true about the conclusions of the classical economists. Hayek and Mises, as well as their teacher Wieser argued that the conclusions of the classical school were sound, but they had been based on fictions (Wieser, 1910; Mises, 1922/51: 512–515; Hayek, 1933).

4 A price worth paying

The interwar experience of the revolt against markets from both the right and the left thus lead to a new way of thinking about markets for Hayek. They require submission and discipline the individual. This is very clear from Hayek's late writings, but as we saw earlier he held these views already during the 1940s when he was working on 'The Abuse of Reason' project of which both *The Road the Serfdom* and the essay on individualism were outcomes. This leads Hayek to a surprising conclusion, especially with our modern view of freedom as the lack of restraints for the individual. Freedom according to Hayek is only possible in a civilized world (an idea, which also according to himself distinguishes him from anarchists). Hayek is aware of a certain paradox contained within this idea of freedom: "Man has been civilized very much against his wishes" (Hayek, 1982: 168). Civilization, in fact freedom itself, comes at a price, the price of submitting ourselves to customs, traditions and values that we cannot rationally understand. As Hayek stresses time and again, his concept of freedom defends the individual from the arbitrary will of others, but it does not defend him from the impersonal forces of the market, social norms, a governing morality or the acceptance of not fully understood and hence incompletely justified norms. It is thus a rather limited or constrained idea of freedom, more limited than the type of freedom Wieser and Schumpeter reserved for the elite, and much more limited than the freedom of life-style that John Stuart Mill promotes in his famous essay *On Liberty*. Hayek argues that these constraints are worth the price, because our intelligence, our civilization depends on it. Even stronger still, our own limitations, our limited rationality and intelligence are the reasons for accepting these restraints in the first place. That is how Hayek concludes his essay on individualism. Earlier in that essay he had summed it up even stronger:

[True individualism] is a product of an acute consciousness of the limitations of the individual mind which induces an attitude of humility toward the impersonal and anonymous social process by which individuals help to create things greater than they know.

(Hayek, 1948: 8)

The acceptance of these impersonal and anonymous forces however, requires submission and acceptance of the individual; it is not free. That analysis has much in common with that of Karl Popper in *The Open Society and its Enemies* (1945). In that book Popper coins the term: 'the strain of civilization'. Popper first comes to speak of the concept in his discussion of Plato who according to Popper: "found that his contemporaries were suffering under a severe strain, and that this strain was due to the social revolution which had begun with the rise of democracy and individualism" (Popper, 1945: 150). The individual responsibility associated with civilization and progress was experienced as a strain by many individuals. Plato – similar to socialist or romantic politicians and intellectuals during the twentieth century – promised to relieve this strain, not realizing that this would destroy that very civilization. Popper believes that Plato was mistaken, like the romantic thinkers of the interwar period: "he erred in his fundamental claim that by leading them back to tribalism he could restore their happiness, and lessen the strain" (Popper, 1945: 151).

Popper makes a distinction between tribal forms of living together and higher levels of civilization, the culmination of which he calls humanitarianism, and that was first achieved by the Greeks. Such a society is an open society, where there is space for discussion, migration, individual choice and responsibility and freedom while the tribal forms of societies are closed societies. As soon as Greek society, or our society, moves away from being a closed society toward an open society the strain of civilization will be felt: "It is the strain of the demand that we should be rational, look after ourselves, and take immense responsibilities. It is the price we have to pay for being human" (Popper, 1945: 154). Hayek and Popper both argue that civilization and freedom come at a price. Hayek primarily sees that price as the submission to traditions, norms and social forces we do not fully comprehend, while Popper argues that the price consists mainly of the responsibility for our own actions and the justification of our individual choices. Popper further emphasizes that an open society also means contact with other people, it means migration and it means that individuals have to accept differences, in other words, it requires tolerance. But Popper too is aware that awareness and acceptance of imperfections is part of that strain:

we are becoming more and more painfully aware of the gross imperfections in our life, of personal as well as of institutional imperfection; of waste and unnecessary ugliness; and at the same time of the fact that it is not impossible for us to do something about all this, but that such improvements would be just as hard to achieve as they are important.

(Popper, 1945: 176)

At this point, it is perhaps good to see how close both Popper and Hayek are to the analysis of Freud. Freud argues: "If civilization is an inevitable course of development from the group of the family to the group of humanity as a whole, then an intensification of the sense of guilt (...) will be inextricably bound up with it, until perhaps the sense of guilt may swell to a magnitude that individuals can hardly support" (Freud, 1930: 122). Replace guilt with responsibility and there is hardly any difference left, except that Freud seems to be suggesting that a highly advanced civilization might be associated with too much guilt, too much responsibility for the individual to bear. He concludes empathically toward those who can hardly bear the load: "it is vouchsafed to a few, with hardly an effort, to salve from the whirlpool of their own emotions the deepest truths, to which we others have to force our way, ceaselessly groping amid torturing uncertainties" (Freud, 1930: 122).

That is not the conclusion that Popper and Hayek draw, they instead attempt to argue that this strain is a price worth paying. It is a strain that is the result of an individual and liberal civilization, but a strain that enables a richer and more open culture to emerge. It is this relationship between tradition and norms on the one hand, and freedom and individualism on the other, that is called paradoxical by the anthropologist Malinowski. In his remarks that serve as the epitaph to this chapter, he points to the paradoxical relationship between traditions and freedom, but we now understand how a wide array of Central-European thinkers come to this conclusion. They learn from the interwar experience, from what Popper calls 'the revolt against civilization', that the market experience is not a natural process, or one that is in line with man's natural inclinations. One might argue that any notion of a civilizing process will stress the difference between nature and culture, and that some element of learning and disciplining is an inherent part of any notion of the civilizing process. But we have seen a clear shift from an early notion of virtues promoted by markets to an emphasis on the disciplinary character of market forces within the Viennese tradition. It therefore makes sense to distinguish between the idea that markets have civilizing effects and the idea that markets have a strong disciplinary force. They at once restrain and enable individuals, as is evident from the two cases discussed in box 1 and box 2 below.

Just take some examples of claims that have been made about markets. Markets punish inefficient and irresponsible behavior. Markets tend to reward those who are industrious and those who save money to increase their future wealth. Market processes ensure that profitable and beneficial projects survive and evolve, while unprofitable and harmful projects disappear. Markets allow individuals to act based on their own knowledge of time and place, and that through the market this knowledge spreads through society. Market transactions also make people realize that they cannot have it all at the same time, that choices are an essential part of human life. The discipline of the market is learning to understand that making one choice, means abstaining from another. If individuals wish to be successful on markets they have to produce goods or services that other people value. The market process also allows individuals to be entrepreneurial and try new things. If such new projects are too costly or not valuable enough for others, these entrepreneurs will incur losses. In the same manner, the market process punishes entrepreneurs who do not adapt quick enough, or make wrong investment decisions. Markets also punish those governments or individuals who have borrowed too much with higher interest rates. Via the same process, those who have failed to

Box 1: The moral effects of markets: the case of interest

Someone we have not yet discussed much, but who was a central figure within Austrian economics was Eugen von Böhm-Bawerk. Economically, he is known as an early critic of Marx analysis of the capitalist economy and for his theory of interest. This theory of interest combined three different explanations for the existence of interest, but his new contribution was that interest had psychological origins. The issue of interest and profit had been the main bone of contention between the socialist authors such as Marx, Lassalle and Rodbertus, who had all argued in various guises that interest and profit originated from exploitation and should really accrue to the workers. Even closer to home, Carl Menger's brother Anton had argued precisely this in a book during the 1880s (Menger, 1886). Böhm-Bawerk and other liberal authors of the period were thus concerned with showing that interest formed a natural part of every economy and society, and was not the result of capitalist exploitation as the socialists claimed.

Böhm-Bawerk offered two psychological reasons for the existence of interest. These psychological reasons, according to him, would hold in any type of society, whether capitalist, feudal or communistic. The first reason is that people are generally situated in poorer circumstances today than they are in the future, and therefore they value present goods higher than future goods. Böhm-Bawerk himself does not fail to point out that this might not be true for all people at all times. Later critics especially concerned with the existence of interest in an economy operating at a constant level of output, therefore generally disregarded this explanation. Within the older Austrian framework of advancing civilizations however it makes more sense.

The second reason according to Böhm-Bawerk is that: "we systematically underestimate our future wants and the means serving for their satisfaction." He in turn, gives three reasons for this underestimation: weakness of the will, our incomplete imagination of future wants and the shortness and uncertainty of life (Böhm-Bawerk, 1891: 254–245). This explanation has been criticized for various reasons, for example, because it seems to be an irrational explanation. One would expect that an economizing individual would learn that he should not systematically underestimate future wants. If we, however, think of the tension Hayek describes between restraining ourselves and our innate instincts, interest has a clear function. The existence of interest directs our wants away from immediate satisfaction to more long-term goals. On the other hand one could say that human nature is such that it wants things as soon as possible, and that abstaining from these wants comes at a price. As such, interest is the reward for abstinence.

This is precisely what later theorists, most prominently Mises, would argue. He formulated what has come to be called a time-preference theory of interest in which the preference of the individual, as consumer, for present goods over future goods is central. A popular description of this theory is that interest is a compensation for waiting; it is a compensation for abstaining from present consumption. A relatively low interest rate can then be interpreted as a sign that people are relatively easily motivated to abstain, and the Viennese students of civilization did not hesitate to consider low interest rate as a sign of an advanced civilization.

Box 2: The moral effects of markets: the socialist-calculation debate revisited

The most important contribution of the Viennese students of civilization of the interwar years is usually considered to be the criticism of economic calculation under socialism, first by Mises and later by Hayek (see Lavoie, 1985). In this debate, Mises first argued that socialists would lack the necessary information to make production decisions. By getting rid of markets the socialists would also get rid of the knowledge captured by market prices. This would cause problems in choices of the appropriate production methods. Should processes that were labor-intensive or that were capital-intensive be chosen? How would one make such a decision without information about the relative prices of labor and capital? Mises was especially worried that socialists would implement policies that would raise consumption in the short run, at the expense of investments in future production (Menger's higher-order goods). Mises was afraid that socialists would give in to our basic instincts to satisfy our wants now, instead of restraining our present consumption in favor of long-term progress.

Socialist engineers were impressed by the objections raised. Oskar Lange even, somewhat cynically, responded that Mises deserved a statue for showing what would be necessary for central planning. The central solution he, along with various others, proposed was to simulate markets to obtain the necessary information or to look at markets that still existed to obtain these prices. Hayek in turn responded by pointing out that markets did not only provide information about prices, but that they were information-processing systems, which processed information much more efficiently than any central planner would be able to do.

One might impatiently ask what this debate has to do with civilization. I think this debate is best understood through Hayek's claim that man did not intelligently design civilization or its institutions, but that man: "became intelligent by submitting to new rules of conduct" (Hayek, 1982: 163). This holds for markets similarly, markets enable individuals to become intelligent, to make well-informed decisions, and not the other way around. We should thus understand Hayek's and Mises objections as expressions of this belief. By getting rid of markets, we are getting rid of some of the most advanced products of our civilization, and hence we are getting rid of one of the most important instruments that make us intelligent. In his essay 'Knowledge and Society' Hayek argues that we do need to know the supply conditions and all those other types of knowledge relevant to our decision, but we only need to know how much the prices rises or falls (Hayek, 1945: 525). What Hayek is in fact claiming is that rational behavior is impossible without markets. If we were to eliminate markets, we would eliminate our primary means of valuation and rationality itself would become meaningless. We would become 'blind' as Menger had put it much earlier.

The other underlying element of their criticism is that markets, just as civilization, is best understood as a process of change and adaptation. If we eliminate these processes, we lose sight of the effects of these changes, and we consequently do not adapt to such changes. Planners think of production decisions as being made at one point, but the Viennese show the importance of processes, such as market processes, which are an essential part of the civilizing process.

pay back loans in the past pay higher interest rates in the future. The market fosters trust if transactions are successfully completed, but can destroy reputations too.

Some of these are easily categorized in the category of market discipline, others in the civilizing category, some are in between. The two strains also remain part of Hayek's work. To understand this it is important how important responsibility and choice are for Hayek: "It is only where the individual has choice, and its inherent responsibility, that he has occasion to affirm existing values, to contribute to further growth, and to earn moral merit" (Hayek, 1962: 45). The market is not only important because it promotes particular values, but also because it provides the scope for the individual to form valuations, to test these valuations, and to develop new values. But those opportunities to express oneself, to develop oneself and to cultivate and affirm certain values is counterbalanced by the discipline and the restrictions that social and market forces impose. On the one hand, Hayek uses the language of cultivation and developing values in his work, but on the other hand he uses the language of discipline. Compare for example, the aforementioned quote on choice and responsibility with: "he [man] had to shed many sentiments that were good for the small band, and to submit to the sacrifices which the discipline of freedom demands but which he hates" (Hayek, 1982: 167–168). This tension can more generally be found in the difference between the language in *The Constitution of Liberty* in which he speaks of the creative powers of a free civilization and the language of discipline and norms to which the individual must submit in 'Three Sources of Human Values', as well as his emphasis on the disciplinary force of the market in 'The Road to Serfdom' and the essay on individualism.

5 Conclusion – discipline and civilization

When Hayek talks about the discipline of cultural and social processes, and of the taming of our animal spirits, he has transformed what a civilization process is. It is no longer the process of Bildung (character formation), deliberation and emancipation that we identified in Chapter 3 as a characteristic of optimistic Austrian liberals in the 1860s and 70s. It has instead become a disciplinary process, in which the market imposes certain type of behavior on individuals.

For the Viennese students of civilization, the market is no longer a sphere where individuals can emancipate themselves away from dependence and superstitions, but it has become a process that disciplines individuals (sometimes against their will). This submission has in the past often relied on religious norms or an overblown respect for authority. We moderns, however, must submit out of free will. With a certain nostalgia Hayek observes that:

> They [members of an exchange society] held an ethos that esteemed the prudent man, the good husbandman and provider who looked after the future of his family and his business by building up capital, guided less by the desire to be able to consume much than by the wish to be regarded as successful by his fellows.
>
> (Hayek, 1982: 165)

Our society is no longer that exchange society, it no longer esteems those values, and therefore we need, according to Hayek, some other institution to instill these values. The crucial word here is *submission*. In certain passages, he even transforms the previous emphasis on restraints to an emphasis on discipline: "Freedom was made possible by the gradual evolution of the discipline of civilization which is at the same time the discipline of freedom" (Hayek, 1982: 163). According to Hayek this is the only type of freedom that is feasible, because only with sufficient discipline are individuals capable of living together in a free and open society.

What the Viennese liberals were attempting to formulate was a self-sustaining liberalism for an advanced civilization. They believed, Schumpeter and Karl Polanyi most famously so, that market societies as existed during their time were destroying themselves, or that they were at the very least under severe attack. The initial optimistic liberalism of the 1860s and 1870s had slowly but surely faded away. Liberalism and the emancipation initially associated with it were no longer conceived as ideals, but liberalism had become in the words of John Gray a 'modus-vivendi', the best alternative for living peacefully together. Civilization is consequently no longer a natural process of progress, but a cultural process with both negative and positive effects. The students of civilization move away from an older belief about natural progress and development. Civilization is no longer a natural process unfolding itself throughout history, but rather a cultural process subject to cultural forces, and hence vulnerable. Civilization and freedom, and in Hayek's account even intelligence (see box 2) become features of culture, of human traditions. This means that he rejects the belief that there is anything natural or inevitable about the process of civilization and freedom. The process of civilization can be, and is in danger of, being undone. It, however, can also be advanced, and we human beings are responsible for these developments (although our powers in this respect are rather limited, and never direct, themes that will be explored in the coming chapters).

Markets consequently are cultural institutions with moral effects, or rather cultural effects. Markets are not natural as is sometimes believed, nor are they designed. Markets do not work because individuals are rational, but markets allow individuals to make rational choices. This means that civilization and human rationality are vulnerable. That means, hence Popper's title *The Open Society and its Enemies*, that our civilization has to be protected in times during which it is under attack.

This pessimistic conclusion is best understood in its interwar context, in which the Viennese liberals felt that civilization they cherished was coming to an end. As Mises once lamented when he walked on Vienna's wonderful Ringstrasse: "Grass will grow right here where we are standing" (quoted in Kurrild-Klitgaard, 2003: 55). Another insight follows from this analysis. The defence of markets is the defence of civilization itself for Hayek and Mises. This means that the defence of markets, given their idea of civilization as constraints, is moral. But moral here is perhaps not the right word, for it suggests that they are engaged in an ethical or political project and that is certainly not how they thought of it themselves. They are genuinely concerned about civilization; this concern is a continuous element in the Viennese tradition of thought. It is present in Carl Menger's work whose idea of higher order goods was clearly linked to higher levels of civilization, and it is important for Mises and Hayek who believe that markets are the central elements of our civilization, both as products of civilization, and as means to preserve that civilization. Now one could call that moral, for them it was their task as students of civilization.

There is another important lesson to draw from this chapter. We have witnessed in the analysis of civilization, mainly during the interwar years, the confrontation of a group of 'economists' with the central problems of modernity. Today, it is usually sociologists who are occupied with this problem, but that only shows how ill our professional disciplines sometimes fit the intellectual concerns of our predecessors. For if one thinks of the group of thinkers analyzed here as students of civilization, it makes perfect sense that they would confront the problems of modernity. The social problem of old communities and sources of values that are breaking up and being superseded by modern, more impersonal communities and forms of human interaction is a central concern to them. This means that habits and traditions that had appeared natural are being unmasked as fictions (or otherwise lose their legitimacy). This destabilizes the culture that enables markets to flourish, and these market thus require new intellectual and moral support. It is in that sense, at least, that the term neoliberalism is correct.

Their view of the market as a disciplinary process is today (at least implicitly) widely accepted. It was for example, generally expected that economic integration in Europe would lead to more discipline in the South-European economies. Or even more basically the disciplinary force of competition forces business every day to improve their production methods, and products. What I have added to that view here is not only that I have shown the origins of this view, but I have also attempted to show that there is a strong moral element to this view of markets and competition as disciplinary processes. Various authors including the historian Burgin have argued that the market is believed to be a morally neutral arbiter by Hayek, but we have seen earlier here that such a view cannot be upheld (Burgin, 2012: 188). I have also pointed out that the word 'moral' is not really appropriate in the framework of Austrian liberal thought. Within that tradition, the study of civilization is not neatly split-up between moral and nonmoral elements. The scholars we have been discussing here are better understood as students of civilization, and whatever is part of that civilization falls within their scope.

Their interwar experiences had shown them how vulnerable civilization can be and hence they sought ways to protect it. They came to be convinced that there was a price to be paid for civilization, the 'strain of civilization'. This strain could also explain the widespread revolt against civilization they saw around them. Hayek concluded from this that individuals should submit to impersonal rules that they cannot fully rationally justify or understand. A skeptic might say that such submission requires a kind of Kierkegaardian 'leap-of-faith', in which the individual willingly accepts this submission, for the greater good it will bring. Both Popper and Hayek, however, believed that in reality there's no real choice. They agree that this strain is part of what it means to be human, and that submission to such restraints is necessary. As Hayek argues:

Man in a complex society can have no choice but between adjusting himself to what to him must seem the blind forces of the social process and obeying the orders of a superior. So long as he knows only the hard discipline of the market, he may well think the direction by some other intelligent human brain preferable; but, when he tries it, he soon discovers that the former still leaves him at least some choice, while the latter leaves him none, and that it is better to have a choice between several unpleasant alternatives than being coerced into one.

(Hayek, 1948: 24)

Or to paraphrase Popper, we can only keep on carrying the cross of being human (Popper, 1945: 176).

Instincts, civilization and communities

The conversation about the individual
and civilization continued

In this chapter, I would like to pursue some of the themes developed in Chapter 3 and 4 a little further. What are some of the questions that emerge from the analysis of the Viennese studies into the relationship between civilization and the individual? And not unimportantly, who are some of the other scholars who have worked on similar themes, sometimes even explicitly connected to the Viennese tradition? It is thus explicitly not my aim here to settle issues definitely, or to conclude, but instead to explore possible ways forward.

To do so, I will explore three themes that I believe have prominently come up during Chapters 3–4. The first is the role of instincts, or natural inclinations in the economy, and to what extent they can and should be tamed. The second theme relates to the cultural norms and institutions. How are these cultural norms supported?[1] We have seen that Hayek and others grew skeptical that such support would be widespread during the twentieth century, and that they attempted to conceptualize the market as self-sustaining. On the one hand, they saw it as one of the most important cultural institutions, but at the same time it had to generate the support for itself and other cultural institutions. Is that perhaps too much to ask? This leads to the third issue, do we perhaps need more to sustain such cultural norms and institutions? In Hayek's account of cultural evolution norms and institutions are imitated within particular groups and communities. This leads to the question: what ties groups of traders together, what unites them, and what are the integrative institutions of such groups.

To do so, I will draw on various sources, some economic and some noneconomic, but I will try to stick most closely to those that I perceive to

---

[1] The more common question to ask is how these norms evolve (Gray 1984, especially chapter 2; Caldwell 2004, chapter 13).

be working roughly in the same tradition as the Viennese students of civilization. They will mostly be social theorists with breadth of vision (economic, social and cultural) who have reflected on an analytical as well as practical level on developments of their own times.

1 Taming the instincts?

We have seen that the literature that emerged around the middle of the twentieth century from scholars with their roots in Central Europe emphasized the importance of restraining our instincts, and the importance of norms, institutions and traditions to discipline the individual. This is, however, certainly not the only way to conceptualize the relation between instincts and cultural restraints. In this section, I would like to discuss three competing accounts of this relation. The first account is a short summary of the Viennese analysis of Chapters 3–4, with some relations to other authors. The second account is represented by the perhaps odd pairing of Keynes and Schumpeter who have argued that human instincts are an important life-source of capitalism, and that capitalism cannot do without these instincts. The final account, which draws heavily on Hirschman's work 'The Passions and the Interests', argues instead that man can be left relatively free in the economic domain because there, the passions cannot do much harm. This account is somewhat critical of the process of civilization; it argues that we should give up attempting to restrain our passions, and that we instead should find specific 'safe' outlets for them.

Before I start describing these accounts, it is perhaps good to spend a few words on why this issue is so important. It is clear that in our contemporary society individuals depend on a great many others, very few of whom they ever get to know. Or as Adam Smith put it: "In civilized society [man] stands at all times in need of the co-operation and assistance of great multitudes, while his whole life is scarce sufficient to gain the friendship of a few persons" (Smith, 1776/1975: 18). The question that follows from this observation is: which institutions enable this cooperation, which institutions allow the individual to benefit from the efforts of others, with whom he is not in direct contact? Or to reverse that question, how do we prevent individuals coming into conflict with one another and how do we prevent predatory behavior? The market and the division of labor occupy such an important place in Smith's book, because he believes them to be institutions that allow individuals to benefit from the effort and skills of one another, without caring directly about one another, or even knowing about one another's existence. This is why Hayek places the market as a culturally developed institution next to language and law that also developed through human interaction, and that also foster mutually beneficial human interaction. Just like books allow us to 'interact' with people at great distance in both place and time, so markets allow us to trade and interact with individuals far away from us. The question we are interested in answering is therefore not one about human rationality, efficient markets or economic growth, although such concerns might come up, but primarily about more or less peaceful and mutually beneficial human interaction and the institutions that enable this type of interaction. I will confront later in this chapter whether posing the question this way opens us up to particular criticisms.

We have seen that in Hayek's account, especially, there was a lot of emphasis on taming the instincts, on restraint. Such restraints could take many forms: self-restraint, social restraints, cultural restraints or economic restraints (imposed by markets). Hayek argued that individual freedom was possible, but only if individuals were willing to submit to market forces, social norms and cultural traditions. The acceptance of these norms would allow them to beneficially interact with others, and within these constraints they would be able to pursue their own ends. Hayek is rightly famous for his emphasis on the dangers of the intrusion of the state into various cultural institutions (especially the market) that enable mutually beneficial human interaction. In Chapter 4 we have, however, seen that he considers social or intellectual currents, at least potentially, just as dangerous to civilization. Given his experiences with war, mass political movements such as socialism and fascism, it is not surprising that he sketches a civilization that is very fragile. While that civilization used to be supported in various ways through civil society, via institutions such as the family, church, associations and even political parties, this support had largely waned during the first half of the twentieth century. Society and political movements revolted against civilization. Or rather, they revolted against certain aspects of it they particularly disliked, putting civilization as a whole at risk. The Viennese consequently emphasized the need for discipline and restraint, in politics, markets as well as in society.

Someone who shares the intellectual and cultural background of Hayek has argued, to the contrary, that the restraint and especially the discipline associated with modern society would ultimately kill the life-force that was still left in capitalism. That person was Joseph Schumpeter, famous for his theory of the entrepreneur. The entrepreneur is the individual who introduces new things to the market, conquers new markets or improves the production process. Especially in the German version of his work on economic development, Schumpeter explores the psychology of the entrepreneur. The entrepreneur is the 'economic leader, a truly, not merely apparent leader, as is the shopkeeper' (Schumpeter, 1912: 172).[2] This man, never a woman in his account, knows no psychological opposition, and by virtue of being a leader is able to shape the world around him, instead of adjusting to it. It is worth quoting Schumpeter at some length here:

They [Men of action] will create the new and destroy the old, they will initiate and execute courageous plans of various kinds, whose originality will surpass the conceivable. They will dominate their fellow citizens, perhaps influence national politics and organizations, they will alter the 'natural' course of the economy by lawful and unlawful means, but never through mere exchange.

(Schumpeter 1912: 157)[3]

In his *Capitalism, Socialism and Democracy* Schumpeter integrates his theory of entrepreneurship into a wider social analysis. He shows that the entrepreneurial function is becoming defunct, and that in an increasingly rationalized and bureaucratized world there is no space for entrepreneurs anymore. His energy is being smothered by the rise of big governments and big firms in which the introduction of new products and methods becomes a routine (Schumpeter, 1943/1976: 131–134). The entrepreneur, the man of action, has no place in a highly advanced civilization according to Schumpeter. His inner will and motivation have been important in the process of development of our modern society, but have lost their place and even their function. This issue is also on the mind of Keynes, in what Schumpeter has once described as Keynes' 'intuitive diagnosis of England's aging capitalism: the arteriosclerotic economy whose opportunities for rejuvenating venture decline' (Schumpeter, 1954: 1171).

In that analysis Keynes discusses the animal spirits that cause much of the instability in economic life:

Even apart from the instability due to speculation, there is the instability due to the characteristic of human nature that a large proportion of our positive activities depend on spontaneous optimism rather than mathematical expectations, whether moral or hedonistic or economic. Most [...] of our decisions to do something positive, the full consequences of which will be drawn out over many days to come,

---

[2] My translation, in German: "Er ist der wirtschaftliche Führer, ein wirklicher, nicht bloß scheinbarer Leiter, wie der statische Wirt."

[3] My translation, in German: "Sie werden neues schaffen und Altes zerstören, kühne Pläne irgendwelcher Art konzipieren und durchführen, deren Originalität aller Erfassung zu spotten scheint, ihre Mitbürger ihrer Herrschaft unterwerfen, vielleicht die nationale Politik und Organisation beeinflussen, den 'natürlichen' Gang der Wirtschaft durch gesetzliche und ungesetzliche Mittel und jedenfalls anders als durch Tausch abändern."

can only be taken as the result of animal spirits — of a spontaneous urge to action rather than inaction, and not as the outcome of a weighted average of quantitative benefits multiplied by quantitative probabilities.

(Keynes, 1936: 161)

Like Schumpeter, Keynes contrasts this urge toward action with the calculation based on risk and expected costs and revenues associated with rational economic action. Perhaps surprisingly, Keynes does not seem to think of them negatively at all, for he continues: "Thus if the animal spirits are dimmed and the spontaneous optimism falters, leaving us to depend on nothing more but a mathematical expectation, enterprise will fade and die" (Keynes, 1936: 162). It is in this respect that Schumpeter and Keynes are quite close to one another. They both believe that without some scope for these animal spirits, for spontaneous actions, capitalism will come to a halt, or rather reach a kind of steady state. Cold calculation would not warrant many of the actions undertaken by entrepreneurs, but they are led to them anyway by their natural instincts. The fact that cold calculation will usually not lead to investment is due to the great uncertainty associated with especially long-run projects, and thus Keynes concludes: "If human nature felt no temptation to take a chance, no satisfaction (profit apart) in constructing a factory, a railway, a mine or a farm, there might not be much investment merely as a result of cold calculation" (Keynes, 1936: 150).[4] For both Keynes and Schumpeter, the animal spirits, the spontaneous urge to action, the energy of the entrepreneurs keep our economy in development. Both are however acutely aware that such animal spirits can also cause instability, through unwarranted optimism (bubbles) or irrational fears about the future.

One might wonder to which extent this is actually different from Hayek's emphasis on restraint. Is there no room for entrepreneurship and reckless initiative in Hayek's analysis? If we study Hayek's theory of the entrepreneur, we indeed find that there are important differences with the analysis of Schumpeter and Keynes. Hayek's theory focuses on the dispersion of knowledge throughout society, and entrepreneurship is primarily considered as a process of searching for and discovery of knowledge and consequently acting upon these additional pieces of knowledge, rather than on spontaneous action (Ebner, 2005). Schumpeter and Keynes argue that innate instincts, an urge to action and (unfounded) optimism have an important role to play in economic development. This contrast is at its starkest when we compare the romantic heroism that is present in

---

[4] The Keynes quotations used here all come from chapter 12 of his 'General Theory', a chapter that is widely praised but not easily integrated into his general theory.

Schumpeter's theory of the entrepreneur with the more restrained picture of economic individuals in Hayek. In his obituary, Smithies explains that Schumpeter was attracted by the rigor and logic of the Walrasian system, but admitted that it lacked 'glamor and passion', something that he instead found in Marx, whom he could never wholeheartedly embrace as an analyst (Smithies, 1951: 17).[5] A similar desire for glamor and passion can surely be found in Keynes, but is wholly absent from the sober analysis of Hayek.

The third position on the relation between our instincts and the market could be considered a combination of the previous two. In his book *The Passions and the Interests* (1977) Albert Hirschman argues that during the seventeenth and the eighteenth century capitalism was mainly praised for its ability to channel human passions away from politics, religion and other spheres of life. Hirschman argues that the authors during this period were well aware that it would be nearly impossible to truly restrain, let alone extinguish these passions, and therefore their main goal instead was to canalize them. As Keynes, characteristically shifting his perspective, would put it:

Dangerous human proclivities can be canalized into comparatively harmless channels by the existence of opportunity for money-making and private wealth, which, if they cannot be satisfied in this way may found their outlet in cruelty, the reckless pursuit of personal power and authority, and other forms of self-aggrandizement.
(Keynes, quoted in Hirschman, 1977: 134)[6]

The economic sphere in this view is not the domain where restraint is promoted as Hayek would argue, but rather a sphere where the passions can exist relatively harmlessly. The passions of one individual are counter-balanced by another through competition, and the passionate pursuit of profits could lead to social benefits.

Hirschman argues that this view resulted from of a period of great political upheaval, during which a need was felt to steer human passions away from politics. One might argue that the period that we have been talking about, the interwar period, is similarly a period during which the passions have been let loose in the political and military sphere. Passionate ideological debates, violent conflict, and deep political oppositions were the

---

[5] In the Viennese novel par excellence *Der Mann ohne Eigenschaften*, Musil reserves much praise for the character Dr. Arnheim who is able to unite the spirit and the economy (Seele und Wirtschaft). This combination was not too far from the aspirations of Schumpeter.

[6] This Keynes quote, although it presents a rather different perspective from the previous one is also taken from his *General Theory* (Keynes, 1936: 374).

order of the day during the tumultuous first half of the twentieth century in Europe. It would therefore not be surprising if intellectuals became critical of such passions or sought alternative outlets for them. Hayek thus might not only have thought of the economic sphere as a sphere that would restrain the passions, but also one of the only spheres where human beings could be left relatively free.

Some commentators have been puzzled by the antidemocratic strand in Hayek's thought, and the Viennese tradition more generally. Given the context of Hirschman's conclusions, we can now perhaps understand why the economic sphere is different from these other spheres in their framework. Hayek makes clear in his criticism of democracy that he believes that 'unlimited democracy' lacks the necessary restraints, and will therefore lead to restrictions of individual freedom or worse. A democratic system (often) does not have the restraining features that characterize a competitive market system. So instead of merely reading Hayek's famous blueprint for a free society *The Constitution of Liberty* as a kind of utopia (which it undoubtedly is), one should perhaps also be reading it as a framework that grants as much freedom to individuals as Hayek believes is reasonably possible. Since the political sphere – especially if it is a democracy *without* a strong constitution – lacks the necessary restraints, the freedom of politicians to alter this framework should be severely limited. Such freedom, on the contrary, can be more safely granted within the economic sphere. This clearly distinguishes the Viennese view from, say, the ideal state sketched in *Anarchy, State and Utopia* (1974) by Nozick.

This leaves the question open whether it is true that the passions can relatively safely be canalized into the economic sphere. I think Hirschman is rightfully critical of the idea that passions can best be canalized to the economic sphere, where they will do least harm, or will even be beneficial. In fact, in a time where we have just witnessed an economic crisis caused by a financial crisis, with severe global consequences, it seems strange to think of economic activity as 'comparatively harmless', as Keynes put it. In fact, it should have sounded just as strange when Keynes wrote this, in the aftermath of the Great Depression, which at least in the public opinion (if not unanimously among economists) was caused by passionate economic activity. Nonetheless I think we should take it historically serious that the economic domain was believed to be an attractive alternative outlet for human passions, after the highly politicized atmosphere, especially on the European continent, of the interwar years. A similar sentiment was more recently expressed by the Hungarian author György Konrád, living in a similar highly politicized state, in his *Antipolitics* (1984). He argues that too much passion and effort have been poured into the political domain leading only to deeper conflicts. Directing these passions into the economic sphere would be liberating he argues.

This discussion hopefully makes us aware that in discussing the pursuit of self-interest and its limits merely talking about rationality and its limits, is equivalent to adopting an impoverished language. A language that, before our discussions circled around the rationality concept, was much richer. It would hopefully also help in overcoming the overly simplistic market-state dichotomy (where the market fails the state has to step in, or the other way around). In the previous chapters, I have demonstrated that cultural and social forces can sometimes just as well tame self-interest.[7] This also opens a discussion about the wider culture needed to support this market society (Storr, 2013). And the cultural and moral effects of markets on that culture (Hirschman, 1982). It might even make us rethink whether the so-called economic laws are really as inevitable as term 'law' suggest, or whether they are also shaped culturally? (Nelson, 2006). Or to take another starting point, to take seriously the argument by McCloskey that especially capitalist middle classes are endowed with excellent virtues for the development of the economy and society (McCloskey, 2006). At the other end of the spectrum, one might think of authors such as Michael Sandel who argue that markets cultivate vices instead of virtues (Sandel, 2012).

An issue that I think has been less explored, certainly by economists, is the balancing act between instincts and drives on the one hand, and our reasonable and more temperate inclinations on the other hand. As Thomas Sedlacek argues: "humans may have left the wild and moved into civilized and more predictable cities, which seem under control, but wildness has not left us. It has moved to cities with us; it is in us" (Sedlacek, 2011: 276). Economists are frequently fond of quoting Smith about the human propensity to truck, barter and exchange, but certainly that is not the only human propensity. There is a wide variety of human propensities that are less benevolent, and that are best restrained if we would like to stimulate peaceful and mutually beneficial human interaction. Economists should be aware of the importance of institutions, norms and cultures that support such interaction. An associated concern to which we will now turn is which sources might promote the type of behavior needed to advance civilization?

---

[7] A recent book by Steven Medema subtitled *Taming Self-Interest in the History of Economic Ideas* (2009) does unfortunately fall back on the classic dichotomy market and state, and the consequent conclusion that self-interest can only be tamed by the state.

2 Sources of civilization

In the discussion about the support for the norms and traditions associated with a market society the Viennese students of civilization somewhat somberly concluded that support was no longer provided by traditional institutions such as the family, the church or civil society, and that it could perhaps only be cultivated by the market itself (Mises, 1922/1951: 511–515; Schumpeter, 1943/1976; Hayek, 1948: 2). High expectations were placed on markets by the Viennese, not only was the market the main cultural institution that needed support, but it was also the institution that should provide this support. It even seemed that Hayek fell here into a kind of economistic thinking that reduces human interaction to market inter-actions, something that he attempts to avoid in his wider body of work. We might consequently wonder what other types of human interaction might breed some of the values and norms that he believes are so vital to our market society? What other institutions or practices might be part of the civilizing process.

To start that discussion, I would like to start with the work of Johan Huizinga, who not only was a contemporary of the later generation of the Viennese students of civilization, but who also shared their pessimism about the development of European culture during the first half of the twentieth century. His book *Homo Ludens*, which originally appeared in Dutch in 1938 opens characteristically: "we humans turned out not to be as rational as a joyful century of worshipping Reason had made it seem" (Huizinga, 1938: vii).[8] As the title of his work suggests Huizinga then introduces the importance of play for human culture. He argues that culture often starts out as play. Various activities, including the more basic ones, are often acted out as play. An aspect of Huizinga's work that is especially interesting for us is that Huizinga argues that play has an important civilizing function. It confronts individuals with situations of uncertainty, in which they have to perform certain tasks within a given set of rules. Huizinga especially emphasizes elements of competition in ana-lyzing play. Competition, he argues, is especially interesting if it is not a mere game of luck, but if it requires the players to exercise dexterity, skill, agility, courage or power (Huizinga, 1949: 46–49). Huizinga even argues

---

[8] My translation, in Dutch: "(Toen) wij menschen niet zo verstandig bleken als een blijder eeuw in haar vereering van de Rede ons gewaand had." For some reason the English translator has rather messed up the first few sentences. He has also decided, probably rightly so, that the century of Reason-worship was the eighteenth century for which no indication is present in the Dutch version.

that competitive play can be at the heart of community life: "The contest as one of the chief elements of social life has always been associated in our minds with the idea of Greek civilization" (Huizinga, 1949: 71). Huizinga, however, does wonder whether such play-elements will slowly disappear with modern societies. He argues that what play is left in our modern culture is mostly an atavism from earlier periods.

I think one might question the disappearance of play in our culture. Contests are still very important in the art and sports world. In fact, Frank Knight has argued that business life, especially in the higher regions, is perhaps better understood as a competitive game rather than as a system of want-satisfaction. At least it seems that many of the 'players' are more interested in gains internal to the game: "It seems evident that most of the ends which are actually striven after in the daily lives of modern peoples are primarily of this character; they are like the cards and checker-men, worthless (at best) in themselves, but the objects of the game" (Knight, 1923: 612). Knight himself is quite skeptical of such pursuits, preferring instead the pursuit of higher values. What is nonetheless interesting for us, is that he points to the character-forming, or civilizing force of such competitive processes. Knight makes it clear that there might be rather close similarities between market processes and games. They are both competitive, constrained by certain rules, and they involve a combination of luck, effort and skill. The rules of the game, like cultural norms, are not fixed forever and always, but some stability and observance of them is necessary for the game or the market process to function. Like Hayek, Huizinga emphasizes that such rules emerge from human interaction. They do not merely civilize by teaching the importance of rule-abiding behavior or the process of competition, but also because rules and norms of, for example, 'fair play' emerge in the process.[9]

If we think of the importance of rule-abiding, it is inevitable to also think of the law (a subject that Huizinga also discusses in relation to play). Hayek argues that laws come about in processes of human interaction, and that there is an important role for the state to punish violations of these rules. In fact, the early liberal constitution in Vienna during the 1860s, Wieser's plea for a constitutional life and Hayek's attempt to formulate a constitution of liberty are all part of the same tradition. A tradition in which

---

[9] A connection with the work of Huizinga and Knight is also suggested in Appendix E of the *Fatal Conceit* (Hayek, 1991). The emphasis on play might also make us think of game theory, but even though the initial game theorists were inspired by actual game playing, game theory assumes rationality rather than attempting to explain it.

some rules are so important for human interaction that they should be fixed in a constitution, but this argument is not grounded in human rights as in many contemporary accounts. The defense is also not directly utilitarian, not all rules will be beneficial to every individual at every single instance. They are instead justified because they provide a clear framework for human interaction. As Wieser makes clear, if these rules are not reaffirmed in society they will be of little value. In fact, Wieser is skeptical that armed force will be very effective in maintaining rules that are not widely shared. The law and the armed forces that protect it might therefore be considered more of a disciplining than a civilizing force.

The civilizing process does not merely consist of rule-abiding. We saw in the previous chapters that Menger as well as Mises and Hayek stressed the importance of valuation. In Menger, this was most closely related to planning for the future and extending our time horizon, or one could say by increasingly valuing our future needs and wants over our present ones. In the work of Hayek and Mises, this comes out most clearly in their criticism of central planning without markets. They argue that without the valuation process occurring at the market, individuals (and consequently also the central planners) would miss essential knowledge to make reasonable decisions. In terms of the civilizing process one might say that the individual, in the absence of markets, would not learn to plan and value competing ends. The feedback process that characterizes market interactions would not occur. Or, as some commentators have argued about education and health care in many Western economies, people do not value or use it in the 'right' quantities because the prices of these goods are so distorted. At the same time, I believe it to be somewhat economistic to think that valuation and evaluation with a feedback mechanism only takes place in the market sphere. Scholars, for example, continually engage in the valuation of the work of others: when they decide what to read, whom to cite, what literature to use in courses, or when they review article or books from their colleagues. Matters are no different in the arts, sports and the culinary world. Valuation takes place in everyday conversations, and more organized discourses. Contributions to those conversations are not without consequence; those whose contributions are valued by others will be regarded highly, they will receive applause, praise and status.

Frequently – as in the arts, sports, or the culinary world – we tend to regard such valuations as more important than the information that comes from the market. We do not only want to view the most expensive artwork, watch the most well-paid sports players, or eat in the most expensive restaurants. High praise and good evaluations of art, sports players or chefs will sometimes lead to high prices, but certainly not always (issues of scarcity left aside). In conversations about these subjects we nearly always distinguish between artistic merit, athletic ability, skill, or more generally quality on the one hand and price on the other. This is especially important to recognize since there has over the past few decades been a strong trend to create markets with prices, which would supposedly measure merit. Looking at valuation more broadly should make us realize that it takes place not just in market processes but in many other domains of human life as well.

This realization brings us back to Max Menger's observation about the cooperatives in which he argued that individuals would learn the skills of deliberation and to subsume their personal interest under the general interest. The associations in a society, often called civil society, are believed to be a civilizing factor. Hayek laments the centralization associated with his time, which tends to destroy this civil society. He praises De Tocqueville and Lord Acton for attempting to resist this tendency toward centralization (Hayek, 1948: 28). This civil society is hardly ever part of our study of the economy, but it can play an important role in this civilizing and valuation process or in setting up the type of institutions that restrain individuals. The work of Elinor Ostrom is one of the few exceptions to this trend; she has studied how civil society provides public goods and deals with common resources (Ostrom, 1990).

I would like to end this section with a few observations. I have shown how various spheres might support the institutions of our civilization, and markets more specifically, but little was said on how this might precisely work. It is one thing to claim that market processes discipline or restrain individuals, it is another thing to show how they do so. The Viennese students of civilization do not write much on this issue. Hayek does observe that individuals working in large corporations might experience little of the discipline of the market (Hayek, 1982: 165). An observation that echoes Coase's theory of firms as islands of conscious power in otherwise competitive processes (Coase, 1934: 388). Such casual observations, however, are only hints toward a more serious study of how markets and other institutions cultivate certain values and how they might erode others. So there is certainly a lot of work left to do, which shows how markets might restrain and discipline behavior, and what specific values they instill.

Secondly, we have presumed so far that there was a positive, civilizing effect from the various sources we have discussed. The Viennese students of civilization, however, were working during a period in which the majority of the intellectuals, of civil society and of political movements were endangering those institutions. This led especially Hayek to study how this revolt against civilization could be explained and prevented. I think much of his work from the mid-1930s onward must be understood as an attempt to understand that revolt and to prevent it in the future. He looked for models of our institutions that would restrain individuals and he sought an intellectual position that would guard against the rationalistic hubris that he felt dominated modern thought. That work should at least make us aware that the institutions discussed here do not necessarily cultivate support for the existing institutions. To give but one example, it is well established that the managers and entrepreneurs within relatively successful firms frequently seek to preserve a current status quo and therefore tend to support for policies designed to protect this status quo rather than to promote competition within their own industry. Historically one might think about the discussion of the role of civil society in the rise of Nazism (Berman, 1997).

3 A shared culture

It is clear that in the work of Hayek and other Viennese concerned about civilization during the interwar period and during WWII there is a sense that there is something to be defended, a culture and a set of values that are endangered, although they deserve to be upheld. As Mises, Schumpeter and Hayek analyzed, the acceptance of such traditional beliefs and norms was declining, and the authorities that supported them were losing ground. That traditional support had to be replaced by alternative processes and spheres in which the appropriate values could be cultivated, but on a more intellectual level they also had to be replaced by modern rational justifications and new ideals. These considerations point the way to the realization that a market society, just like other cultures, depends on a shared set of values. Of course individual interpretations of these values will differ and consensus on these values will never be complete, but there is a shared culture that underlies a market society. The disintegration of the Habsburg Empire and then later of Europe made the Viennese acutely aware of the importance of such a shared culture. It is no coincidence that Hayek argued for a United States of Europe in his 'The Road to Serfdom'. But what will integrate the individuals in a market society? Are some of the central values, such as restraint, capable of doing this?

The Viennese students of civilization all agreed that restraint was an important value, within the economy but also within politics. Max Menger early on argued that individuals would learn to restrain themselves within cooperatives and Wieser lamented how various new political parties were unwilling to compromise and restrain their group interests. Böhm-Bawerk praised the role of interest in restraining our tendency to value our current wants higher than our future wants, and for Mises it is even what makes us human:

Man is not a being who cannot help yielding to the impulse that most urgently asks for satisfaction. Man is a being capable of subduing his instincts, emotions, and impulses, he renounces the satisfaction of a burning impulse in order to satisfy other desires. He is not a puppet of his appetites.

(Mises, 1949/2007: 16)

Would this mean that human beings would also restrain themselves? How would this value of restraint be cultivated? In the previous section, we saw how it might be cultivated or instilled by market processes, but could restraint also become an ideal, something that unites people, a shared value?

There are religious communities in which restraint, as in fasting or a complete disregard for material possessions, is practiced and held up as an ideal. This is, however, surely not what the Viennese students of civilization are after; they are not seeking to promote asceticism. Even on restraint, there should be restraint. It seems however that such a restrained restraint is hardly a value that will unite people. Its practical value can be demonstrated, we can agree that it is not always realized, but it is hardly an ideal that will unite us. Even stronger, in 'Three Sources of Human Values' Hayek argues that restraint and submission to the values that make up civilization might come at the expense of the individuals involved. Individuals are asked to submit themselves to these values in the name of civilization, but why would they do so? Wieser faced a similar problem around the turn of the century. He observed that the Austrian liberals had failed to develop ideals after the constitution of 1861 was realized. Wieser suggested that a continued affirmation of this constitution might provide the liberals with a kind of identity. This continued affirmation of the constitution is done with some success in the United States, but elsewhere the constitution does not seem to have the power to serve as a continued ideal.

A similar issue is raised by Anthony O'Hear in a discussion of the work of Karl Popper, who we will discuss in more detail in Chapter 7. O'Hear too is worried about the ties that might bind an open liberal society. He argues about Popper's ideal of an open society: "to think that a disposition to criticize might on its own be enough to hold a community together is itself utopian, and it could be as destructively utopian as some of the other utopias Popper correctly criticizes" (O'Hear, 2009: 209).

Kenneth Boulding suggests that these issues point to a deeper problem for economists. They have always suffered from a neglect of what he calls 'integrative relationships'. Economists have paid excessive attention to exchange relationships, but they have largely ignored other types of relationships (Boulding, 1963).[10] While market relationships are usually (but not exclusively) exchange relationships, integrative relationships usually take place outside the market in families, associations, clubs, schools and politics.[11] Considered as such we can understand Hayek's attempt to argue how the market might cultivate its own support as an argument that market relationships can also be integrative relationships. We all know this to be true to some extent, integrative relationships take place within firms between colleagues, between customers and shopkeepers, or more generally between two parties who trade frequently. But, as Boulding points out:

> It has been the precise weakness of the institutions that we think primarily of as economic, that is, associated with exchange [. . .], that they easily lose their legitimacy if they are not supported by other elements and institutions in the society which can sustain them as integral parts of a larger community.
>
> (Boulding, 1969: 10)

In other words, a market society needs integrative relationships or institutions that sustain the economic relationships. The strength of the cultural analysis of the Viennese students of civilization is that they recognize that markets cannot be taken for granted, they are not natural phenomena. Markets are cultural phenomenon and they need a shared culture which sustains them. There is, so to say, 'a commons', without which a market society cannot continue to exist. This gives rise to two questions: what do cultures in which the market is prominent share, and how can these 'commons' be sustained?

---

[10] He also considers threat-relationships, which I will not discuss here.

[11] I believe it is also possible to develop from Boulding's recognition of integrative relationship a separate category of goods, which comes about mainly in such integrative relationships instead of exchange relationships. Goods such as a conversation, a music festival, a dinner party, choir practice, sports matches or more generally games are created in integrative relationships, not in exchange relationships. Of course metaphorically we can say that in a conversation we exchange stories, anecdotes, arguments and attention, but what really happens is probably better described as coproduction. This is also why many of these goods cannot be bought (or traded) on the market; nonetheless they are very important in our lives. Klamer has suggested calling such goods social or shared goods.

Both questions cannot be fully answered here, but it is important to realize how different the Viennese tradition is from that of, say, mainstream economics. There the questions of whether something 'common', a shared culture, is necessary for the operation or existence of markets is never posed. Within the Viennese tradition it becomes a central issue to find out how market societies can be sustained. The Viennese too, however, only partially pursue this issue. They do not really consider what integrates a community and what sustains a shared culture. Surely Max Menger's and Wieser's call for a 'Verfassungsleben' can be understood as an attempt to form a liberal community, but in their wider analysis such issues are not given much prominence. They realize that a market society needs a market culture, or liberal culture if you like, but they hardly consider seriously how such a community would come about, or how it would be sustained. They do not explore what such a community would share, what type of identity it would provide for the individuals.

Hayek does not completely ignore such issues, in his later work he does focus on the evolution of social norms within groups, but he mainly approaches that topic from an evolutionary angle and he does not consider issues of identity-formation. This is perhaps all the more surprising since the issue of national identities had been so prominent a problem within the Habsburg Empire. We have seen in Chapter 3 how the Viennese liberals were frustrated with the fact that newly enfranchised or emancipated groups did not develop into liberal, patriotic citizens. These groups instead developed a variety of other identities, most prominently religious and ethnic. Even closer to home the early Viennese students of civilization must have remembered or would have been told that the liberal movement in Vienna had started around the celebration of German cultural heroes such as Goethe or Schiller (Franz, 1954: 116). Communities can never be sustained without a shared identity and shared symbols.

Kenneth Boulding points economists in the direction in which they are perhaps most reluctant to go. He points them toward a consideration of identity, to discard their idea *homo economicus* as identityless individual, devoid of birth-place or even life-span. He asks them to consider actions, even economic actions, as resulting not from cost-benefit analysis, but from a sense of identity.[12] The parents caring for their child, because it is *their child*, the soldier willing to risk his life for his country, because he is a

---

[12] Needless to say that such a conceptualization of identity would be quite different from the recent work by Akerlof and Kranton (2010) and possibly more along the lines explored by Davis (2011).

soldier and it is his *country,* the economist seeking the truth, for he is a *scientist.* This is not to say that parents, soldiers, or economists would never act otherwise, but rather that such actions arise from their identity rather than a cost-benefit analysis. Boulding is aware that the idea of identity is not only neglected by economists, but that is also at odds with much of what economists argue. He believes that the strongest criticism of the idea of reasonable decision-making comes from those who attach more importance to their identity. He contrasts what he calls the 'heroic ethic' with the reasonableness and prudence emphasized by economists or more broadly by liberals: "we have to recognize that there is in the world another type of decision-making, in which the decision-maker elects something, not because of the effects that it will have, but because of what he 'is', that is, how he perceives his own identity" (Boulding, 1969: 9). The acceptance of moral norms central to a market society, as promoted by Hayek, is a commitment of the same kind.

Boulding is quite right to argue that we need both the heroic and the reasonable in our life. Or in his eloquent way of putting things: "Economic man is a clod, heroic man is a fool, but somewhere between the clod and the fool, human man, if the expression may be pardoned, steers his tottering way" (Boulding, 1969: 10).[13] Hayek is not blind for the need of a shared identity, consider for example, what he writes about Germany after WWII: "nothing will be more conspicuous than the powerlessness of good intentions without the uniting element of those common moral and political traditions which we take for granted" (Hayek, 1944/1992: 202).

One contemporary of the Viennese students of civilization Vilfredo Pareto similarly struggled with the issue of how what is rational or reasonable comes to be accepted. In his sociological work he distinguishes between logical and nonlogical action. He argues that social action is frequently of the nonlogical type based on 'residues' such as conservatism, integrity or sexual drives rather than of the logical type (means-ends relationships). It would take us too far here to explore his theory, but his theory suggests that more might be at stake in justifying our actions than rational arguments only. The theme of justification has more recently been explored by Boltanski and Thévenot in their *On Justification* (2006), in

---

[13] Boulding expresses the hope that the heroic ethic will fade, although I doubt he really hoped that: "My personal view is that, especially at his present stage of development, man requires both heroic and economic elements in his institutions, in his learning processes and in his decision-making and the problem of maintaining them in proper balance and tension is one of the major problems of maturation, both of the individual person and of societies" (Boulding, 1969: 10).

which they explore various rationalities or 'economies of worth' as they call them. These might be directions in which the central question of how to justify a market order might take us.

The Viennese students of civilization faced the problem of delegitimization and disintegration time and again. They, however, seemed unwilling or unable to come to grips with it. More than merely an animal spirit, or an atavistic element of our culture, this need for an identity, and thus to be part of a shared culture seems to be fundamental. Indeed to think of markets, language and the law, and various other institutions as forming a culture, a civilization, means thinking of them as something we have in common, something which unites us. While market societies might stimulate human interaction, economic development, peace, they should also seek to find a way to maintain this common culture, and be strong enough to inspire a sense of belonging, of pride in the individuals who make up such a culture.

6

Therapeutic nihilism or the humility
of the student

On the limitations of the student of the civilization

No person can escape death; yet the recognition of this necessity certainly
does not force us to bring about death as quickly as possible
—Ludwig von Mises, *Nation, State and Economy*, 1919

Though we cannot see in the dark, we must be able to trace the limits
of the dark areas
—Hayek, *Constitution of Liberty*, 1960

The next three chapters will deal with the position of the student of
civilization vis-à-vis his or her civilization. This relation, in the form of
the social scientist vis-à-vis society, has been conceptualized in different
ways over time. Especially influential has been the idea that the social
scientist studies society as objectively as possible. He or she formulates
factual statements and theories about the object of his studies, from which
predictions can be derived. These theories and the knowledge of relationships between different variables allow him to give policy advice to the
policy maker, who sets the ends of these policies. Mark Blaug has compared the role of the economist in this perspective to that of the technocrat,
a technocrat who, free of personal and political values can give scientific
policy advice, based on objective knowledge (Blaug, 1992: 128–129). The
technocrat – in this perspective that emerged in the first half of the
twentieth century – passively accepts the goals of the policy maker and
provides advice on the most efficient way to achieve these ends. In this
manner, the technocrat will help increase efficiency and consequently the
welfare in a given society. An even stronger variant has held that social
engineers would be able to rationally manage society toward society's
desired goals. The softer and stronger engineering view can be found in
such disparate thinkers as Otto Neurath, Thorstein Veblen and Ragnar
Frisch and Jan Tinbergen, and has become the standard perspective in

economics. A modern instance of this perspective is the idea that economists can design markets (see for example, Roth, 2002).

A variation of this position can be found in Pigou's introduction to his famous *Economics of Welfare* (1921). There, he compares economics to human physiology, a science whose primary interest lies in bearing fruit, rather than bearing light: "there will, I think, be general agreement that in the sciences of human society, (. . .) it is the promise of fruit and not of light that chiefly merits our regard" (Pigou, 1921: 4).[1] Pigou therefore compares the economist to the doctor, seeking cures for the individual or society as a whole. Pigou is neither the first nor the last to compare the economist to the doctor, or the economy to a patient.[2] Typical is an argument such as relatively recently made by Romer, who compares the economist to the doctor: "You can let the pastor, the legislator, the family and the philosopher struggle with the moral question of whether to actually stop the treatment, but what you want from a doctor is correct scientific statements about what will happen if" (cited in Uchitelle, 1999).[3] For Romer, too, the economist is primarily a neutral observer, who, based on expert knowledge, can advise on the effects of various treatments. The judgment of the desirability and the goals of such treatments will be left to the pastor, the legislator, the family or the philosopher, although the comparison with the doctor suggests that deciding on such goals will be pretty straightforward. Or take the title of a paper by Hahn 'Economic Prescriptions for Environmental Problems: How the Patient Followed the Doctor's Orders' (1989). Just like the doctor is supposed to cure the patient, so the economist is supposed to heal the economy, or at least to be able to predict the effect of various cures. Keynes even dreamt of economists who would be regarded as dentists: "If economists could manage to get themselves thought of as humble, competent people on a level with dentists, that would be splendid"

---

[1] Bearing fruit and bearing light are also the two goals Samuelson identifies in the introduction to his classic *Economics* textbook.

[2] Peter Groenewegen has examined various economists who were trained and/or worked as physicians (Groenewegen, 2001).

[3] Or, to use another example from an interview in the New Yorker by John Cassidy with John Cochrane: "The other reason I've been against the stimulus: it's pretty clear what the problem with the economy was. For once, we know why stock prices went down, we know why we had a recession. We had a panic. We had a freeze of short-term debt. If somebody falls down with a heart attack, you know he has a clogged artery. A shot of cappuccino is not what he needs right now. What he needs is to unclog the artery. And the Fed was doing some remarkably interesting things about unclogging arteries. Even if (the stimulus) was the solution, it's the solution to the wrong problem" (Cassidy, 2010).

(Keynes, 1930/1963: 373). To sum up, a comparison of the economist to an engineer or doctor seems to lead easily to the corollary that the economist can prescribe the appropriate policies or cures for the economy.[4]

This chapter will challenge that view. I will argue that although the medical metaphor was popular among the Viennese students of civilization, they adopt a different professional position. Rather than believing that they were able to heal the patient, they preferred to study the patient (the economy), and to focus on the limits of their healing powers. More broadly the Viennese students of civilization challenged the view that society could be engineered (by the technocrat) or healed through interventions (by the doctor). Instead they emphasized the autonomous and inevitable development of the economy and society, and they preached the importance of acceptance of such developments. Rather than providing cures, the student of society would only be able to help us understand the forces around us. Or to continue the medical metaphor, they argued that before we can heal a sick body, we must learn to understand why such a complex organism functions in the first place (Hennecke, 2000: 135). To develop this perspective they could build on a wider Viennese tradition in which the doctor or more broadly the intellectual was mainly engaged in understanding, rather than curing. A medical and intellectual perspective sometimes negatively referred to as 'therapeutic nihilism'. As one cultural historian of Vienna has described it, therapeutic nihilism is: "diagnosing social ills without prescribing remedies for them" (Janik, 1985: 49).[5]

In the Viennese perspective the forces of society move (almost) completely beyond our control, and the social scientist is consequently not the master of such forces but merely its student. This perspective in which the powers of the social scientist are virtually nil would come under serious criticism during the late 1930s, even within the Viennese tradition. Both Hayek and Popper would identify such a perspective as too deterministic. They come to reject the fatalism they associated with it and would

---

[4] In the essay quoted earlier, Roth shares such optimistic sentiments: "Just as chemical engineers are called upon not merely to understand the principles that govern chemical plants, but to design them, and just as physicians aim not merely to understand the biological causes of disease, but their treatment and prevention, a measure of the success of microeconomics will be the extent to which it becomes the source of practical advice, solidly grounded in well tested theory, on designing institutions through which we interact with one another" (Roth, quoted in Roth, 2002).

[5] I am aware of one other author who makes the link between therapeutic nihilism and the Viennese economists (Müller, 1998). He however does not make clear what the term means for him, nor does he make the connection between the phenomenon in medicine and in economics.

conceptualize civilization and its development as cultural phenomena, for which citizens and intellectuals bear a shared responsibility. To do so they, however, had to refute the older Viennese perspective that we will examine in this chapter.

1 Therapeutic nihilism in medicine

The Medical Faculty of the University of Vienna enjoyed great prestige during the majority of the nineteenth century, and it attracted students from all over Europe. Ignaz Semmelweis developed his theories on child-bed fever there, and the discipline of pathological anatomy was greatly advanced there, especially under the leadership of Karl von Rokitansky (1804–1878). Rokitansky alongside his close colleagues Joseph Dietl (1804–1878) and Josef Skoda (1805–1881) are most commonly associated with therapeutic nihilism.[6] In an increasingly professionalizing field these men wanted to found a scientific study of medicine, which would replace the individualistic and sometimes idiosyncratic methods that had prevailed under the old system. To this end a group of doctors had recently founded 'der k. und k. Gesellschaft der Ärzte in Wien', which enjoyed some independence from the Medical Faculty at the university. The major outlet of this society was their periodical and it was in the second issue of this journal that Dietl published the article, which led others to accuse him, and his followers, of therapeutic nihilism.

In the article, Dietl argues that instead of focusing on finding practical cures, doctors should start to focus on knowledge. Medicine, according to him, is a 'filia ante matrem', a daughter without a mother, a field where cures have come before knowledge. The development of cures without a theory of either medicine or the human body has been misguided he argues. The main goal of a doctor should be not to find practical cures, but to study the forces of nature, just as natural scientists do:

Why do we not ask from the astronomer, that he turns day into night, from the physicist that he turns winter-cold into summer-heat, from the chemist that he turns water into wine? Because it is impossible. That is, it is not possible according to the laws of his science.

(Dietl, 1845: 14)[7]

---

[6] For a full discussion of the second Viennese Medical school, see Lesky (1976).

[7] My translation, in German: "Warum verlangt man nicht vom Astronomen, dass er Tag in Nacht, vom Physiker, dass er Winterkalte in Sommerhitze, vom Chemiker, dass er Wasser in Wein umwandle? Weil es unmöglich, d.i. weil es nicht im Principe seiner Wissenschaft begründet ist. " The similarity with the position of Wieser discussed in previous chapters is striking.

The doctor and the natural scientist are thus in a similar position according to Dietl. The role of the doctor is not to be a healing artist, but he should be a student of nature. From a close study of the forces of nature, one can then perhaps suggest some cures, but the primary aim is *understanding* not healing, light not fruit. This was a head-on challenge to his colleagues and especially to the practical doctors who in 1845 still dominated the medical profession in Vienna and most of Europe.

According to Dietl this change of goals would have important consequences for the claims doctors could make. They would have to stop pretending to possess powers they did not have, and to acknowledge what they did not know: "Let us avow openly the limits of our sphere of influence, which precisely therefore, that this sphere is based on the principles of science is fully justified" (Dietl, 1845: 12).[8] This would, according to Dietl, consequently also mean that a doctor is judged not on his success rates in healing, but rather on the amount of knowledge he possesses. Whether a patient ultimately heals depends on nature, and not on the treatment. The doctor might often lack the courage to admit this, but it is only nature that has healing powers: "Whether a treated illness finally cures, is not dependent on the treatment of the doctor, rather it is dependent on the relevant forces of nature that determine the outcome of the illness" (Dietl, 1845: 15).[9] Dietl makes clear to his colleagues that just as the natural scientist cannot bend the laws of nature, but can only tell us how to make use of these laws, so the doctor cannot heal incurable diseases, he can only diagnose which forces of nature are at work.

The strong emphasis on knowledge instead of healing, combined with the conviction that the healing powers of the doctor were limited by the laws of nature, have led many critics of Dietl to call him a 'therapeutic nihilist' or somewhat more positively a 'therapeutic skeptic'. The critics specifically criticized Dietl and his associates for adopting too much of a hands-off approach at the bedside and for taking a far too fatalist attitude toward illness. The critics argued that Dietl and his allies should not call themselves doctors since they merely wrote 'Meditations on Death' (Risse, 1997: 64). The response to such charges is telling, Clarke who promoted the Viennese perspective in the United States responded:

---

[8] My translation, in German: "Bekennen wir vielmehr offenherzig die Beschränktheit unseres Wirkungskreises, die eben darum, weil sie im Principe der Wissenschaft begründet ist, ihre volle Rechtfertigung findet."

[9] My translation, in German: "Ob die behandelte Krankheit in Genesung übergehe oder nicht, liegt nicht an der Behandlung des Artzes, sondern an bestimmten Naturgesetzen, welche den Ausgang der Krankheit bedingen."

But, if the men that are fond of the phrase therapeutic nihilism, mean by it that our creed is that of *laissez faire,* that our attitude by the bedside is one of folded hands, that, in short, we are willing waiters and not workers, we may well plead to the indictment.

(Clarke, 1888: 199)

The group around Dietl, Rokitansky and Skoda preferred the term 'Naturheilkunde'. They argued that it is Nature that ultimately does the healing, not the doctor or the treatment. Their proposal of 'Naturheilkunde' sounds strange to the modern ear. A modern dictionary will quickly equate it with homeopathy, a so-called *unscientific* healing method. It is, however, important to realize that Dietl and his colleagues were arguing for exactly the opposite, a more scientific study of medicine.

The dispute between the therapeutic skeptics and their opponents was not merely about knowledge and methods, but also about the relation between the doctor and his patients. Dietl was after a change of attitude among his colleagues, a goal we will also find in the work of the Viennese students of civilization. Dietl, in one of his later books 'Der Aderlass in der Lungenentzündun' (1849), explains that the minimum prerequisite for any treatment should always be that it does no harm, or at least that it does more good than it does harm. By the end of the book he has sharpened this into the aphorism that modern medicine turns the doctor into wise advisors who: 'if they cannot help, at least do no harm' (Dietl, 1849: 113).[10] This went directly against the motto of his colleagues who preferred the maxim: 'it doesn't hurt to try'.[11] Courage for Dietl meant the mental strength to admit one's limitations and be frank about them. To be able to say no to a patient, and to admit the limits of one's knowledge and one's healing powers. Courage for many of his colleagues had always meant the courage to try new methods and to experiment on the patient.

The final aspect of Dietl's position to which we should pay attention here is his reverence for nature. Dietl does not only expect that most of the healing will be done by nature, he calls it the highest of all healing powers. He also argues that wherever nature can perform the healing process, we should let nature run its course. Even stronger he argues that the primary task of the doctor is to study the healing powers of nature, and their limits. Only when those limits are reached is there a role to play for the doctor and medicine. This reverence for nature and the skepticism, that much can

[10] My translation, in German:"[der] wenn er nicht nützen kann, wenigstens nie schadet."

[11] A plaque above Freud's desk would later read : 'En cas de doute, abstiens-toi', (In case of doubt, don't), a phrase commonly attributed to St. Augustine (Francis and Stacey, 1985: 93).

be done about the course of its development, will be a prominent feature when we will examine this type of attitude among the Viennese students of civilization.

For clarity's sake let us sum up what the position of Dietl entails in five elements: new criteria for knowledge, a strong belief in the healing powers of nature, an emphasis on the limits of human knowledge and consequently of our healing capacities, a reverence for nature and its healing powers, and finally a redefinition of professional courage: from experimenting with new treatments, toward admitting the limits of the expert's knowledge and his ability to heal.

2 Therapeutic nihilism as a cultural phenomenon

The best way to introduce therapeutic nihilism as a cultural phenomenon in Vienna is perhaps with a quote from the Viennese novelist Joseph Roth's novel *The Radetzky March*:

> The district captain himself was never sick. Getting sick meant dying. Sickness was merely nature's way of getting people accustomed to death. Epidemics—cholera had still been feared in Herr von Trotta's youth—could be overcome by some people. But when diseases simply came sneaking along, striking only one person, he was bound to succumb—no matter how many different names were applied to those complaints. The doctors, whom the district captain called medics, pretended that they could heal patients—but only to avoid starving.
>
> (Roth, 1932/1996: 140)[12]

As a description of the therapeutic nihilist stance, this is about as concise as one can get: the prominence of nature's will, the futility of fighting diseases and the depiction of doctors as quacks, only after money. It is hardly a description of a cultural phenomenon however. Nonetheless, Roth's purpose of this passage is best understood as an allegory on the fate of the Habsburg Empire, which is the central theme of the novel. Roth describes three generations of Trotta's; the district captain referred to in this passage is of the second generation, still firm and never sick. His father, the first generation Trotta, is well known as the hero of the Solferino, because he saved the Emperor's life. The son of the district captain on the other hand is constantly suffering from ill-health, growing alcoholism and a lack of purpose. The story of these three generations is symbolic for the fate of the Empire, as one of the characters in the novel puts it: "This empire is doomed. The instant the Kaiser shuts his eyes, we'll crumble into a

---

[12] Translation by Joachim Neugroschel, 1995.

hundred pieces". At the end of the novel, both the district captain and the Emperor do pass away and hence symbolically the Empire itself.

This theme of an Empire in decline, and a loss of values, is also captured by Hermann Broch, novelist and critic of Viennese culture. He has labelled the period leading up to WWI the 'gay apocalypse'. A carefree attitude combined with an acute awareness of a crisis. In fin-de-siècle Vienna Broch senses a loss of the older values, and a withering belief in progress. Whereas the therapeutic nihilism of the doctors had still been associated with a belief in the healing powers of nature, and a moderate belief in the advancement of knowledge, Broch describes an intellectual atmosphere in which this belief in progress is quickly fading. Therapeutic nihilism in his work is no longer a passive belief that Nature will ultimately heal, but rather the belief that the Empire is suffering from an incurable disease, while the Viennese intelligentsia are nothing more than passive onlookers. They lack any inclination to heal, instead they rejoice in diagnosing the patient. Just as the autopsy on dead patients became a favored method at the Viennese Medical school, so the intellectuals in Vienna engaged in a kind of cultural autopsy. The Empire – while still alive – was dead for all practical purposes, and the intellectuals could ponder over the causes of death. Indeed Broch compares Vienna at the time to a kind of museum, a dead city and the Viennese citizens to the spectators in this museum, or rather to the spectators in their Viennese theaters (Broch, 1948/2002: 178–183).

Prominent among these Viennese intellectuals is a duo, which especially through subsequent scholarship, have come to embody much of what characterizes Vienna around 1910. That duo consists of Karl Kraus and Ludwig Wittgenstein. The former was the most prominent Viennese satirist who would exercise a strong influence on the work and ethic of perhaps *the* philosopher of the twentieth century: Wittgenstein. Both thinkers are as much part of Viennese culture as they are critics of it, and especially Kraus excelled in exposing the hypocrisy of his fellow Viennese. For Kraus, the Viennese civilization is indeed all but dead, as is exemplified by his most famous play *The Last Days of Mankind*. In the periodical that he published single-handedly, he described the satirist as standing on 'the death-bed of the age' (Kraus quoted in Timms, 1986: 226). That Kraus was as much part of this culture, as he was its critic is best exemplified by Bertolt Brecht's tribute to Kraus: "When the age came to die by its own hand, he was that hand" (Brecht quoted in Timms, 1986: 230). Kraus, one could say, adds another dimension to therapeutic nihilism. He is no longer merely the passive onlooker, but he suffers from that same disease. It becomes an acute question for him how to face the moral decline honorably and with integrity.[13]

Janik and Toulmin in their *Wittgenstein's Vienna* argue that this integrity is the central element in the work of Kraus and Wittgenstein. About Kraus they argue: "He concerned himself with the integrity of the individual writer. It was not a matter of ideology or literary schools; it was always a question of the unity of form and personality" (Janik and Toulmin, 1973: 81). The philosopher or the critic had to be one with his work, he had to live it, and rather than being true to his civilization or an external set of moral values, he had to be true to himself. This gave philosophy an important moral and personal dimension, philosophy was no longer a kind of occupation, but an extension of one's personality. In the value vacuum identified by Broch the philosopher can only be true to himself. This has none of the lightness of the gay apocalypse; it requires the intellectual to look fate straight in the eye, and to face it with integrity and dignity. It is a moral precept with similarities to the moral dimension of Dietl's therapeutic nihilism. His call for the courage to admit what we do not know, the integrity to admit what we cannot achieve is mirrored in the call for integrity of Kraus and Wittgenstein. They require a relentless truthfulness from the intellectual, a perspective in which the limits of our knowledge are as important as that knowledge itself. Or as Kraus summed up the futility of writing in one of his aphorisms: "Why does a man write? Because he does not possess enough character not to write" (Kraus quoted in Janik and Toulmin, 1973: 201).

Just as Dietl sought to redefine courage as admitting one's limits, Kraus here argues that a man of character and courage does not write at all. The cowardly doctor would keep prescribing cures, and the cowardly author would keep on publishing his works, despite the fact that both are aware of their own futility. Perhaps the most quoted aphorism by Wittgenstein argues similarly for an explicit awareness of our own limits: "Whereof one cannot speak, thereof one must be silent." Integrity required of the philosopher not to transcend the boundaries of what can be said, just as the doctor should not transcend the boundaries of what he can do. The doctor could not change nature, only attempt to understand it, and the philosopher could not change the fate of our culture, he could only dissect it.

---

[13] Karl Polanyi once compared the Viennese attitude to that of the Prince of Denmark in the play Hamlet: "If challenged to choose between life and death, he [Hamlet or the Austrian] would be undone, since he cannot deliberately choose life" (Polanyi quoted in Johnston, 1972: 180).

The charge of fatalism could therefore also be directed at Wittgenstein, especially regarding the power of language. The power of language is strictly limited, and it is the philosopher's moral task to show these limits. Although Janik and Toulmin do not explicitly connect this element to the wider situation of the Habsburg Empire, I think it should be understood in that context. In an Empire in decline intellectuals are faced with the question, whether this decline can be avoided. They become acutely aware of the superstitions and illusions on which civilization was built. The response of some will be to look for new foundations while maintaining as much as possible of the old civilization. Others, however, adopt openly fatalist positions, accepting the decline of their beloved world, as we will see Schumpeter do later in this chapter.

The most common response was to search for new foundations. Peter Hall argues that the central question to Viennese composer Arnold Schönberg was, whether: "it [was] possible to strip away the traditional props of tonality that had supported music, and still create something with integrity and balance?" (Hall, 1998: 167). I believe that this question extends to other domains, and indeed Janik and Toulmin argue that Schönberg, Kraus Wittgenstein and Loos were engaged in similar projects in different spheres. They sought to strip away the old props, the old illusions but without giving up the goal of creation, integrity and balance. Kraus sought to eliminate the 'effects' and 'illusions' from theatre, Loos sought to eliminate unnecessary ornaments and facades from architecture. They did so not in attempts to eliminate beauty, but to distinguish clearly between beauty and truth, between aesthetics and function; knowledge of which can be spoken, and that which can only be shown.

So what can we conclude about therapeutic nihilism as a cultural phenomenon? Johnston in his extensive analysis of 'the Austrian mind employs the term to a wide variety of thinkers (Johnston, 1972). By doing so, the term becomes rather empty, and, as Janik forcefully points out, primarily confusing (Janik, 1981). I hope, on the contrary, to have shown here that the various elements that can be defined by examining its proponents in the Viennese Medical Faculty, can be traced in the cultural criticism of Vienna. The Empire is the patient, the intellectuals instead of trying to reform it, rejoice in picking it apart, and critically analyzing its components. Many of them recognize that the prevention of the decline of the Empire is impossible, the patient is incurably ill. For Wittgenstein and Kraus this means that the intellectual should come to grips with his own futility, with his own limitations. A slightly more optimistic group of intellectuals attempts to preserve what they can. They attempt to restore the civilization of the Empire, without 'the Emperor', whose authority, they have to admit rested on illusions. We saw an example of such an attempts in Hayek's nostalgia for the discipline of the gold standard (in Chapter 4). The gold standard he admitted rested on an illusory belief in gold, but the discipline associated with it could perhaps be restored through competitive currencies. In other words, the criteria for knowledge change, the powers of the intellectual are very limited, and they should have the courage to admit this. What is different compared with the work of Dietl is that the situation has become gloomier, the Empire is in decline, and there seems to be nothing that can bring this decline to a halt.

3 Therapeutic nihilism among the Viennese students of civilization

As in the wider Viennese culture, the attitude of therapeutic nihilism only slowly became prominent among the Viennese students of civilization. In fact early on, they had been mildly optimistic about the possibilities of improving society. Let us first examine the initial positions to show how this attitude developed.

The most elaborate statements on this issue are to be found in Menger's *Investigations into the Method of the Social Sciences* (1883/2009), which was written during the Methodenstreit with his German colleagues. Much of Menger's discussion is about law, which was also the broader faculty in which economics was studied at the time in Vienna. He compares the lawyer or the economist to the farmer or the physician who study the laws of nature in order to influence the course of things in a beneficial way (or in Pigou's words more fruit than light). The task of the lawyer, Menger warns is not merely to preserve what has come about organically, but to look for gradual improvement of the law. He argues:

But never, and this is the essential point in the matter under review, may science dispense with testing for their suitability those institutions which have come about 'organically'. It must, when careful investigation so requires, change and better them (. . .). No era may renounce this 'calling'.

(Menger, 1883/2009: 234)

This statement comes at the end of a discussion in which Menger has compared the historical tradition of Burke and Savigny that he praises for having shown the importance of organically grown institutions. In fact, he argues this was a necessary correction to the rationalism of the classical school of Adam Smith: "what characterizes the theories of Smith and his followers is the one-sided rationalistic liberalism, the not infrequently impetuous effort to do away with what exists" (Menger, 1883/2009: 177).

So, even though Menger argues that the economist or student of law has a calling to improve existing institutions, laws and policies, he has to do so with a great sense of moderation, and respect for them, since they contain the wisdom of previous generations.

The position of Wieser differs somewhat from that of Menger. Critical of the laissez-faire attitude of the classical liberal school, he argues: "the liberal economic school has behaved like a doctor, who has recognized the excess of the old therapy, falls into the other extreme and teaches, that Nature must always be left alone, and the doctor should not intervene" (Wieser, 1910: 141).[14] Wieser, like Menger, warns against the attitude of natural scientists and technocrats who think that society can be rationally transformed, in words very similar to those of Dietl:

The engineer scoffs at those, who expect from him the miraculous power to lift a weight, without having the necessary power available; that is how the sociologist should scoff at the oft-repeated plans to create the largest social changes, before the necessary historically prepared powers of sufficient power are available.

(Wieser, 1910: 144)[15]

Wieser and Menger seem to differ in their evaluation of the classical school, but they share the concern that the economist should caution for both overtreatment and neglect.[16] Menger believes it is the calling of the economist and the student of law to gradually improve existing institutions, while Wieser warns against an extreme overreaction to earlier mistakes. The practical economist should not conclude from previously failed attempts to improve, that all such attempts are bound to fail. They share a mild therapeutic optimism.

---

[14] My tranlsation, in German: "Die liberale wirtschaftliche Schule hat sich benommen wie ein Arzt, der, weil er das Übermass der alten Therapie erkannt hat, in das andere Extrem verfällt und lehrt, man müsse stets die Natur allein wirken lassen, der Arzt dürfe nichts dazu tun."

[15] My translation, in German: "Der technischen Fachmann spottet über den Laien, der von ihm das Wunder verlangt, eine Last zu heben, ohne die nötige Kraft parat zu haben; so muß auch der Soziologe über die immer wiederholten Vorschläge spotten, welche die größten gesellschaftlichen Wirkungen hervorbringen wollen, ohne geschichtlich vorbereitete Mächte von genügender Stärke zur Verfügung zu haben."

This trope is repeated by Machlup in the 1930's when he argues: "The economic laws hold also when, the minister, the banker, and the politician do not know or recognize them. Just as the laws of physics hold, whether some technician observes them or not" (Machlup, 1932/2005: 69).

[16] This could be due to the fact that Wieser is talking more about policy prescriptions that under the influence of the Manchester school were reduced to the well-known 'laissez-faire, laissez-passer', while Menger is more concerned with differentiating between a rationalistic basis for policy, versus historically grown institutions.

Just after, or even during WWI the prevailing attitude changed. There was a widely shared feeling that the war, and wartime planning, had paved the way for the coming of socialism. In Vienna, the socialization of the economy had started, while not very far away in Bavaria the revolution had begun with the short-lived experiment of the Bavarian Soviet Republic. Consequently both Mises and Schumpeter saw themselves forced into more fatalist positions. It certainly was not because they welcomed the rise of socialism that they saw no other way out, in fact Mises compared what was happening to the fall of the Roman Empire. In his analysis of the situation just after WWI, there was little hope left that the coming of socialism could still be prevented:

> Marxism sees the coming of socialism as an inescapable necessity. Even if one were willing to grant the correctness of this opinion, one still would by no means be bound to embrace socialism. It may be that despite everything we cannot escape socialism, yet whoever considers it an evil must not wish it onward for that reason and seek to hasten its arrival; on the contrary, he would have the moral duty to do everything to postpone it as long as possible. No person can escape death; yet the recognition of this necessity certainly does not force us to bring about death as quickly as possible.
>
> (Mises, 1919/1983: 217)

At first it might seem that Mises claims we have a moral duty, to do something about the coming of socialism. Upon second reading, Mises, more than anything identifies the tension described earlier. He argues that we should not hasten the arrival of socialism, but despite everything, its coming might be inevitable. If we are to do something about it, our efforts are probably completely futile.[17]

Schumpeter was actively involved in the socialization of the economy after WWI, first in Berlin and later as finance minister in Vienna, and one might thus expect a different response from him to the situation. When he was afterward asked about his political role in these years, he responded (once again in medical terms): "If somebody wants to commit suicide, it is a good thing if a doctor is present" (Schumpeter quoted in Allen, 1994: 163). Like Mises, Schumpeter clearly considers the socialization process a disaster, an attempt at suicide. His various biographers have pointed out, however, that Schumpeter was not completely negative about these measures; he also saw it as an opportunity to improve inefficient state

---

[17] Some years later, he regained some hope and argued that: "No one can find a safe way out for himself if society is sweeping towards destruction. Therefore everyone, in his own interests, must thrust himself vigorously into the intellectual battle" (Mises, 1922/1951: 515).

enterprises. So, when Schumpeter compares himself to the doctor, he does see some positive role for himself, perhaps to alleviate some of the worst pain. Whatever way we look at it, the position of the liberal economist helping to socialize the economy remains a curious one. As Allen writes in his biography, Schumpeter behaved more like a doctor 'handing a pistol to the potential suicide', than like a doctor trying to alleviate the worst pains (Allen, 1994: 163). Another way to understand Schumpeter's ambivalence is to realize that he genuinely believed that the coming of socialization was inevitable. He therefore was assisting in an inevitable process. The inevitable coming of socialism is a thesis to which Schumpeter returns repeatedly in his work. He does so in an article that explains the policies that he wants to pursue as finance minister, 'Die Krise des Steuerstaats', which is based on a lecture he gives in 1919 (Schumpeter, 1919/1950). And he does so more extensively in his *Capitalism, Socialism and Democracy* (1943/1976). In that book, he clearly explains that he admires the capitalist system, but that it will inevitably have to make way for socialism.[18] He argues that capitalism eradicates the social support for its system and it will ultimately have to stand trial: "before judges who have the sentence of death in their pockets". He no longer believes that this lamentable situation can be cured and continues: "They are going to pass it, whatever the defense may hear" (Schumpeter, 1943/1976: 144). Schumpeter adopts a truly fatalist position, even though he does so in a book, which according to some commentators contains the best defense of capitalism ever written.[19] He became a doctor, who could do nothing but wait for the patient to die. It might look cowardly to some, but for Schumpeter it was a matter of dignity and integrity. He had to accept what he could not change.

Mises and his fellow intellectuals sought to find a response to socialism, and especially how to prevent the coming of socialism and the destruction of civilization that they associated with it. The first thesis that came out of

---

[18] Schumpeter was to some extent also interested in a genuine attempt at socialism. In his recent biography McCraw describes a conversation between Max Weber and Schumpeter about the Russian Revolution. "Schumpeter said: 'but it will be a good laboratory to test our theories'. 'A laboratory heaped with human corpses!' said Weber. 'Every anatomy class is the same thing', replied Schumpeter" (McCraw, 2007: 94). An interesting conversation, especially because of the reference to the anatomy class, which had also been so prominent within the Viennese Medical school. But in the light of this conversation one might explain Schumpeter's role as minister of finance as an experiment on a body (economy or civilization) that was already dead.

[19] See for example, McCloskey (2006).

these discussions was the idea that any type of interference with the free market system, would via a logic of interventionism inevitably lead to socialism. This idea is also suggested by the title of Hayek's book 'Road to Serfdom' (although less by its actual content). According to Mises once the government starts to intervene the shortages or surpluses this will create will create a call for more interventions: "either capitalism or socialism; there is no middle of the road" (Mises, 1926/1977: 26).

The analysis of monetary policy for which the Austrian school has become famous in contemporary debates shows clearly how they believed that government cures would only lead to more serious problems. When the central bank lowers the interest rate, or otherwise expands the money supply, this would lead to (artificially) cheap investment funds. Additional investments, based on these artificially low prices, would be undertaken by entrepreneurs, but when interest rates would return to their normal level, these entrepreneurs would realize that their investments were not profitable enough to justify the investment, and they would incur losses. These losses could only be prevented by keeping interest rates at their artificially low levels, that is, more interventions. If the economy is considered as the patient in this analysis, then we can certainly speak of overtreatment, in fact the patient becomes addicted to the drug of cheap money. Or as Hayek would put it some decades later: "there is, indeed, more than a mere superficial similarity between inflation and drug-taking" (Hayek, 1960: 330).

Another good illustration of this attitude is found in a newspaper article by Fritz Machlup from the 1930s. In response to the attempts by the Austrian government of the time to save some from firms and industries from bankruptcy, he argues: "The drowning man clings to all those who still have their head above water, and pulls them with him. But if we want to save the others, we should suppress our pity, and let the drowning man drown" (Machlup, 1932/2005c: 117). If we would not do so, the first intervention would soon lead to the need to support other firms and industries as well. Instead of keeping unprofitable firms alive through interventions and cheap credit, we should help the industry as a whole, by letting the selection process do its work.

Mises returned to a strong belief in the healing forces of nature, with which the government and the economist should not intervene. Just as Max Menger, Carl's brother, had argued during the 1860's that socialist plans would not work since they did not respect the laws of nature, so Mises now argued that any type of interference with these competitive forces would make the economy sick instead of healing it. This passive, hands-off attitude, and its associated resignation is what ultimately unites Schumpeter, Mises and other Viennese intellectuals. Mises is more of an activist in his defense of capitalism than Schumpeter, but there are also periods when he is devoid of any hope, and can only opt for resignation. For example, when in his recollections, written during the early years of WWII, he writes:

> Occasionally I entertained the hope that my writings would bear practical *fruit* and show the way for policy [...]. But I have never allowed myself to be deceived. I have come to realize that my theories explain the degeneration of a great civilization; they do not prevent it. I set out to be a reformer, but only became the historian of decline.
>
> (Mises, 1942/1978: 115)

In one sweep, Mises sums up the argument of this chapter: from an initial optimism to an unwilling acceptance of the futility of his work – from an initial calling to improve policy to the realization that social scientists are powerless in steering the development of a civilization. There are, however, some elements of Dietl's work that are more easily found in Hayek's work of this period than in that of Mises or Schumpeter. While Mises is aware of the limits of human knowledge, Hayek develops this insight in more detail. And even though Mises and Schumpeter pay attention to the role of the economist, it is Hayek, to whom we will turn in the next section, who most clearly identifies the moral dilemma of the economist: offering tentative treatments, or admitting his limitations.[20]

4 The limits of economic knowledge

Hayek begins to develop his views on policy, at least in print, during the early 1930s. Of special interest is his address at the LSE 'The Trend of Economic Thinking' (1933). He challenges Pigou and his emphasis on bearing fruit head on. Hayek's essay contains a very similar structure to that of Dietl from 1845. Hayek, too, first explains how economists are very prone to jump from the investigation of causal relationships to practical conclusions, and policy proposals. He then continues to demonstrate that the economic process is much more complex than was believed by earlier economists. Hayek shows that the economist should marvel at the processes of the market:

---

[20] Historian of Vienna and Austria, Edward Crankshaw suggests that resignation is typical of Vienna: "The gaiety of Vienna is, indeed, a peculiar mixture of fact and myth. Nowhere is found more resignation and nowhere less self-pity" (Crankshaw, 1938: 48).

It was only incidentally, as a by-product of the study of such isolated phenomena, that it was gradually realised that many things which had been taken for granted were, in fact, the product of a highly complicated organism which we could only hope to understand by the intense mental effort of systematic inquiry.

(Hayek, 1933: 123)[21]

In a similar vein, Dietl had claimed we should have great respect for the healing powers of nature. The economist, just like the doctor is quickly criticized if he does not show how such knowledge (light) could bear practical solutions (fruit): "And he [the economist] is bitterly reproached if he does not emphasize, at every stage of his analysis, how much he regrets that his insight into the order of things makes it less easy to change them whenever we please" (Hayek, 1933: 124).

Hayek integrates this (very early on in his career) into what would become his central idea of civilization: restraint of our innate instincts. He argues: "The existence of a body of reasoning that prevented people from following their first impulsive reactions [...] occasioned intense resentment" (Hayek, 1933: 125). From that point onward Hayek increasingly adopts the medical metaphor. He explains the attraction of the solutions of the German Historical school was mainly caused by their conclusions justified 'the treatment of practical problems'. Not much later, he compares practical policies that bring short-term solutions, but cause serious long-term harm to 'palliatives and quack remedies'.[22] In this early article, Hayek still emphasizes the differences between economic thinking and lay-thinking, and hence the tension between lay understanding and expert understanding. In his later work on the subject he increasingly contrasts the attitude of the social engineer and that of the economist, and hence he focuses on the tensions that every student of human affairs faces.

He picks up this theme again in the essays that would together become *The Counter-Revolution in Science* (1952). There he argues that the strong faith in the rational powers of human beings, combined with the innate urge to create order according to a plan, has led to a revolution in the social sciences. This revolution in the social sciences has to be countered. The counter-revolution[23] that Hayek proposes is based on the

---

[21] In a later essay, Hayek argues even more strongly: "I have deliberately used the word 'marvel' to shock the reader out of the complacency with which we often take the working of this mechanism [the market] for granted" (Hayek, 1945: 527).

[22] In yet another instance of the medical metaphor, Fritz Machlup speaks of Monetary Quackeries and he concludes: "Legal experiments of the worst kind will lead to a vivisection with the entire economy" (Machlup, 1932/2005b: 72–74).

[23] On the intricacies of the use of the concept counter-revolution, see n. 2 of chapter 8.

recognition of limits, both in terms of what we can know, and what one individual can achieve:

The individualist approach, in awareness of the constitutional limitations of the individual mind, attempts to show how man in society is able, by the use of various resultants of the social process, to increase his powers with the help of the knowledge implicit in them and of which he is never aware; it makes us understand that the only 'reason' that can in any sense be regarded as superior to individual reason does not exist apart from the inter-individual process in which, by means of impersonal media, the knowledge of successive generations and of millions of people living simultaneously is combined and mutually adjusted.

(Hayek, 1952: 91)

An excellent example of such knowledge that cannot be known by any one individual but that is communicated via social institutions, is the value of a good. Each individual values such a good individually, and by buying the good, or abstaining from this, he makes his valuation known to others on the market. The price that comes about on the market contains the valuation of all these individuals. This price, however, does not allow us to trace back the precise individual valuations that went into creating it. This shows clearly that the knowledge of any one individual is always limited, but that he becomes more knowledgeable than he would otherwise be through social institutions such as language or markets. It should come as no surprise that for both Hayek and Mises the lack of such information, the lack of prices, would cause insurmountable problems for (socialist) central planners. The most important task of the social scientist in a rational age is, according to Hayek, not to show how the world should be improved. Instead, the most important task of a rationalist should lie: "in recognizing the limits of what individual conscious reason can accomplish" (Hayek, 1952: 203).

Where Menger was calling for recognition of the limits of rationalism, but combined this with a call for the improvement of organically grown institutions, Hayek places most emphasis on the former. In an age of 'scientism' the primary purpose of the rationalist lies in showing the limits of rationalism: the limits of what we can know, what we can design and what we can achieve. Rather than attempting to mirror nature in our theories, or worse attempt to shape nature, it is the scholar's task to hold a mirror in front of human beings, of social scientists, and make them recognize their own limitations. Wittgenstein had earlier been calling for recognition of the limits of language, in a similar vein Hayek calls for recognition of the limits of rationalism and human reason in the study and improvement of society and specifically of markets. Hayek combines this with an attempt to redefine the role of the economist, just as Dietl was doing. The social scientist has to suppress his instinct to improve, to recognize the limits of his rational powers. As the medical student Clarke wrote when he defended the therapeutic nihilists in the United States:

Doubtless there is something captivating in the phrase [therapeutic nihilism] itself for it stands out in evident contrast to the general instinct of humanity, to do something for the sick. Whether to do something is necessary or not, whether it is wise or not, whether it may not be even harmful, we all understand that it is expected of the physician, by common consent, to do something.

(Clarke, 1888: 199)

Similarly Hayek demands of the economist to repress his instincts and the social pressure to do something. He should admit that he often lacks the knowledge, and that if he had the knowledge he would often lack the necessary power to improve the situation.[24] This is not an easy task by any means, since improving the world around us is and was an essential element of what it means to be an economist, as Hayek points out in his address to the LSE (Hayek, 1933: 122–123). Hayek considers it his task to show his fellow economists that their 'sphere of influence' and their sphere of knowledge is limited.[25]

That is not an easy task for the economist (a moral scientist): "It is because the moral sciences tend to show us such limits to our conscious control, while the progress of the natural sciences constantly extends the range of conscious control, that the natural scientist finds himself so frequently in revolt against the teaching of the moral sciences" (Hayek, 1952: 100). The writings of the Viennese therapeutic nihilists do not teach us how to cure the disease. They teach us instead to accept disease as a force of nature, a force to be accepted rather than resisted.[26] This is a very different perspective from the standard economic account, in which the outcomes of markets are known and interventions have definite effects. The Viennese students of civilizations instead argue that interventions will hardly ever result in the predicted or desired effects; in fact often they will not have much effect at all. Such a perspective is at odds with the idea of improving the world through specific interventions, and more generally with the idea that the economist can fully grasp what is happening in markets. The contribution of the Viennese students of civilization is,

---

[24] As such, the popular term 'dismal science' to describe economics is very apt.

[25] This is also the main argument of his Nobel Prize address *The Pretence of Knowledge* (Hayek, 1975).

[26] One more similarity: competition is not an evil to be fought, but a force of nature to be accepted, and perhaps to be used to our advantage. This argument is already present in Max Menger (1866).

however, not merely negative. They also show us the power of the forces of society that work to our benefits. Language, markets and laws all make human interaction possible and mutually beneficial, and it is for this reason that Hayek argues that we should 'marvel' at the workings of the market.

5 Conclusion – acceptance and courage

In this chapter, I have shown that the attitude of the Viennese students of civilization is perhaps best exemplified by the redefinition of courage that Dietl sought. For Dietl, courage meant the ability to know one's limitations and be frank about them, thus to be able to say 'no' to a patient. Courage for many of his colleagues had always meant the courage to try new methods and to experiment on the patient. Both Dietl and the Viennese students of civilization were working in an era full of reformers and idealistic (if not Utopian) plans to improve the world and human well-being. Both Dietl and the Viennese students of civilization believed that these attempts, although often undertaken with the best intentions, would frequently lead to disasters.[27] Ignaz Semmelweiss, the doctor known as the 'savior of mothers' for his emphasis on the importance of hygiene in obstetrical clinics, would later in life, after a failed career, attempt to convince pregnant women in the street, to give birth at home; convinced as he was that the doctors and medical institutions in Vienna did more harm than good. In the same spirit, various Viennese students of civilization were telling politicians not to listen to social scientists who sought to engineer society. At the same time, they were telling their fellow scientists that they should be more aware of their own limitations.

This put them in an odd position, which is well illustrated by the description the Dutch economist Jan Pen gives of them during the 1960s. He calls the later members of the Austrian school of economics sour, and Mises only concerned with what is not possible and how things should not be done. He describes them as full of rancor, about their own frustrated ambitions, and frustrated with the development of society (Pen, 1961). The ironic aspect of his description is that there is an unintended truth to that description. The Viennese students of civilization are indeed frustrated with the development of society and social science. They were indeed reacting to, in their eyes misguided, attempts to improve society. They

---

[27] This is further exemplified in the emphasis on unintended consequences in Austrian economic thought.

were indeed concerned with showing what could not be done, and what could not be known. On the other hand, Pen fails to understand them completely because he thinks of the economist as someone who should be primarily concerned with bearing fruit. Pen's optimistic view of economics and the possibilities of rationalizing society did not allow him to really understand what the Viennese were after. To continue our metaphor of fruit and light, it was not so much that the Austrians were only concerned with shedding light, instead they were concerned with what could not be illuminated, what could not be known. Or in Hayek's words: "Though we cannot see in the dark, we must be able to trace the limits of the dark areas" (Hayek, 1960: 23). As such, their perspective is also very different from the call for a focus on positive economics as put forward by their British associate Lionel Robbins.

Robbins argued for positive economics, and objective economists, who would stay away from any discussions about ends. He, however, hardly paid attention to whether economists would be able to provide the accurate assessment of means. In Robbins' methodology, the economist remained a technocrat (however much Robbins was influenced in other respects by the Viennese). In the 'early' Viennese perspective we examined here, the scholar is merely a student of society. The emphasis on unintended consequences and the inexact nature of economic predictions within the economics in the Austrian tradition fit within the perspective in which the economist or social scientist is acutely aware of his own limitations. These limits are threefold, he can never know all the relevant facts, he is unable to foresee the precise effects of various changes (or cures), and he is unable to change the outcomes of market processes much. I have chosen to call this the perspective of the student, to contrast it with that of the technocrat or the doctor prescribing cures. Recently, I have come across a similar distinction in the work of Peter Boettke, who distinguishes between the economist as student and the economist as savior. He too argues that there has been a prominent tradition within economics that thought of the economist as a social engineer: "equipped with the appropriate scientific/ engineering tools to right social ills and guide the ship of the state," which he contrasts to the economist as: "a student of society, teacher of the knowledge gleaned from his or her study, and at times social critic of existing practice in the citizen capacity" (Boettke, 2012: 53).

As becomes evident from reading economics or any social science, it has proven very hard for any scholar to retain this humble position of the student. That difficulty becomes especially great for the Viennese students of civilization during the 1930s when they increasingly feel that the civilization they so cherish and have studied is about to collapse. The earlier Viennese saw an Empire in decline, and later a civilization under siege, and they were aware of the limited powers of humans to influence these developments. They accepted what was going on; they came to grips with the fact that they could not change such developments. This, however, became an increasingly uncomfortable position for a younger generation of Viennese intellectuals.

Both Hayek and Popper therefore emphasize the openness of the future, and the responsibility of individuals to shape their own future. More importantly perhaps, they move away from thinking about social and economic forces as natural forces. They increasingly come to think of such forces as cultural, and hence at least partly shaped by human actions. Without wanting to run ahead of our argument, we can say that they reject (important parts of) the older passive strain of acceptance in Viennese thought, in favor of a more activist stance. Stronger yet, they realize that support for their ideals is mainly dependent on what they can promise for the future. To fight the Utopian visions of the future of the socialists they develop alternative long-term perspectives, alternative ideals. Instead of accepting the decline of liberalism and their civilization as Schumpeter does, they decide to act as its custodian, and ultimately to fight back.

7

The student as defender of civilization

Or Scipio's tears and the fate of a civilization

Nichts bringt das Verlorne zurück
—Rudolf Sieghart, 1932

Human reason needs only to will more strongly than fate, and it is fate
—Settembrini in Thomas Mann's, *Magic Mountain*, 1924

Scipio Aemilianus Africanus minor was the adopted grandson of the Roman general Scipio Africanus maior, who had defeated the great warrior Hannibal Barca, the most famous of the Carthages. He was sent by the Roman Senate to finally destroy the city of Carthage, which had already been deprived of its Spanish Empire during the Second Punic War. During the Third Punic War Scipio Aemilianus led the army that would end the civilization of the Carthages. After completely destroying the city and slaughtering most of its citizens, Scipio did not feel victorious, instead he is said to have shed tears. He explained to his friend Polybius, the Greek historian that he wept over the demise of the city. In Appian's *Roman History* from the second century, the episode is described as follows:

Scipio, beholding this spectacle, is said to have shed tears and publicly lamented the fortune of the enemy. After meditating by himself a long time and reflecting on the rise and fall of cities, nations, and empires, as well as of individuals, upon the fate of Troy, that once proud city, upon that of the Assyrians, the Medes, and the Persians, greatest of all, and later the splendid Macedonian empire, either voluntarily or otherwise the words of the poet [Homer] escaped his lips:

> 'The day shall come in which our sacred Troy
> And Priam, and the people over whom
> Spear-bearing Priam rules, shall perish all'

Being asked by Polybius in familiar conversation (for Polybius had been his tutor) what he meant by using these words, he said that he did not hesitate frankly to name his own country, for whose fate he feared when he considered the mutability of human affairs.

Scipio had shed his tears not only because he had destroyed the city and civilization of the Carthages, but more importantly because he realized that the same fate would one day fall upon his beloved Rome.

One might wonder why we start a chapter on Viennese students of civilization, with this tale about the tears of Scipio. I do so, because this comparison is made by the Viennese historian, and pupil of Carl Menger, Rudolf Sieghart in his *Die letzten Jahrzehnte einer Grossmacht* (The Final Decades of a Great Power, 1932).[1] In this book, he describes and laments the decline and destruction of the Habsburg Empire. He compares the downfall of the multinational Empire and civilization of the Habsburgs to the destruction of Carthage. Understandably, Sieghart argues, one sheds a few tears over this destruction, the loss of the work of so many statesmen, of so many generations. Those tears are praiseworthy: "just as we still praise the tears, which Scipio shed on the rubble of Carthage" (Sieghart, 1932: 443). Those tears, for Sieghart too, take on a second meaning for they should serve as a warning for the fate of Europe. The old Habsburg intellectuals, scholars and historians fear that the same fate might befall other parts of the western world. Or, as Hayek writes to his new Anglo-Saxon audience in the introduction of his *Road to Serfdom:* "The following pages are the product of an experience as near as possible to twice living through the same period" (Hayek, 1944: 1).[2]

A wider circle of Viennese scholars had the feeling of witnessing the same development as they had seen in Austria and previously in the Habsburg Empire. They felt that they were witnessing the collapse of a civilization, the end of an era, for a second time. Just as Scipio had realized that the fate of Carthage would one day befall Rome, so the Viennese believed that the decline of their civilization would also befall the rest of the Western world. Amidst the rubble of the Empire, they were not only shedding tears for the deceased Emperor Franz Josef and his destroyed Empire, but also because they realized that this fate would not be limited to the Habsburg Empire. It is in this spirit, that Sieghart concludes that even more important than weeping over the fate of Carthage or our own fate is to seek to prevent this development for other civilizations.

---

[1] A recent study of the Austrian school of Economics includes Rudolf Sieghart as one of the students of Menger (Schulak and Unterköfler, 2011: 60). Mises favorably reviewed the book in 'Economica' (Mises, 1932).

[2] Hayek also attempted to write a fairy tale based on his experiences in Austria. This fairy tale was about an Empire which after a war loses some of its provinces and then drifts into socialism. It was to warn the readers about the dangers of this march into socialism (Hennecke, 2000: 199).

The acuteness of these sentiments was increased by two developments of the 1930s and 40s. The first development is already alluded to in the previous paragraph, the (often forced) migration of intellectuals from Vienna. The students of civilization tended to end up in the Anglo-Saxon world, while many of the more socialist-minded Mitteleuropaer sought refuge in France first. This migration meant that they would be writing for a different audience, in a different language than they had done so far. It also meant that they came into contact with new groups of scholars and new intellectual currents. The second development was the rise of fascism and the outbreak of WWII. This increased the feeling of a crisis and the potential of an actual destruction of Western civilization enormously. Consequently, various Viennese scholars described their intellectual work during that period, as their 'war effort'. For some, it brought new successes as well, especially for Hayek and Popper. Both the *Road to Serfdom* and the *Open Society and Its Enemies* would become cornerstones of postwar political thought and both sold well to their new audiences.[3]

This chapter will explore and analyze a double transformation in the work of the Viennese students of civilization, especially the work of Hayek and Popper. A transformation away from the perspective of therapeutic skepticism we analyzed in Chapter 6. Hayek and Popper both attempt to refute historicist modes of thinking in which the future is (more or less) determined, and argue that the future is open. This means that they also start thinking of the development of civilization as an open process. The development of civilization is no longer a more or less inevitable and natural process. This cultural process is ultimately shaped by human interaction, they argue, and they consequently both take on the responsibility to act as custodians or defenders of their civilization, and decide to write political books in which they sketch out alternatives for the future. This also means that as 'students' they trespass their sphere of competence, which leads to them ask existential questions about the role of the scholar in a world in decline. They refuse to accept the fate of their civilization as symbolized by Scipio's tears, but they attempt to prevent a similar fate for

---

[3] Popper is perhaps the odd man out in the sense that he is usually considered to be a philosopher of science, rather than part of the Austrian school of economics. Various scholars, however, have identified the similarity between his and especially Hayek's work during this period (1940s). It was also during this period that Popper and Hayek corresponded frequently and Hayek ultimately managed to secure a position for Popper at the London school of Economics where they could collaborate. Their solutions to the problem might not always have been identical, but their diagnosis was very similar or as Hennecke expresses that they were working on parallel fronts (Hennecke, 2000: 128).

other civilizations – as Sieghart claimed they should be doing – but they accept this new role reluctantly.

1 Broch and the power of literature

The tension we have just identified between acceptance of social and cultural developments and the moral duty to attempt to steer those in a right direction, is one of the central themes of Hermann Broch's novel *The Death of Virgil* (1946b). Broch started writing this novel in 1938 while imprisoned in a German concentration camp, and unsurprisingly the novel is frequently interpreted as an allegory on the period through which Broch was living. The novel describes the final day in the life of Virgil. The book starts when Virgil, the Roman poet, arrives on a ship that has brought him from Athens to Brindisium. Virgil has brought with him the manuscript of his *Aeneid*. When Virgil arrives in Brindisium, the Roman republic has collapsed, and the first contours of the Roman Empire are becoming visible; a clear reference to the collapsing European culture, out of which a new civilization had to be formed (Bailes, 2012: 174–175). When Virgil is carried through the city he is struck by: "people's profound capacity for evil in all its ramifications, their possibilities for human degradation in becoming a mob, (. . .) never had he perceived the savagery of the masses with such immediacy" (Broch, 1946b: 23). These masses, these violent masses, make him doubt the worth of his poetry, the value of his work. Virgil realizes that these are the people he had glorified in his work, those for whom he has written. He suddenly becomes uncertain about the meaning of his poetry.

In the second part of the book, Virgil further reflects on his life. He "laments that he has failed as an artist and that the Aeneid is a product of his vanity and has no use to humanity" (Bailes, 2012: 176). His conscience in fact tells him to burn the Aeneid. This, however, does not happen, mostly because in the third part, two old friends and Caesar Augustus attempt to persuade Virgil that the Aeneid is of great value. Especially Augustus is unwilling to let Virgil destroy the manuscript, for he argues: "your poem is the very spirit of Rome, and it is magnificent (. . .) You have interpreted Rome and therefore your work belongs to the Roman people and the Roman State which you serve" (Broch, 1946b: 314–315). Augustus' pleas initially make Virgil even more reluctant to hand over the manuscript, he seems doubtful about the Roman people and especially about the real purposes that Augustus has with his work. Broch lets Augustus orate about his relation to the Roman people and their need for discipline and leadership with clear similarities to the 1930s fascist rhetoric.[4] Virgil finally gives up the manuscript, when Augustus accuses Virgil of jealousy of his position. But Virgil's real motivation for handing over the manuscript remains obscure in the novel. Is it his long friendship with Augustus, or is it fate that is stronger than Virgil? Is he the poet despite himself, as Hannah Arendt described Broch? (Arendt, 1968). This interpretation is favored by Virgil scholar Thomas, who argues that Broch seems to be speaking as much about himself as about Virgil. Or as Thomas puts it: "Broch effectively becomes Virgil, in a moment of literary brilliance that has the effect of eliding the millennia between the two writers, and eliding the gap between the two Caesars under whom each of them lived" (Thomas, 2004: 262).[5] Virgil's reluctance to hand over the manuscript of the Aeneid is thus compared to Broch's own reluctance in writing *The Death of Virgil.*

The concern with the futility, the powerlessness of art is heightened in the face of tyranny, as Broch shows in the novel. This made Broch turn toward science later in life, but he could not resist also working on literary projects. Broch believed that only firm knowledge, science, could be effective in the long run, but he kept returning to literature, or mythos as he called it. In fact, passages of the novel suggest that it is only through mythos that we can expect any effects (Heizmann, 2003: 189). At other times, Broch is unsure whether literature could ever achieve real insight: "literature is only impatience on the part of knowledge" (Broch quoted in Arendt, 1968: 116). Broch's choice for the story of Virgil itself is interesting, because Virgil and the Aeneid had often been abused by political leaders, including the fascists in Germany.

---

[4] There are other, perhaps even stronger, examples of this in the novel, but the discussion about piety between Virgil and Augustus is especially interesting. Virgil argues: "He who is pious, Augustus, is already in awareness; he lives in the memory of the law given by the forefathers (. . .) Piety is that knowledge by which men escape their inescapable loneliness; piety is seeing to the blind and hearing to the deaf, piety is the perception of the simple". To which Augustus responds: "Piety and the state are one, to be pious is to serve the state and to coordinate oneself with it; the pious person is one who serves the Roman state with his whole being and the whole of his works (. . .) I want no other kind of piety; but this one is a duty from which neither you, nor I, nor anyone is excluded" (Broch, 1946b: 375–376). This example is also discussed in the first comprehensive commentary on the novel by Weigand (1947).

[5] Another compelling interpretation of this episode is offered by Lipking. He argues that Virgil finally decides to give the manuscript when Augustus becomes angry, and thereby human instead of imperial. Giving the manuscript then becomes an act of friendship to 'Octavian' rather than a tribute to Augustus and the Roman people (Octavian is the given name of Emperor Augustus, and the name that Virgil in their relationship as friends prefers) (Lipking, 1981: 133).

Broch felt that he wrote at the end of civilization, in fact Broch's novel arose from an attempt to write an essay about *Die Kunst am Ende einer Kultur* (Art at the End of a Civilization) (Heizmann, 2003: 188).[6] I will argue that in the work of the Viennese students of civilization, especially in that of Hayek and Popper, we can find the same two tensions identified here. The tension between on the one hand, the strong conviction of the futility of science or art in the face of tyranny, and on the other hand, the feeling that one has the moral duty to do something in the face of evil; a balance between, on the one hand, the moral duty to fight evil, and on the other hand, the futility of such attempts. Or as it is expressed by Virgil in the novel:

hoping against his inner conviction that the might of beauty, that the magic of song, would finally bridge the abyss of incommunication and would exalt him, the poet, to the rank of perception-bringer in the restored community of men [...] such vain and presumptuous dreams of grandeur, a flagrant overestimation of poetry![7]

(Broch, 1946a: 134–135)

In other words, the tension between our weak-hearted hope that we can make a difference and the acceptance so prominent in the perspective discussed in Chapter 6.

The other tension identified by Broch, the tension between mythos and logos will also occupy a central position. Not as in Broch's work, as a tension between poetry and objective knowledge, but rather as a tension between the attempt to change the world through political books and the more scholarly work of these authors. We will see that the Viennese students of civilization all apologized for the 'political' nature of their work, which diminished in their view their long-term value. Rather ironically, these books have often become the books for which they are remembered most. This tension between writing for one's peers and a wider public can be considered a special instance of the tension between mythos and logos that Broch describes.

2 Defeatism?

The charge of defeatism was leveled at the Viennese students of civilization at various moments. A particularly prominent instance was after the

[6] Broch also wrote an insightful essay on the relation between free will and historical forces (Broch, 1946a, see also Schlant, 1971).

[7] Bailes argues: "This passage is autobiographical of Broch's own experience" (Bailes, 2012: 215).

publication of Schumpeter's *Capitalism, Socialism and Democracy* (1943/ 1976). Readers of his book felt that the combination of his thesis that capitalism was being killed by its own achievements, and that the coming of socialism was inevitable added up to a kind of defeatism. They apparently felt that Schumpeter had given up the hope that socialism could be avoided. Worse yet, it seemed that he had given up the fight against it. Schumpeter himself objects to this interpretation of his work, he argues that a piece of analysis can never be defeatist in itself: "the report that a given ship is sinking is not defeatist". Only our attitude to this conclusion can be defeatist according to Schumpeter, it would be defeatist if: "the crew [would] sit down and drink" (Schumpeter, 1946/1976: 413). It is not beyond imagination, however, that readers interpreted the dispassionate analysis of Schumpeter, his vivid dissection of a moribund capitalism, as just that. He might not literally be drinking and cheering while the ship is going down, he is certainly not looking for ways to fix the ship. The ever elusive Schumpeter does not let himself be pinned down too easily though; the final sentences of his defense are (almost) cryptic:

Defeatist is he who, while giving lip service to Christianity and all the other values of our civilization, yet refuses to rise in their defense –no matter whether he accepts their defeat as a foregone conclusion or deludes himself with futile hopes against hope. For this is one of those situations in which optimism is nothing but a form of defection.

(Schumpeter, 1946/1976: 413)

What are we to make of this defense? Schumpeter's words could be understood within the framework of Chapter 6. Schumpeter here is the anatomist, the dispassionate analyst, diagnosing capitalism. He is not the doctor healing capitalism. He has diagnosed capitalism as fatally ill, and even though we might rise in its defense, such actions are foolish at best. Deep down we know that we are acting against our best knowledge, that we are fighting fate. In Schumpeter's words, it is hoping against hope. Hoping despite the fact that we have given up hope. Or, as Broch lets Virgil express it 'hoping against our inner conviction'. Following the logic of Chapter 6 one might say that we are better off accepting those changes and that is probably what Schumpeter would advise us to do.[8] Optimistic readers,

---

[8] For an interesting discussion of the issue of defeatism and cultural determinism in relation to the theme of civilization, see Leslie A. White (1949). He claims, for example: "To be sure, understanding culture will not (...) alter its course or change the 'fate' that it has in store for us, any more than understanding the tides will change them. But as long as man remains an inquiring primate he will crave understanding" (White, 1949: 359).

however, might find in the same quote a reluctant call to arms, a call to rise in the defense of our civilization.

A similar tension is evident in the work of Mises as we have seen in Chapter 6, but he is also acutely aware of the tension between mythos and logos:

> The defeat of the liberal ideology could not long be postponed. Liberalism has anxiously avoided all political artifice. It has relied entirely upon the inner vitality of its ideas and their power to convince, and has disdained all other means of political conflict. It has never pursued political tactics, never stooped to demagogy. The old Liberalism was honest through and through and faithful to its principles. Its opponents called this being 'doctrinaire'.
>
> (Mises, 1932/1951: 462)

Mises forcefully rejects any kind of political demagogy, and argues that liberalism has always relied on rational modes of persuasion only. If the people refuse to listen, the liberal theorist is powerless:

> if they do not hear, whether because they are deaf or because the warning voice is too feeble, one must not seek to seduce them to the right mode of conduct by tactical and demagogic artifice. It might be possible to destroy society by demagogy. But it can never be built up by that means.
>
> (Mises, 1932/51: 463)

A younger generation of Viennese, however, is unwilling to accept defeat. Especially Popper and Hayek attempt to find ways around this fatalism.

3 The flaws of historicism

The major enemy that both Popper and Hayek identify is historicism. Scholars who have written on Popper and Hayek have observed that their tracts against historicism are somewhat curious. The historicism against which they are arguing seems like an elusive, perhaps even a nonexistent school of thought. It is thus not directly clear against precisely what they are so opposed. Historicism was a strand of thought earlier criticized by Mises who described it as the methodological belief that there are no universally valid laws, and that each epoch has its own unique laws and regularities. Mises associates it closely with the historical economist Werner Sombart and his predecessors of the German historical school. The main reason for Mises to pay so much attention to historicism is that he thinks that economics is a universal science based on causal laws, independent of time and place. Popper and Hayek are more reluctant to embrace such a strong belief in a universal social science, and they are not primarily interested in a criticism of relativism.

This historical relativism, while perhaps dangerous, for it might undercut the belief in universal values and truths, is not the main problem with historicism for Popper and Hayek. They both argue that a fundamental tenet of historicism is its prophetic character. For Popper and Hayek, historicism is not mainly associated with the German historical school and its aversion to theory, but rather to the Hegelian tradition of universal historical laws, discoverable by the historian. This type of historicism, while it contains a similar type of relativism between epochs, is much more ambitious. It claims to be able to discover the laws of development of society as a whole, and it has led many historicists to prophetic claims about inevitable developments in the future. Thus Popper defines historicism as consisting of three elements: historical relativism, determinism and holism. Determinism, according to Popper, is that aspect of historicism that stresses that there are inevitable historical developments, that the laws of the development of society are immutable, *and* discoverable by the historian.

The addition of holism to the set of historicist beliefs is particularly crucial for Popper. Popper's own theory of science stresses the need for (refutable) predictions, and at first sight this is precisely what the prophetic theories of historicists seem to do as well. Popper, however, argues that the type of predictions he is looking for are small-scale predictions under controlled circumstances not the holistic prophecies of the historicists, which he compares with those of soothsayers.

Popper emphasizes the limits of social knowledge, when he asks rhetorically: "Is it within the power of any social science to make such sweeping historical prophecies?" (Popper, 1945: 3). Hayek is similarly critical of the historicists. When he discusses the errors of Comte and Hegel, he argues that they believe: "the central aim of all study of society must be to construct a universal history of all mankind, understood as a scheme of the necessary development of humanity according to recognizable laws" (Hayek, 1952: 196–197).[9] Hayek then continues to show that such claims are 'arrogant' and beyond the capabilities of the human mind. Just as Popper – whom he applauds for his treatment of historicism – Hayek discusses the fact that for Hegel and Comte, history leads to a predetermined, and thus inevitable, goal. This according to Hayek, implies a "thorough fatalism: man cannot change the course of history" (Hayek, 1952: 200). It was this kind of fatalism, this acceptance that we identified as

---

[9] While published in 1952, Hayek developed these arguments during WWII, as he describes in the preface to 'The Counter-Revolution in Science' (Hayek, 1952).

typical of earlier Viennese thought. So, in a sense, rather than fighting just historicism, Popper and Hayek were also forcing a break with their own tradition.[10] Popper is quite aware of this when in the preface of the Open Society he claims that we must be outspoken in our criticism of what "admittedly is part of our intellectual heritage".[11] It is this fatalism that Popper and Hayek have recognized, even in some of their close allies, which they seek to overcome. When Popper reads the *Road to Serfdom*, he is especially struck by the sense of duty from which Hayek has written it: "I felt that you were driven by fundamentally the same experience which made me write my book" (Popper quoted in Hennecke, 2000: 174).

This does not mean that Hayek and Popper themselves are necessarily immediately very far removed from the historicist position. This similarity, or at least, close resemblance between their own position and the position they criticize, is also pointed out by some students of Popper. They have pointed out that Popper's description of open and closed societies and especially the transformation from the closed to the open society contains (more than) a 'whiff of historicism' (Watkins, 1999). The study of history, however, leads both Popper and Hayek to see that historical developments are never unidirectional or inevitable. Both stress the struggle for ideals that were going on in the past, Popper in his study of the Greeks, and Hayek in his study of the history of English liberalism. They come to realize that the advent of liberalism and freedom were neither inevitable nor natural. That is the message they would like to get across to their contemporaries: the fate of our civilization is in our own hands, rather than in the hands of history. As Popper puts it in the preface: "The future depends on ourselves, and we do not depend on any historical necessity" (Popper, 1945: 3). In this respect, it is worthwhile to quote the analysis of Hacohen, Popper's biographer, of this part of Popper's work:

The West could either fulfill that which it was already by definition – rational, humanitarian, cosmopolitan – or decay into the Other, its origin. Popper seemed to discount diverse patterns. This was historicism, but it was innocuous because it was nondeterminist and nontriumphalist. Progress was possible, but regress, given

---

10 The manifesto of the German counterpart to Viennese group, the Ordo-liberals, many of whom would later join the Mont-Pèlerin Society, starts similarly with an attack on this belief in inevitable historical laws and the associated fatalism (Bohm, Eucken and Grossmann-Doerth, 1936/1989).

11 The structure of Popper's argument bears close resemblance to Hayek's attempt to distinguish between a true and a false individualism, which are both prominent parts of our intellectual heritage.

history, more likely. The narrative's major problem was not Western superiority but potential defeatism. Whence hope? From nowhere, said Popper, but we must fight nonetheless.

(Hacohen, 2000: 426)

What immediately stands out is Hacohen's emphasis on defeatism. Popper and Hayek had witnessed the defeatism in many of their contemporaries. They had witnessed it in their intellectual enemies, fascists and socialists, but more importantly they had witnessed it in many of their fellow liberals. Undoubtedly they had experienced it themselves on more pessimistic days. To convince themselves and their allies that there was still something worth fighting for, they had to show that the future was open, that there was hope despite despair.

4 The need for a defense

The other element that stands out in the description of Hacohen is the emphasis on the fighting spirit present in the work of Popper. This spirit also strikes us in the title of the Popper's book *The Open Society and its Enemies*. Popper and Hayek describe their books from this period as their 'war effort' (Popper, 1976: 115; Caldwell, 1997: 37)[12]. Both Hayek and Popper were well aware that they were transcending, or trespassing, the traditional boundaries of scholarly activity.

Schumpeter still claims that: "this is not a political book and that I did not wish to advocate anything" (Schumpeter, 1946/1976: 412–413).[13] Hayek on the contrary argues: "When a professional student of social affairs writes a political book, his first duty is to plainly say so. This is a political book" (Hayek, 1944: 6). Popper: "The systematic analysis of historicism aims at something like scientific status. This book does not. Many of the opinions expressed are personal" (Popper, 1945: 3). They make clear that they write these books to defend their civilization. Once more Popper: "if we wish our civilization to survive we must break with the habit of deference to great men" (Popper, 1945: 4). Hayek, who argues that

---

[12] The fighting spirit of Popper is very evident from the drafts for a new preface to the *Open Society and its Enemies* (Popper, 1950/2008: 169–179).

[13] Mises writes his *Omnipotent Government* in the same period that Hayek and Popper work on their books. As might be expected, Mises' account is more resigned and diagnostic, but he too emphasizes that historical forces are not inevitable: "The ordeal through which mankind is going in our day is not the outcome of the operation of uncontrollable natural forces. It is rather the inevitable result of the working of doctrines and policies popular with millions of our contemporaries" (Mises, 1944: 9).

we have to take a stand: "When the course of civilization takes an unexpected turn – when, instead of the continuous progress which we have come to expect, we find ourselves threatened by evils associated by us with past ages of barbarism" (Hayek, 1944: 10). Or take Michael Polanyi: "[Between 1935 and 1940] the ideas of Liberty, which at the end of the period were to divide the world in a struggle of life and death, were left almost uncultivated" (Polanyi, 1940: 5). These scholars write their books with political goals in mind, they hope to steer civilization in a different direction. At the same time, they realize that it is unlikely that their books will do much to alter the course of an entire civilization. Hayek expresses that tension beautifully:

I have every possible reason for *not* writing this book. It is certain to offend many people with whom I wish to live on friendly terms; it has forced me to put aside work for which I feel better qualified and to which I attach greater importance in the long run; and, above all, it is certain to prejudice the reception of the results of the more strictly academic work to which all my inclinations lead me.

(Hayek, 1944: vi-vii, emphasis in original)

Hayek makes clear that this book is written despite himself. He becomes a defender of civilization despite thinking of himself as a student. He is afraid that it will damage both his relationships and the reception of his future work. More importantly, it seems that he is uncertain of the effects of his work. He puts aside more scholarly work that he believes is of more value in the long run. In fact, his hope that this work might change the course of events seems idle if we consider what Hayek writes elsewhere around the same time about 'true' individualism:

[it] is a product of an acute consciousness of the limitations of the individual mind which induces an attitude of humility toward the impersonal and anonymous process by which individuals help to create things greater than they know.

(Hayek, 1948: 8)

Civilization is precisely such a phenomenon that we help to create, but can never completely understand, let alone steer in a particular direction. Polanyi, with whom Hayek corresponds at the time seems even more uncertain about the effect of the collection of papers he publishes around the time under the title *Contempt of Freedom* (1940). After he has written about the ideals of Liberty (his capital L) and humanity, and particularly about the anxieties and danger surrounding them, he comes to a humble conclusion: "looking back on these essays with this in mind, I am of course aware of their insignificance" (Polanyi, 1940: 6). Popper is, perhaps characteristically, less modest about the effects he hopes his work might have.

But even Popper phrases his hopes with some restraint. He hopes that his work will contribute to the analysis and understanding of totalitarianism, and hopes it will have significance in the 'perennial fight against it'.

These scholars, these students, nonetheless publish these books; they speak out instead of submitting themselves to these developments. Where does this hope come from?

It should come as no surprise that Popper and Hayek consider the theory of socialism and especially that of Marx to be of the historicist type. In Marxist theory, the class struggle would ultimately resolve itself in the rule of the only remaining class, the proletariat. The proletariat would rule in the socialist world, which would inevitably follow capitalism. It was this type of theory that was embraced by Schumpeter, although in a modified form (he believed that capitalism would collapse from a lack of social support, rather than expecting a proletarian revolution caused by exploitation). In fact, at certain points, the Viennese students of civilization were all convinced that while socialism was fundamentally flawed, it was also inevitably coming. What these prophetic theories however did not account for was the rise of fascism. Many socialists at the time attempted to write fascism off as the last phase of capitalism: its last convulsion before its final demise. Popper and Hayek on the contrary saw fascism and socialism as related; they were both collectivist and totalitarian ideologies. More importantly they had seen that various intellectuals had discarded socialism and placed their faith in fascism. This provided a glimmer of hope for Hayek and Popper.

This change is most evident in Hayek's analysis of socialism in these years in the article 'Freedom and the Economic System' (1939), which would lay the groundwork for *The Road to Serfdom*. In that article, he argues that the socialists have succeeded in capturing the popular imagination. He argues that the socialists realized that: "if the ideals and tastes of the great majority are determined by factors which are under human control, we might as well use this power to turn their thoughts into what we think a desirable direction" (Hayek, 1939: 35). As such, Hayek is merely restating an observation that can be found in the work of Schumpeter and Mises, but he, from then on, also actively engages in attempts to recapture this popular imagination.[14] Compare that to what Mises writes in

---

[14] Regarding the views on the masses, Hayek's thought is in line with the views we explored in Chapter 3. In *The Road to Serfdom* he argues, for example: "Probably it is true enough that the great majority are rarely capable of thinking independently, that on most questions they accept views which they find ready-made, and that they will be equally content if born or coaxed into one set of beliefs or another. In any society freedom of

Omnipotent Government, which he writes during the war: "It is hopeless to expect a change in the near future (...) Liberalism failed because the intellectual capacities of the immense majority were insufficient for the task of comprehension" (Mises, 1944: 282–283).

Hayek and Popper on the contrary asked themselves: If socialism and fascism have succeeded why could liberalism not succeed once again? Fascism and socialism were cultural forces, strong forces, but nonetheless they were not natural developments. So Hayek argues: "If in the long run we are the makers of our own fate, in the short run we are the captives of the ideas we have created" (Hayek, 1944: 2). And Popper: "The responsibility of this tragic and possibly fatal division becomes ours if we hesitate to be outspoken in our criticism" (Popper, 1945: 5).[15] The change is not immediately apparent, but Popper and Hayek transform socialism from an inevitable social development into an ideology, a cultural development. The rise of fascism makes them realize that they are fighting a cultural ideal, instead of a natural force. In the long run it might be possible, if unlikely, to change that cultural ideal. Instead of passively accepting the inevitable changes of their time, Popper and Hayek argue that it is their personal responsibility as intellectuals to resist these changes and especially the mistaken beliefs underlying them.

This shift was also slowly taking place among the Viennese liberal economists in the 1930s. Richard Strigl, member of the Mises Kreis, in 1932 already wonders, employing the medical metaphor once more, whether if all cures have been tried we should perhaps not wonder whether the real problem is psychological; which leads him to wonder whether we should reconsider the ideas that currently underlie our economic policies (Strigl, 1932/2005: 110). Fritz Machlup, too, argues that the problem is not so much that we do not know what to do, but that politicians refuse to do it. He argues that if we compare economists to doctors then we should recognize the crucial difference that while patients typically take the medicine prescribed to them: "the sick economies, however, refuse to take their medicine" (Machlup, 1933/2005: 204).[16] The articles by Machlup and Strigl are part of

---

thought will probably be of direct significance only for a small minority" (Hayek, 1944: 168).

[15] Such sentiments remained the most important driving force behind Popper's work, see especially the introduction to Popper, 1994. There he writes: "*The future depends upon ourselves. It is we who bear all the responsibility*" (Popper, 1994: 8).

[16] In an argument that is highly reminiscent of the price of civilization argument of Chapter 4, Machlup continues that politicians instead prescribe themselves sweet pills, and then complain to the economists when these do not work.

a campaign by members of the Mises Kreis and Geistkreis associated with the business cycle institute to educate the public in economic matters and to alter economic policy in Austria, which during this period abandons the gold standard and introduces various tariffs (Klausinger, 2005).

A second cause for renewed hope was undoubtedly their migration to the Anglo-Saxon world. They felt that the harmful developments in the 'new world' had not yet progressed as far as on the continent, and that perhaps the trend could still be reversed in their new home countries. This belief comes out most clearly in the introduction to the Hayek's 'Road to Serfdom' in which he makes clear to his British audience that he has already lived through the development of thought that the Anglo-Saxon world is currently experiencing. He wishes to warn his audience that if they continue on this path, they will ultimately end up in the situation of the European mainland. Hayek argues: "history never quite repeats itself, and just because no development is inevitable, we can in a measure learn from the past" (Hayek, 1944: 1).

If socialism and fascism are cultural developments, and if they are successful because of the utopian images they sketch for the future, they have to be fought on this ground. To the attentive reader this will sound familiar, for this is what Wieser had argued in 1910. In the series of lectures, he had called for a new kind of liberalism. He had compared his age to the glorious days of the liberal hero Schiller. Back then, he argued, people were working together on a shared project, a shared ideal, the ideal of freedom, under the banner of liberalism. Wieser argues that the end of an era has come, and that a new one is beginning: "Politically also a better time will come, with new values, new hope, and a new belief in freedom" (Wieser, 1910: 154).[17] In this new era, Wieser suggests that we might need to get rid of the concept of liberalism, especially since it is surrounded by so much controversy. Even if the word liberalism is given up, however, the wish for and belief in freedom should be kept alive. It is this task that Hayek and Popper now take up.

5 Renewed ideals?

One of the Viennese liberals who recognized early that new ideals were needed was Peter Drucker. A man, now best known for his work in management, was trained as an economist and like his fellow Viennese

---

[17] My translation in German: "Auch politisch wird eine bessere Zeit kommen, mit neuen Werten, mit neuen Hoffnungen, mit neuen Freiheitsglauben."

intellectuals he tried to make sense of fascism and socialism in the 1930s. From the introduction of his *The End of Economic Man* (1939) it becomes clear that he is writing with a similar purpose as Hayek and Popper, to warn the Anglo-Saxon world for the dangers of socialism and especially fascism. The first sentence is the typical disclaimer: "this is a political book (...) it has a political purpose to serve: to strengthen the will to maintain freedom against the threat of its abandonment in favor of totalitarianism" (Drucker, 1939: xv). In this book, which is cited twice in a positive way by Hayek in his *Road to Serfdom*, Drucker argues that alternative ideologies were bankrupt at the time when fascism was on the rise. The liberals had given up most of their fundamental beliefs during the Great Depression, while socialism in Central Europe had collapsed. In Russia, it had become clear that equality and freedom could not be achieved through socialism. Drucker therefore argues that there is a need for new ideals, in a world of bankrupt ideologies. The appeal of fascism can only be countered by offering an alternative positive program.

Drucker argues that both socialism and capitalism were based on the idea of economic man, for whom economic satisfactions alone appear socially important and relevant. In both philosophies: "Economic positions, economic privileges, and economic rights are those for which man works. For these he wages war, and for these he is prepared to die" (Drucker, 1939: 43). This prominence of economic man has led to the dominance of a purely economic logic and purely economic ideals. Neither liberalism nor socialism was able to realize these ideals completely, and there was an increasing dissatisfaction with the emphasis on the economic side of life. Fascism, on the other hand, was successful because it set up noneconomic ideals, such as that of the heroic man, the courageous individual willing to sacrifice himself for the greater good. According to Drucker, though, even fascism has trouble explaining what this individual sacrifice is supposed to be for; sacrifice might sound plausible for the individual, but not for society as a whole. Sacrifice always presumes some higher goal, a goal that fascism fails to offer. So he argues the future of Europe depends on whether we are able to come through this crisis to find a new (noneconomic) domain in which the fundamental Christian/European values of freedom and equality can be realized.[18]

---

[18] As with so many of the Viennese thinkers, and this is especially true of their postwar reception, this political dimension of Drucker's work was largely ignored. But Drucker's work on organizations after the war was envisaged as a possible solution to such political problems.

Hayek is quite critical of this part of the analysis of Drucker. In what I believe to be the most important chapter of the 'Road to Serfdom', he responds to Drucker's thesis. In that chapter entitled 'Material Conditions and Ideal Ends', Hayek fiercely attacks the idea that economic ideals could or should be less important: "Economophobia would be a more correct description of this attitude than the doubly misleading 'End of Economic Man', which suggests a change from a state of affairs which has never existed in a direction in which we are not moving" (Hayek, 1944: 203). According to Hayek, individuals have always been concerned with wider ideals than mere economic ones, but he is especially critical of the idea that the 'economic' will lose its importance. The denial of basic economic laws and the denial of the importance of material welfare for the realization of our ends are according to him dangerous threats to civilization. Such denials suggest wrongfully that we are able to shape the economy according to our wishes, or that human flourishing can be realized without a flourishing economy. More importantly, still, is the fact that the ends of individuals are always varied and heterogeneous, so society should not concern itself with the realization of such ends. The deliberation of ends should be left to individuals, for which the economic sphere will provide them the (appropriate) means and freedom. Just as he had earlier stressed in the article 'Freedom and the Economic System', the coordination of such individual ends could only occur in a decentralized system, such as the market. If it were attempted in a centralized manner, this would inevitably lead to totalitarian control: "individual freedom cannot be reconciled with the supremacy of one single purpose to which the whole society must be entirely subordinated" (Hayek, 1944: 211). He argues that even a goal such as 'full employment' which Drucker suggests, cannot and may not ever be the single or primary goal for which society strives.

Hayek believes that Drucker gives in too easily to the socialist criticism of our civilization. Drucker emphasizes the need to do something about the 'despair of the masses'. He suggests the need for more (job) security and an enduring peace. Hayek, on the other hand, approvingly quotes Benjamin Franklin: "Those who would give up essential liberty to purchase a little more temporary safety deserve neither liberty nor safety" (Hayek, 1944: 133). Hayek's 'solution' is problematic to say the least, because it hardly provides consolation for those who suffer from this insecurity.

Popper and Hayek believe, as we have seen in Chapter 4 that the revolt against civilization as embodied by socialism and fascism is caused by the 'strain of civilization'. The uncertainty associated with an open and free society, the burden of individual responsibility, and the unwillingness to accept certain unavoidable ills. Instead of attempting to decrease this strain as Drucker suggests, and as social-democracies arguably attempt to do, Hayek argues that we should submit ourselves to: "conventions which are not the result of intelligent design, whose justification in the particular instance may not be recognizable, and which to him will often appear unintelligible and irrational" (Hayek, 1948: 22).[19] Or in other words, we should accept the strain, but for *what* Drucker would reply? What justifies this sacrifice?

Hayek's book does not provide an answer to that pressing question. Many readers of his book are indeed surprised that very few positive ideals are suggested. Hayek finally hopes to remedy this in his *Constitution of Liberty*: "If we are to succeed in the great struggle of ideas that is under way, we must first of all know what to believe" (Hayek, 1960: 2). And he asked his colleagues at the Mont Pèlerin Society, to have the 'courage to be utopian' (Hayek quoted in Burgin, 2012: 217). The tension between analysis and political ideals, between science and politics, between mythos and logos, remains present also in his most idealistic book 'The Constitution of Liberty'. Like *The Road to Serfdom* this book starts with a warning: "This book is not concerned mainly with what science teaches us" (Hayek, 1960: vii). Hayek explains that he wants to sketch an ideal, and how this ideal can be achieved. He seems more optimistic than ever and willing to sketch ideals for the future. The reader, however, soon discovers that this is far from easy for the skeptic Hayek. Instead, he more cautiously attempts to restate old truths for new generations. He argues that these truths and principles have been almost completely disregarded over the past century. The true novelty of his *Constitution of Liberty* is that Hayek stresses the necessity of a 'wide consent on certain fundamental values', or as he also puts it, the importance of: "our ability to rally a sufficiently strong part of the world behind a common ideal" (Hayek, 1960: 2–3). In other words, Hayek emphasizes more strongly that a liberal society consists of individuals who share certain values as well as ideals. A similar shift has been noticeable in liberal political philosophy, for example, in the work of John Rawls (Rawls, 1971; Rawls, 1996). Whereas Hayek earlier had stressed the divergence of individual aims and values, he now argues that such a

---

[19] This quote is from 'Individualism: True and False', but in chapter 14 of the 'Road to Serfdom' one can find similar arguments: "It was men's submission to the impersonal forces of the market that in the past has made possible the growth of civilization which without this could not have developed; it is by thus submitting that we are every day helping to build something that is greater than any one of us can fully comprehend" (Hayek, 1944: 204), see also Chapter 4.

divergence can only exist and be fruitful if there is also some overlap in values and ideals. This combination of a lively discussion by those who shared a certain fundamental outlook would also be the starting point for the Mont Pèlerin Society (Hayek, 1947/1967). That society, however, would similarly run into difficulties whenever it attempted to formulate a positive program for the future, as Burgin has shown recently (Burgin, 2012).

Hayek's claim for a return to older values raises the question whether this would be at all possible. In Chapter 4, we have seen how Hayek himself was skeptical about this. Once the gold standard had been unmasked as a fiction, it could no longer serve the function it once had; and that was true also of many Christian values. Schumpeter was deeply convinced, as we saw earlier, that hoping for a return to such values was wrongheaded. Virgil, in Broch's novel, realizes that the *Aeneid* promotes republican values, values that belong to the past and values that would be out of place in the new Empire. Virgil concludes from this in the beautiful phrase 'No longer and not yet', that his work as poet is futile, because it comes too late and too early at the same time. Too late, for it attempts to resurrect a culture that is dead and too early because a new republican moment has not yet come (Lipking, 1981: 132–134).

In that sense, Popper is more daring, he offers ideals for the 'Open Society' of the future. He suggests that the adoption of scientific values, such as a critical attitude and cosmopolitanism could inspire a new generation. His ideal of piece-meal social engineering offers an alternative to totalitarianism on the one hand, and laissez-faire on the other. Popper is less reluctant to fill in what the future might look like, even though that is sometimes at odds with his scientific skepticism. In the introduction to his book he suggests that what his work owes to the scientific method is mainly an awareness of the limitations of scientific knowledge (Popper, 1945: 3).[20] At the end of the first volume, however, he offers a program of

---

[20] Popper himself was far from humble, see for example, the reminiscences of John Watkins of the many personal conflicts he got involved in (Watkins, 1997). But in his political philosophy, he kept arguing for fundamental humility and awareness of our limitations. When he reflects on his generation, he for example, argues that it was not that his generation was clever, but wicked, but rather that they were "quite good-natured and well-intended, but also intellectually lazy and hazy and altogether pretty stupid" (Popper, 1963/2008: 232). The main difference with Hayek is that Popper places much more emphasis on our duty and ultimately our ability to do better: "[the next generation] must try to become less stupid than we were; in other words it *must try to learn from our mistakes*" (Popper, 1963/2008: 233, emphasis in original).

humanitarianism and faith in reason, and offers the Great Generation of the Greeks as an ideal community to aspire to. Sometimes, he cautions against the fanatic and feverish urge to improve the world, which should be sufficiently tempered by an awareness of the limits of our knowledge, a sense of individual responsibility, and the acceptance of our own fallibility it. At other moments he is optimistic that his program for the future of the 'Open Society' offers a constructive and comprehensive program for the postwar world.

Even if they do so in different ways, both Popper and Hayek attempt to point the way forward for our civilization, instead of lamenting its decline. As Popper puts it: "We must go on into the unknown, courageously" (Popper, 1945: 177). This is no longer the courage to admit our ignorance, to know our own limitations; this is once again the courage to hope, the courage to experiment and help build something new. It is perhaps no coincidence that Broch in the new world devoted most of his time to helping fellow émigrés, and developing a program of universal human rights. Vienna had not left these scholars. Hayek, in the introduction to the *Constitution of Liberty* even explains to his American readers that his mind had been formed in 'my native Austria', but they could now use their knowledge of a civilization in decline, to help build one that might be resistant to those forces that had brought it down: a civilization that could defend itself from its enemies.[21]

6 Conclusion-fate and civilization

The study of the theme of fate is not common in economics, or the history of economics. In sociology, it is somewhat more common; Liebersohn for example, examines how German sociologists have dealt with the theme of fate between 1870 and 1923. He describes a belief in fate as a "serious conviction that impersonal forces ruled the world" (Liebersohn, 1990: 3). This description makes it instantly clear how central this theme remains in Hayek's work. In his later work, as in his earlier work, he thinks of the market as a sphere where impersonal forces govern. Popper and Hayek's critique of historicism criticizes the belief that impersonal forces

---

[21] There is a great lack of studies that seriously deal with this migration and its impacts, both negative and positive. The one great exception is Reisch (2005), who examines the migration of the members of the Wiener Kreis. The study by Vaughn *Austrian Economics in America* (1994) does unfortunately not deal with these years following the migration, but rather with the reception of Austrian economics in the 1980s.

(historical, cultural, economic, or otherwise) determine history, but it does not mean a rejection of impersonal forces altogether. It should rather be seen as a renegotiation between these impersonal forces and the power of humankind to alter such forces. These impersonal forces, or fate if you like, cannot be shaped, designed, and sometimes they cannot even be altered, but they are ultimately shaped by human interaction, they are cultural.

Liebersohn perceptively argues that the recognition of fate, even during the pessimistic first decades of the twentieth century did not always imply a withdrawal from politics.[22] Sometimes it led to action in perceived harmony with those forces, a position to which Schumpeter comes close at times.[23] More generally the emphasis on fate and impersonal forces might be especially strong during periods of decline.[24] In fact, when we see the transformation from thinking about civilization and its development as purely determined by impersonal forces, toward a shared responsibility for our civilization in Hayek and Popper this coincides with a period of new hope. New hope caused by on the one hand, their (forced) migration, and on the other hand, because the coming of socialism did no longer look as inevitable as it once had.

The novel by Broch about Virgil demonstrates the tension for the authors during this transformation. Virgil's wish to burn the *Aeneid* because it represented the values of a dying civilization is mirrored in the reluctance of a younger generation of Viennese students of civilization to write political books. On the other hand, these authors feel a moral duty to do something about the developments of their time, to alter fate. In that sense, the new world is liberating to them, for they could once again contribute to a living civilization. Hence Hayek dedicates his *Constitution of Liberty* to "the unknown civilization that is growing in America"

---

[22] Schorske in his intellectual history of Vienna emphasizes the process of withdrawal from politics (Schorske, 1980). An interesting example of such withdrawal during the interwar period is the development of Karl Menger, the son of Carl Menger, described in meticulous detail by Leonard (2011). For mathematical economists, it was perhaps also easier to escape into an aestheticism than for the more politically minded economists we study here. That being said, it cannot be denied that there is a tendency toward aestheticism and a search for pure foundations in Mises major work on praxeology. He considered the manuscripts he wrote during this period his 'posthumous works' so in a sense he felt he had withdrawn himself from the world (Mises quoted in Hülsmann 2007: 802).

[23] Congdon suggests for example, that this is the way to understand the work of György Lukács (Congdon, 1991).

[24] For more on the relation between the development of civilization and theorizing about it, see the Postscript in Norbert Elias (2000) especially section VII.

(Hayek, 1960). The Viennese students of civilization reconceptualized the future as open, and its course as a shared responsibility for mankind. They felt that they had a responsibility to contribute to this future in a positive manner, although they remained skeptical of the value of their contributions. As Hayek put it: "When we do not dare to hope anymore, there remains that one hope, that the influence that the academic teacher has on the thought of the next generation at least can partially make up for what many of our predecessors have so heavily transgressed" (Hayek quoted in Hennecke, 2000: 119).[25]

---

[25] My translation, in German: "Wen wir schon nicht mehr hoffen dürfen, so bleibt doch immer die eine Hoffnung, daß wir mit dem Einfluß, den der akademische Lehrer auf das Denken der folgenden Generation hat, wenigstens zum Teil das wieder gutmachen können, worin sich manche unserer Vorgänger schwer versündigt haben."

8

The student of civilization and his culture

On the relationship between the scholar
and his object of study

He saw the world going under, and it was his world
—Joseph Roth, *The Radetzky March*, 1932

Grillparzer, the nineteenth century Austrian poet and playwright whose aphorism on freedom I quoted before, was intrigued by Napoleon. As Claudio Magris explains in his discussion of Grillparzer and Napoleon, Grillparzer thought of Napoleon as the symbol of an age, who had destroyed the 'religio of tradition'. His subjective hubris of a revolution combined with nationalism disregarded reality and most importantly the importance of tradition. "For Grillparzer, Napoleon, with his assertion that in the modern age politics have replaced destiny, represents totalitarianism, life seen as totally political". This is contrasted by Magris with the rule of Joseph II "the loyal servitor of the state, who does his duty with self-abnegation, but who also defines the limits of political interference, defending the distinction between the public and the private spheres" (Magris, 1989: 80). Napoleon's totalitarianism, the pursuit of a single idea for which everything else must be sacrificed, is contrasted by Grillparzer with the Austrian tradition of "the tangible detail, the unique particular, that side of life which cannot be reduced to a system" (Magris, 1989: 80). In his play *King Ottocar: His Rise and Fall* Grillparzer contrasts these two types of leadership by presenting the kings Ottocar and Rudolph. Ottocar is the leader who attempts to Germanize the regions Bohemia and Moravia, to lead them forward into the future. Ottocar is proud, easily enraged and concerned with honors and powers ("[He] who even challenged Nature as his foe"), while Rudolph is the humble leader who primarily practices patience and prudence. Where Ottocar dreams of greatness, Rudolph merely wishes to contribute to a tradition that is far older and greater than he is ("And we are mindful of our ancient line").[1] There is no better way to introduce the difference between the role that the Viennese students of civilization envisioned for themselves and the role they believed that modern social scientists adopted.

The Viennese students of civilization imagined themselves to be like Rudolph, humble with attention for the particular and the unforeseen, and fully aware that they could never fully understand let alone control that land of which they were supposed to be the ruler. They believed that modern social scientists had started to act like Napoleon, subsuming their subjects to a single goal that they would objectively and rationally organize. Not surprisingly in Grillparzer's play, Ottocar's fall is caused by his arrogance and hubris. And perhaps also not surprisingly Hayek would trace this transformation of the position of the social scientist back to the spirit of the age of Napoleon, early nineteenth century France: to the thought of Saint-Simon and Comte. It is tempting to even interpret the title of his book as suggestive of the idea that social science is in need of a counter-revolution, along the lines of the political counter-revolutionary movement of Burke and others. But matters are not as simple. The only time that Hayek explicitly refers, except in the title of his book, is indirect and dismissive.[2] Even so, it is quite useful to think of Hayek's plea for the limits on reason, as a counter-revolution to the revolution of Reason (with a capital R). As such his counter-revolution is the reaction to the intellectual project of positivism in the social sciences. In what follows, I will explore three important themes that emerge from this counter-revolution: an alternative type of knowledge, the responsibilities of the student of

---

[1] The two quotations are taken from the translation of the play by Arthur Burkhard (Grillparzer, 1823/1962: 14 and 113).

[2] The origin of the idea of a counter-revolution in science is interesting in itself. Hayek cites a reference in the work of Werner Sombart to the phrase coined by De Bonald (Sombart, 1908: 54). Sombart in that particular chapter argues that following the French Revolution, a more realistic and historical theory of the state, was founded as opposed to the rationalist theory (presumably the social-contract theorists) by Savigny, Guizot, Schleiermacher and others who could build on a more historical sense found in Montesquieu, Burke and Vico. These counter-revolutionaries argued that the constitution of a state could never rest on mere rational arguments, but has to be grounded in the current power relations in society. These men argued for a 'Verfassungsleben', a phrase frequently (and positively) used by Wieser. It is clear that Hayek's interpretation of the phrase is negative. And Sombart thinks of these men as the founders of the historical school, needless to say that the Viennese students also did not want to be associated with that school. But Menger and Hayek's own emphasis on norms and traditions is certainly not out of step with the goals of these counter-revolutionaries, and they frequently referred positively to many of the individuals associated with this movement by Sombart.

civilization and the extent to which the Viennese managed to live up to their own ideals of humility and acceptance.

1 Therapeutic and edifying knowledge

In the introduction of this book, I suggested that what particularly struck me about the Viennese students of civilization were statements that floated somewhere between prudent advice, methodological criticism and moral principle. In his German biography of Hayek, Hennecke quotes a typical one by Hayek: "The economist is the Cassandra of the modern world by occupation. His unfortunate, and mostly hopeless, task is, to shatter illusions" (Hayek quoted in Hennecke, 2000: 119).[3] My question then, as now, was how we are to understand such statements, what type of knowledge is this, does it have any value? I think that they do contain knowledge; I will argue that this knowledge is best understood as therapeutic knowledge. The discussion of Rorty in Klamer's *Speaking of Economics* inspired me to explore this notion (Klamer, 2006: 75–76).

Rorty, like the Viennese students of civilization, is intrigued by the relationship between the social scientist and the accumulated body of knowledge, or in his case the relationship between philosophers and philosophy. Rorty explains how he was taught that studying philosophy was equivalent to studying its progress; especially the progress in the philosophical discipline epistemology. But during his studies, he hit upon a group of philosophers that did not easily fit into the traditional systems. This other group was, however, at least as useful for him as were the more traditional philosophers. This leads him to distinguish two groups of philosophers, the first group he labels 'systematic' and the second one 'edifying'. He argues that systematic philosophers typically argue: "Now that such-and-such a line of inquiry has had such a stunning success, let us reshape all inquiry and all of culture, on its model" (Rorty, 1979: 376). Rorty associates this view with scientism, in an analysis that bears striking resemblances to that of Hayek. Systematic philosophers build and add on, edifying philosophers on the other hand: "destroy for the sake of their own generation (...) [they] are reactive and offer satires, parodies, aphorisms. They know their work loses its point when the period they were reacting against is over" (Rorty, 1979: 368–369). One of Rorty's favorite edifying

---

[3] My translation, in German: "Der Nationalökonom ist nun einmal die berufsmäßige Kassandra der modernen Welt. Seine ungluckliche – und meist hoffnungslose – Aufgabe ist, Illusionen zu zerstören."

philosophers is Wittgenstein, whom he quotes in the epigraph to his *Philosophy and the Mirror of Nature*: "Philosophy has made no progress? If somebody scratches where it itches, does that count as progress? If not, does that mean it wasn't an authentic scratch? Not an authentic itch?"

This idea seems to describe the work of Dietl and some of his close associates rather well. Dietl and his contemporaries were fond of aphorisms and reacted to the overtreatment common in their time. The function that Hayek envisages for himself is not much different. He wants to temper the rationalism of his age, the naïve belief in science, the belief in progress and the possibilities of politics and planning. These edifying philosophers according to Rorty: "refuse to present themselves as having found out any objective truth" (Rorty, 1979: 370). They rather point to the limits of our current knowledge or aspirations. As such, Hayek's argument should be understood historically (the counter-revolution to the revolution) against certain aspirations present in his time and day. This is also reflected in the working title he had for his great work on knowledge in the 30s and 40s; the first part would be called the 'hubris of reason' (largely covering the nineteenth century and its influence) and the second period would be characterized by the 'nemesis of the planned society' (or the road to serfdom) (Ebenstein, 2003: 112). A period of human presumptions and arrogance about individual knowledge (hubris), would lead to a period of retribution, the failure of the planned society (nemesis).

Rorty puts much emphasis on the fact that this edifying, or therapeutic role as he calls it elsewhere, should not be accompanied by a call for the implementation of a new system. I am not convinced that this is not so important, in his early work, Wittgenstein was attempting precisely to construct a new system, and as we saw, so is Hayek in his later work. Besides, the notion of 'edifying' itself suggests that there is also a positive element to their work, in the way they raise awareness, and make us aware of certain tensions. Or as Rorty puts it: "[Their] work is therapeutic rather than constructive, edifying rather than systematic, designed to make the reader question his own motives for philosophizing rather than to supply him with a new philosophical program" (Rorty, 1979: 5). Rorty argues that edifying knowledge, instead of teaching us about the world (description), helps us to cope with the world. Popper's concept of the strain of civilization is not a call to end this pain, but rather to recognize it as a price worth paying for the benefits of civilization. It is not primarily a constructive attempt to improve the world, but to help us to cope with the world, and to recognize what we cannot change. This edifying function of knowledge helps us to realize what our limits are. They have a moral function similarly to the short prayer, popularly known as the 'serenity prayer':

> *God, grant me the serenity*
> *To accept the things I cannot change,*
> *Courage to change the things I can,*
> *And wisdom to know the difference*[4]

Not surprisingly, Rorty compares the function of edifying knowledge to the function of poetry, as opposed to science. Edifying knowledge helps us to become aware, it helps us to pursue attainable goals, rather than giving us a description of the world. Along this line of thought, economics is not a dismal science for the descriptions it gives about the world, but because it emphasizes scarcity and the responsibility associated with making choices. The economist is often forced to take the role of pointing out that resources are scarce, choices costly, or that there is no 'free lunch'. These insights are part of the therapeutic knowledge of economics. As Rorty also claims, they are an essential part of the humanist education, which is not about how the world is (the domain of science), but rather what we can and should pursue. They are as much about us, as human beings, as they are about the world out there, but most of all they are about our relation to the world.

This edifying and therapeutic element is what differentiates the Viennese style of thinking from other styles of thinking within economics, and more generally the social sciences during the twentieth century. Hayek, placing a slightly different emphasis, recognizes this, when he describes his own efforts as: "The psycho-analytical treatment of our times. This treatment can help to bring into our consciousness, that which without our knowledge controls our thinking" (Hayek quoted in Hennecke, 2000: 119).[5] Hayek emphasizes the therapeutic element of this exercise, it helps us to realize unconscious elements of our thought. For both Rorty and Hayek this does not mean that edifying and therapeutic knowledge should somehow replace scientific knowledge, they are both essential parts of human knowledge, more importantly they complement one another. As Rorty points out, the therapeutic philosophers are often parasitic on the

---

[4] An alternative version in a more medical direction: For every ailment under the sun/ There is a remedy, or there is none / If there be one, try to find it / If there be none, never mind it.

[5] My translation, in German: "Die psychoanalytische Behandlung der Zeit. Sie kann uns dazu verhelfen, uns vieles zum Bewußtsein zu bringen, was ohne unser Wissen unser Denken beherrscht."

traditional scientific knowledge. Like court jesters who exist by virtue of kings, so therapeutic thinkers exist because there is scientific or otherwise privileged knowledge. These therapeutic thinkers demand corrections, they seek to change what the systematic scientists are pursuing, and they attempt to change the content of our economic knowledge. They moreover make us aware of the moral character of our intellectual pursuits.

Now that we are aware of this other type of knowledge (a therapeutic insight), it is also easier to understand the calling to which Carl Menger was referring, analyzed earlier in this book. The introduction to his book on method now appears in a new light. Menger argues that developments in other fields such as political science and jurisprudence had led to promising results, which led various political economists to attempt to apply these methods in economics. In doing so, they overlooked the differences between those fields and political economy, a claim of 'scientism' once again (Menger, 1883/2009: 30). Menger thinks of himself as correcting these flaws; he will be the critic whom German political economic thought has missed for so long. And he concludes morally, but not very humbly: "All great civilized nations have their specific mission in the development of science (. . .). Political economy, too, cannot dispense with the single-minded cooperation of the German mind. To contribute to bringing it back to the right paths was the task of this work" (Menger, 1883/2009: 32). The Austrians would keep attempting such corrections: from Böhm-Bawerk's reaction to Marx, to Mises' reactions against Werner Sombart and German socialists and historicists, to Hayek's criticism of rationalism. Some parts of their work were constructive, but important parts of their work can only be understood in response to corrupting trends they saw around them. One could call it reactionary, the derogatory label for the counter-revolutionaries of the nineteenth century, and some of the Viennese thinkers would not have been very offended, but edification and therapeutic knowledge captures better what they were after.

Their contributions are sometimes therapeutic when they lay bare unconscious elements in the tradition of economic thought and they are edifying to the extent that they help guide us, and cope with the world. This opens up the question whether there is a larger therapeutic and edifying tradition in economics. Within economics figures such as Bernard Mandeville and Thorstein Veblen come quickly to mind, but I hope that this notion will make us aware of a different kind of knowledge that is existent throughout the social sciences. This other type of knowledge is usually neglected, or worse frowned upon, because it supposedly does not add to the accumulated body of knowledge. I hope to have shown here, that such neglect is unwarranted.

2 The responsibility of the social scientist

At the very start of this book, I introduced the painting *Late Visitors to Pompeii*. In that painting, Carel Willink had depicted himself on the left, suspiciously looking over his shoulder toward the viewer. This led me to wonder whether he believed that he bore some responsibility for the demise of the culture depicted in the painting, or whether he perhaps believed he had some role to play in reviving it. This can quite easily lead to somewhat grotesque claims about the role of the painter, or in our case that of the student of civilization, as if it was in his or her powers or to change the fate of a civilization. I hope that the previous chapters have shown that the students of civilization we have studied are far from thinking that this is within their powers or indeed within their scope. They did nonetheless believe that their responsibilities consisted of more than objective analysis.

We find Hayek struggling with this tension, when in 1944 he addresses a gathering of historians at King's College Cambridge. His tone from the very first words is serious and dramatic: "Whether we shall be able to rebuild something like a common European civilization after this war will be decided mainly by what happens in the years immediately following it" (Hayek, 1944/1992: 201). He then explains that the fate of Europe to a large extent depends on the fate of Germany. If older liberal ideals can be re-established there, there will be hope. He argues that the British historians – who make up his audience – can play a role in re-establishing these ideals. Hayek is aware that any overt attempts to do so, through imposed historical textbooks for example, will probably only have counterproductive effects. British historians can nonetheless play a vital role through international collaboration, and especially through the recognition and appreciation of valuable work done in Germany itself. Furthermore, they can help to (re-)establish the "cultivation of certain common standards of moral judgment" (Hayek, 1944/1992: 208–209). The historian, Hayek argues, has a responsibility to contribute to this project, even if he is reluctant to do so, for: "whether he wills it or not, the historian shapes the political ideals of the future" (Hayek, 1944/1992: 214).[6]

---

[6] For more on Hayek's theory of intellectual change see Burgin (2012).

Such a claim clearly runs counter to the traditional image of the historian, or more generally the objective social scientist. It is miles away from the technocratic perspective – which we explored in Chapter 6 – in which the expert is given a goal by the policy maker and then advises on the most appropriate or efficient means to achieve this goal (Robbins, 1932: 149; Berger and Kellner, 1982: 121–142; Blaug, 1992: 128–131, see also Hutchison, 1964: 108–116). This simplistic model has been frequently criticized not in the least by the Viennese students of civilization for the scientism it implies (see also Berger and Kellner, 1982: 121–131). But even if one is somewhat critical of this simplistic technocratic model it is yet another step to accept the idea that the historian or social scientist should help to promote certain ideals. Nonetheless this is what Hayek argues and it was with this goal that he set up the Mont-Pèlerin society (Hayek, 1947/1967). So, is this just a type of ideological activity we should reject as scholars?

I am tempted to concur, but doing so feels unnatural. If students of the economy have established that certain organically grown institutions help to foster human interaction with mutually beneficial outcomes, should they not attempt to promote and protect these institutions? And to what extent are such efforts different from the advocacy of an optimal institutional arrangement that works in theory. The latter perhaps runs the danger of turning into a naïve perfectionism, but the former might lead to too much caution.

It is telling that Hayek seeks to anchor his defense of certain parts of our culture in both intellectual as well as practical traditions. For him, at least during his more humble moments, the defense is a combination of the pragmatism of that which has proven its worth with an attempt to ground this defense in intellectual traditions. His attempt to formulate a *Constitution of Liberty*, on the other hand, tends more toward the perfectionism that Hayek so criticizes in others.

I believe there is an additional reason to believe that it would be wrong to think that economists, sociologists or political scientists should stick to a discussion of means only. Over the past decades, we have seen, especially in economics, a shift away from the metaphor of foundations (as in Samuelson's defining *Foundations of Economic Analysis*) to the metaphor of principles. More recently, we have seen a stream of books that demonstrate the economic way of thinking (Cowen, 2007; Frank, 2008, see also Heyne's textbook of the same name first published in 1973). In this tradition, which at least goes back to Wicksteed's emphasis on the 'common sense' of political economy, but probably further back to

Mandeville, the economic way of thinking is a particular understanding (and critical perspective) on the world: the need for choices (and trade-offs) in a world of scarcity, the emergence of exchange (or social cooperation) under certain institutions, the importance of property rights and incentives within these institutions and the function of prices within the market process. In a recent book, in which Boettke makes a similar point, he argues that these principles are what make up the economic way of thinking (Boettke, 2012: 17–32). Following Henry Simons, Boettke argues that these economic principles provide a kind of prophylactic against a variety of popular fallacies.

This view is in accordance with the view that the sociologist Berger expounds about the sociological way of thinking. Berger argues that sociology is perhaps best understood as a form a consciousness, a way of thinking. This way of thinking according to him consists of three elements: a willingness to look for different levels of meaning of human life, especially those that are hidden from our everyday consciousness (a kind of unmasking), secondly a willingness to look at the unrespectable, to those parts of behavior that are regarded as 'vulgar' or 'unrespectable' or that are too easily taken for granted, and thirdly an awareness of the relativity of identities, ideas and values in the modern world (Berger, 1963: 25–53). It is particularly striking that the first two elements seem to be completely in-line with the recent stream of popular economics books who all unmask our everyday reality ('the hidden reality behind everything' or 'discover your inner economist'), and are prone to look at the unrespectable (cheating teachers or sumo-wrestler, or just realize that the entire idea of studying business was rather unrespectable for many centuries). Berger emphasizes also that these insights might work well to counter various popular fallacies. In that sense, we can perhaps understand Hayek's plea to the historians as a call to awareness that the influence of the historical consciousness has been particularly strong in Germany, and that this historical consciousness is to a large degree the responsibility of the historians.

The 'way of thinking' or principles approach seems to implicitly embrace the idea of therapeutic knowledge. It emphasizes the aspects of knowledge in a particular tradition that help us to understand and cope with the world around us. Another element that at least the economic and the sociological consciousness have in common is the emphasis on the negative: the need for trade-offs, showing what is not true, what should not be taken for granted. One could call it an eye for the tragic elements of human life. In Hayek's own work, this element is of course even stronger when he suggests that economists show men: "how little they really know about what they imagine they can design" (Hayek, 1988: 76). Among historians a similar tradition exists, consider for example, Pocock: "historical inquiry is anti-paradigmatic, in the sense that it multiplies without theoretical limitation the problem-situations, contingencies and contexts in which any historical occurrence may have been situated, and therefore performs the liberal-conservative function of warning the ruler on the one hand, and the revolutionary on the other, that there is always more going on than either can understand or control" (Pocock, 2009: xiii). Similar sentiments might be found in the work of Quentin Skinner and of course, in that of Lord Acton and Tocqueville, the two thinkers after which Hayek originally wanted to name the Mont-Pèlerin Society.[7]

The final step we have to take to realize that the student of civilization is in a position to defend certain institutions, or at least to warn against certain wrong-headed attempts to change these, is that the emphasis is on the student element.[8] Within the technocratic model, a clear separation is made between the individual as scientist (who as an expert can advise on means) and the individual as citizen (who has a personal opinion on ends). When we instead think of the scholar as a student of society, a student of human culture, such a neat separation becomes more problematic. Berger's book *An Invitation to Sociology: A Humanistic Perspective* (1963) on which I drew earlier, and the recent stream of economics books that focus on a certain economic consciousness, consciously adopt a democratic perspective. They hope to show the reader that everyone possesses this particular consciousness (hence the invitation), but that some are more aware of it and have cultivated it further than others.

In other words, economics or sociology is not (just) a substantive body of expert knowledge on how to govern, but rather an awareness from which every citizen can benefit. Not surprisingly this is how Berger ends his book:

---

[7] Some scholars have observed that in both Hayek and Popper the criticism of the social engineering stems from epistemic arguments (see for example Gray, 1984, especially 134–136). I too draw heavily on such epistemic arguments here, the 'student'-perspective emphasizes the skepticism about (the possibility of) certain knowledge.

[8] In the *Fatal Conceit* Hayek emphasizes this defense of the status quo: "An understanding of cultural evolution will indeed tend to shift the benefit of the doubt to established rules, and to place the burden of proof on those wishing to reform them. While it cannot prove the superiority of market institutions, a historical and evolutionary survey of the emergence of capitalism helps to explain how such productive, albeit unpopular and unintended, traditions happened to emerge" (Hayek, 1991: 20–21).

Box 3: A combination of sensibilities

The awareness of the existence of the various sensibilities that we can cultivate also makes us aware that any single one of them will only give us partial insight, might even mislead us. So, we can to a large degree agree with Keynes when, in his obituary of Alfred Marshall, he argues that the: "master-economist must possess a rare combination of talents not often found together. He must be mathematician, historian, statesman, philosopher-in some degree" (Keynes, 1924: 322). But, instead of emphasizing this high standard of his skills, or indeed the idea that there can be 'master-economists', we should perhaps talk of sensibilities. The economist has generally cultivated his sensibility about costs and benefits of a variety means very far; he knows how to do things efficiently. Efficiency only, however, gets us nowhere, as Menger already claimed, without deliberation about ends such efforts will be blind. The historian, as Pollock points out, has usually cultivated his sensibility of contingency and the importance of context very far, but might lack the understanding of certain principles that underlie almost all human behavior. The sociologist, as Berger argues, has cultivated his sensibility of differences in perception between individuals very far, but they might overemphasize this relativism. What all the various students of particular subjects ultimately require is balance, an understanding that their sensibilities are not the only ones, that they are contributions to a wider (cultural) conversation. These sensibilities do not necessarily divide easily into ends and means (if such a distinction is tenable at all since ends are usually means in a longer means-ends chain). When economists praise the economic growth of the past two centuries (the means), they know fully well that that is not the end of the story about human well-being (the end), but they do rightfully feel that economic growth has contributed to it. The awareness of contingency and context will make the historian skeptical not just of certain means, but also of certain ends.

We have the possibility of stopping in our movements, looking up and perceiving the machinery by which we have been moved. In this act lies the first step towards freedom. And in this same act we find the conclusive justification of sociology as a humanistic discipline. (Berger, 1963: 176)

When Baumol and Blinder first introduced the modern principles approach to economics, they called these principles ideas for beyond the exam and Cowen even links the discovery of our inner-economist to the future of civilization. Boettke argues, following Buchanan, that "economics is a public science in that basic knowledge of the discipline improves the ability of the students to be informed participants in the democratic process" (Boettke, 2012: 64). The responsibility of the student of civilization is then not a kind of professional duty, but a civic duty – a duty to speak up given that certain principles or critical insights are ignored. These authors, in other words, appeal to edifying character of economic and sociological knowledge.

This brings us back to the student of civilization and their responsibilities. They have those firstly as teachers, because they cultivate and pass on of the existing body of knowledge. But another responsibility comes about because they possess a certain sensibility. Next to their occupation as teachers and scholars, students of civilization are participants in conversations about human well-being, governance and more broadly the good life. As participants to these debates they have a responsibility to point to successful cultural institutions and warn against proposals they believe to be misguided. They might even have a somewhat privileged position in the democratic debate, precisely because they have studied civilization more than others, but ultimately they are just that, participants. A student should want no more, or should he?

3 On the humility of the Viennese students of civilization

In the previous chapters, I have characterized and in various ways praised the humble position that the Viennese students of civilization take. Now it is time to consider whether they actually practiced this ideal. To examine this, I would like to start what I believe to be one of the most potent criticisms of this self-proclaimed humility by Philip Mirowski, a criticism to some extent shared by John Gray.

Mirowski argues that Hayek hit upon a 'double-truth doctrine' according to which: "the masses will never understand the true architecture of social order, and intellectuals will continue to tempt them to intervene and otherwise mock up the market" while Hayek and other neoliberals would have the power to *"define and institute* the types of markets that they (and not the citizenry) were convinced were the most advanced" (Mirowski, 2009: 443–444). Mirowski is particularly worried that under a Hayekian regime an elite would be able to create the institutions they had found were most beneficial (private property rights, rule of law and constitutional limits) while the citizens would be told that markets and other cultural institutions could never be fully understood (or outperformed) and that they therefore had to be accepted as facts of life. This criticism is compelling for various reasons. We have already seen the contempt with which the Viennese students of civilization wrote and talked about the masses and intellectuals. Secondly, it would certainly be problematic if it turned out that Hayek, who condemned the social engineering of others, was in fact in favor of his own type of social engineering. Thirdly, it hits upon a deeper tension in the work of the Viennese students of civilization who rely heavily on epistemological arguments to criticize the philosophies of others, but seem to put a rather definite plan forward themselves. For Mirowski, there is a fourth reason why this argument carries so much force, because he believes that Hayek and others have set up, through the Mont-Pèlerin society and its various offshoots, a new 'technology of persuasion'. The way in which Hayek and especially some other neoliberal thinkers have disseminated their ideology through think-tanks, academic departments and business elites is further evidence for the idea that this elite has functioned in a very different way from which they describe markets or other cultural institutions. While the dissemination of their ideas, according to Mirowski, has taken place through concerted (and centralized) efforts, in their theories they instead describe a decentralized process of interacting individuals with dispersed and incomplete knowledge.

So what are we to make of this claim by Mirowski? I believe there are two points at which Mirowski's interpretation goes seriously wrong. He greatly overestimates the power of the scholars involved in the Mont-Pèlerin society to shape both the internal coherence, and secondly, the message communicated to the outside world. The recent history of Burgin shows the absence of such internal coherence. More importantly Burgin's history shows that during the mid and late 1950s, Hayek seriously considered to disband the organization that had been set up to foster international cooperation in a period of intellectual isolation. Burgin describes this plan for disbandment as a curious mixture of triumphalism and despair. Triumphalist because the intellectual isolation was disappearing, but despair caused by: "the continued failure of the society's internal debates to fulfill his [Hayek's] original aspirations" (Burgin, 2012: 124). Burgin shows that similar problems plagued the society's outside communication, members could not agree on the message or even the appropriate channels.

This leads to a more serious problem in Mirowski's account of Hayek's role in the Mont-Pèlerin society. Mirowski, in contrast to Burgin, seems to neglect the despair of liberal intellectuals in interwar Europe about the political, social and economic developments. Mirowski, instead of emphasizing this context as prime moving force behind the intellectual project, sneers at the 'refined European tastes' and emphasizes the strong antidemocratic strand in for example, Hayek's thought. That strand is certainly there, but can only be understood against the Weimar and Austrian experience of collapsing democracies giving way to fascism. Even more serious than neglecting the historical context of this movement is perhaps that in characterizing neoliberalism Mirowski seems to willfully neglect Hayek's attempt to position the market between 'the natural' and 'the constructed' (point 1 and 2 in Mirowski, 2009: 434–435). When Mirowski attempts to identify the view of markets within the society, he only contrasts markets as natural entities with the idea of markets as man-made or rather state-made constructs. Hayek's attempt consists in showing that markets are cultural; they are neither designed nor natural. One may certainly believe that Hayek fails to convincingly show this, but to simply neglect it is unfair.

Does that mean that Mirowski's criticism is completely invalid? I tend to think it is not, but to understand the real tension in Hayek's thought it does not help to claim that Hayek "hit upon the brilliant notion of developing the 'double truth' doctrine of neoliberalism—namely, "an elite would be tutored to understand the deliciously transgressive Schmittian necessity of repressing democracy, while the masses would be regaled with ripping tales of 'rolling back the nanny state' and being set 'free to choose'" (Mirowski, 2009: 444). As I showed in Chapter 4, Hayek is frank about the fact that paradoxically freedom can only come about through restraints on that same freedom. One might not agree with this idea or ideal of freedom, but it was certainly there for everyone to read. The tension that is however present, is that between the Viennese students of civilization as critical observers and the Viennese students of civilization as liberal theorists, or even liberal utopians. Or, the tensions between the rationalist and the skeptical aspects of their work, as John Gray once described it (Gray, 1984: 139).

Humility implies mainly the skeptical attitude and only very careful constructive proposals. As humble students, they would focus on under-standing and the therapeutic aspects, but in much of their later work Hayek and Popper go much further. They attempt to formulate theoretical political insights that are at odds with the uncertainty and skepticism that is so central to their work (and critique of socialism).

The tension described in Chapter 7 between mythos and logos, between political ideals and understanding is central in their entire body of work. It is this tension, with which they struggled so deeply, that explains the tension in their work between an emphasis on uncertainty in their theor-etical work, and the conviction of their political work. Different Viennese students of civilization responded differently to these challenges. Some went back to their more theoretical work in various disciplines. One could think of Michael Polanyi (who also stopped attending the Mont-Pèlerin Society). Others hardened into a deep pessimism if they had not already acquired this pessimism earlier. One could think of Joseph Schumpeter and Ludwig von Mises. Hayek, on the contrary, perhaps spurned onward by the public success of the *Road to Serfdom*, pursued his political work further, into directions, I have mentioned *The Constitution of Liberty* earlier as an example, which certain did not sit easily with his own skepticism and emphasis on uncertainty.[9] At times, he indeed consciously adopted the strategies that he deplored in others; a striking example is when he asked his fellow liberals to have the "courage to be utopian" (Hayek, quoted in Burgin, 2012: 217). Or, when he writes as a memo to self: "what is missing today, is a liberal utopia (. . .) a liberal radicalism (. . .) which does not limit itself to what today seems politically possible" (quoted in Hennecke, 2000: 248).[10] As the previous chapters have shown, such utopian courage would run counter to the perspective of the student and the Viennese tradition of which Hayek was such a great representative.

In these three chapters, we have seen that the Viennese students of civilization did not strictly stick to the humble position they advocated in their criticism of others. They attempted to formulate (utopian) ideals for the future, especially since they believed this to be one of the reasons for the success of socialism. The way to understand these pursuits is through the tension in their attitude toward civilization, toward the cultural institutions they studied. They were convinced that cultural institutions such as language, law and markets are indispensable for peaceful and beneficial human interaction. The Viennese students of civilization increasingly felt that a purely passive attitude toward the decline of civilization no longer was a responsible position. This led them to write, what they called political books, which explicitly defended these cultural institutions. This is arguably still consistent with their position as students, but to turn the tide they needed new or reinvigorated ideals for a brighter future. They needed to provide hope. Such attempts led to a tension in their theoretical work also, between the rationalism or even constructivism associated with their plans for the future and the more humble emphasis on uncertainty and skepticism in their theoretical work. I have tried to show that in the process they went through an existential crisis in which they transformed from students of civilization to custodians or defenders of civilization, often 'despite themselves'. Occasionally, they even slipped into utopian formulations, with themselves cast in the role of masters or saviors of civilization.

---

[9] In a recent controversy over the results about the relation between debt-levels and economic growth of Reinhart and Rogoff Tyler, Cowen nicely captured one aspect of this tension: "There is a genuine tension between becoming (and staying) 'famous' and expressing all the appropriate levels of agnosticism on issues" (Cowen, 2013).

[10] My translation, in German: "Was uns heute mangelt ist eine liberale Utopie, (. . .) ein *liberaler Radikalismus,* daß sich [nicht] auf Dinge beschränkt, die heute politisch möglich erscheinen."

9

Meaning lost, meaning found

The migration and initial reception of the Viennese students of civilization in the United States

They operate with modes of argument that differ from those of the poet, but
they share with the poet the assumption that words gather and engender
responsible apprehensions of the truth
—George Steiner, *The Retreat from the Word*, 1961

They were deferred to as authorities; they were mistrusted as intellectuals
—Joseph Horowitz, *Artists in Exile*, 2009

One of the central arguments of this book is that context matters. What
happens to the Viennese students of civilization during the 1930s is one of
the most dramatic shifts in context one could imagine. They choose or are
forced to migrate from Vienna. Initially, there are several options including
a variety of other European countries but sooner or later the United States
becomes the preferred destination. In Chapter 7, we already saw how that
shifting context provided new hope for a younger generation of Viennese
students of civilization. It is thus only logical that we ask how this change
further impacts their work.

In some sense, it looks almost like a natural experiment: what happens
when you take some Central-European social scientists out of their context
and place them in an entirely different one? But matters are unfortunately
not as simple, even if we would restrict our focus on how the Viennese
were received in the United States. Unfortunately that all important condition that other things remain more or less equal does not hold in our
case. The way that economics, and more broadly social science was done,
and what was considered as social scientific knowledge was changing
rapidly during this period. Within economics there was the rise of Keynes-
ianism, which with or without Keynes approval, quickly transformed
economics into an engineering science. A transformation further spurned
on by the war effort and enormous financial support to empirical

economics (Buck, 1985; Bernstein, 2001: chapters 3 and 4; Mirowski 2002: chapter 5; Amadae, 2003). The United States was quickly taking over the leading role in (social) science from Europe. Furthermore, it was not clear what the next step would have been for the Viennese students of civilization had they stayed in Vienna. Various commentators have argued that the development of Austrian economic theory had come more or less to a standstill in Vienna, although that verdict may alter significantly if we adopt the civilization perspective of this book (Caldwell, 1988; Klausinger, 2006). And perhaps more importantly the political-economic and social context was far from stable. The 1930s had brought fascism, the 1940s the war and reconstruction and the 1950s the emergence of the Cold War.

So even without the forced migration, we would expect significant changes to have taken place. What further complicates matters is that while some of the Viennese scholars found a new audience in their new home countries, others found the transition less easy. They had to fight for recognition or failed to obtain positions in their new countries. Some found their work fitted in well to the themes and methods pursued in the postwar world, others had a much harder time fitting in.

That being said, to understand the emergence of the two distinct legacies around the work of the Viennese students of civilization, that we identified in the introductory chapter, we should examine the way in which the Viennese tradition was received and transformed when it crossed the ocean. Those different and distinct legacies have come about in part because the migration had different effects on individual Viennese students of civilization. The more senior among them Schumpeter, Mises and Hayek obtained professorships in the United States (Hayek first in London) that left them relatively free to pursue their own established research interests. And while Schumpeter had earlier parted ways with the Viennese students of civilization, Hayek and Mises now also increasingly pursued different projects. Fritz Machlup and Gottfried Haberler, who were of the same generation as Hayek, born at the turn of the century, became more or less modern economists, with an Austrian flavour. Morgenstern, who had already distanced himself from the Mises Kreis in Vienna, obtained a position at Princeton and went on to contribute to an entirely new field of economics: game theory (Leonard, 2010).

During these processes, the meaning as well as the intent of their work changed. When Hermann Broch wrote in *The Death of Virgil* "No longer and not yet" he captured well the feeling that dominated during the first years of exile. Ludwig von Mises even described his work during this period as his 'posthumous work' (Hülsmann, 2007: 802). Hansjörg

Klausinger has described these initial years, adopting a characterization first used by Ludwig Lachmann, as "in the wilderness" (Lachmann, 1982; Klausinger, 2006). Klausinger's account is the most complete account we have of this period. He emphasizes that soon after Hayek left for London, Morgenstern already steered the Institut für Konjunkturforschung in a direction that was more in line with the empiricist mode of social science, propagated for example, by various members of the Wiener Kreis. Morgenstern expressed his growing discontent with the Mises Kreis and Geistkreis strongly in his correspondence, about Machlup he wrote: "He should eventually start doing *science*" (Morgenstern quoted in Klausinger, 2006: 625, emphasis in original). Of the other prominent members, including Hayek and Mises, he similarly believed that their methods were out of line with the demands of modern social science.

These developments prefigured what would occur in America. The main problem, in this new context, for the Austrians was not, as one might perhaps expect, the English language. They were all conversant in English, even though writing in a different language always involves some adjustment. The real language barrier was emerging from the rise of mathematics in economics. A young generation of British and American economists, as well as those Austrians associated with the Mathematical Colloquium of Menger and Morgenstern were formalizing economics into a mathematical language. The Viennese students of civilization lacked the mathematical skill to contribute to this effort, or even to formulate their own theories in this new language. Moreover, given their methodological convictions they were frequently hostile to the use of mathematics in the social sciences in the first place.

Along with this new political language a new ethos of economists emerged. As Michael Bernstein has shown in great detail American economists positioned themselves as detached and objective experts working in the national interest (Bernstein, 2001). That ethos was very different from the ethos of the Viennese as student or defender of civilization (Chapters 6 and 7). And it was in this particular constellation that the branches of the Viennese tree would start to split off. The work of Hayek and Popper, which was inspired by the work on socialism and interventionism by Ludwig von Mises, was of great importance in the formulation of the Cold-War rhetoric of the struggle between the West and the totalitarian rest. This discourse was important in shaping the context of national interest and public service under which major transformations took place in economics. But that was only the outer, ideological if you will, layer. Underneath that rhetoric a kind of economics emerged that focused on macro-economic engineering science as well as strategic military planning, and the exact study of the allocation of resources. A type of economics that was fundamentally at odds with the Viennese tradition. So, while on the surface it looked as if the work of Hayek and Popper was greatly influential, this was surface only, because beneath the surface a different kind of economics was being forged, one in which the Austrian tradition would come to occupy only a marginal role.

1 Social science in America

In a stimulating essay on the emergence of Cold War science historian of science Theodore Porter argues that the Cold War context for social science: "tended rather to depoliticize it, adding one more incentive for scholars and university administrators to emphasize technical tools of science and to insist on its independence and detachment" (Porter, 2012: ix). It is this narrative of depoliticization and a focus on technique, in economics frequently referred to as formalism (Weintraub, 2002), which has become the standard narrative about postwar economics and social science more generally. In that story, positivism, another intellectual movement that migrated from Europe, is an important actor. The new social sciences sought a clear methodology and an ethos that pronounced them as value-free. As Porter points out, this neutral stance was also important when it came to speaking to policy-makers. But that neutrality came at a price as one critic of these developments argued at the time: "newly escaped from the era of over-easy theory-building into the world of patient empiricism and quantification" they easily accepted "institutional things and their associated values as given" (Lynd quoted in Cravens, 2012: 118–119; see also Novick, 1988). Earlene Craver and Alex Leijonhuvud, in an essay on the influence of European economists on American social science, sketch a similar development. They venture that European economists, having just escaped the European crises, were particularly drawn to the empirical and econometric work because its associated methods provided a "bulwark against the intrusion of political ideologies into the social sciences" and they were more ready to "take the physical sciences as the epistemological model for a 'scientific' economics" (Craver and Leijonhuvud, 1987: 181).

There are at least two reasons to be critical of that story. Firstly, positivism in its European guise was indeed preoccupied with the methods of the natural sciences, but it was far from an ideologically neutral program. And secondly American postwar social science and economics could only claim its nonpolitical nature because of the widespread consent over a national interest. In the formulation of that shared national interest the 'war books' by Popper and Hayek would be of great importance, but meanwhile social science was turning away from the direction that the Viennese envisioned: in content, style as well as organization. But let us start with the depoliticization of positivism to examine how social science in the Cold-War American context was different from that in Central Europe in the interwar period.

In his book on the Vienna Circle and its migration to the United States, George Reisch does an excellent job of showing how logical positivism and its ideals were transformed by this migration (Reisch, 2005). He demonstrates how the ideal of the Unity of Science as a philosophical ideal to unite human knowledge, but also as a practical ideal of collaboration between scientists from different fields and a political ideal of the spread of knowledge and the emancipation of the working classes, is at the heart of the philosophy of the Vienna Circle, especially of its more activist left wing. Reisch shows that the positivist program was not merely a philosophical program, but primarily a social and political program: "the unity of science program transformed from a practical, collaborative goal to a more narrow academic thesis (...) it became an empirical hypothesis about science (...) after it was decoupled from the ideal of active collaboration" (Reisch, 2005: 375–376). We must not forget that the Wiener Kreis was not just a philosophical movement, it was also intimately connected to various social projects, of which the unity of science was just one. Many of its members were active in organizations that promoted the emancipation of the lower and middle classes through knowledge (Dahms, 1995; Dekker, 2014).

This is not the place to debate the merits of the unity of science thesis or these other social projects. What is interesting for us is the shift Reisch describes away from these social goals, toward purely philosophical and academic goals. He contrasts the idea that philosophy underwent: "a development or maturation through which twentieth-century philosophy (finally) acknowledged a fundamental and proper distinction between philosophical research and political partisanship," with his own view that questions of philosophy and epistemology could (and should) inform public debates and individual decision making, or in his words: "a more scientifically and epistemologically informed public, and possibly a more peaceful, economically stable and just world" (Reisch, 2005: 369–388). Reisch is not the only one with this sentiment; Janik and Toulmin in their study of Wittgenstein's Vienna also lament the professionalization that made the position of therapeutic philosophers in modern intellectual life increasingly difficult (Janik and Toulmin, 1973: 249–262). Both Reisch and Janik and Toulmin recognize that within the Viennese tradition there is no clear separation between science and politics or philosophy and life. They argue that for the Vienna Circle and for Wittgenstein political goals went hand in hand with scholarly concerns, just as we saw was the case for the Viennese students of civilization.

That is a very different conception of the purpose of scholarly pursuits, from the one that dominates in the Cold War era. The latter period, is the period of science done in projects, within firmly autonomous disciplines within government-funded universities. The disciplines that make up the social sciences all proclaim that they are absolutely value-free during this period. This leads to a curious constellation, where politicians get to decide on the goals and practical use science, but scientists are completely free to inquire in the domain of truth. This constellation is well captured by the technocratic ideal we encountered in Chapter 6. The neutral experts help to further political aims; aims any intellectual would have at least liked to reflect on.

The shift is well captured in an article by Adorno in which he reflects on his experience in the United States. The contrast in Theodor Adorno's, a critical German philosopher, case is perhaps sharper than it would be in most cases, but I believe it is illuminating nonetheless. Adorno recounts how he enters a project that studies the effects of radio on the American public, which is overseen by Paul Lazarsfeld. As in other cases, Adorno is not at liberty to set the terms of his migration. Or as he puts it, collaboration in this project is a precondition for a 'speedy migration' (Adorno, 1969: 340). Adorno admits to not knowing what a 'scientific project' was before he arrived in the United States. He soon discovers that the project consists of the collection of large portions of data through surveys and experiments: "which were supposed to benefit the planning department in the field of the mass media, whether in industry itself or in cultural advisory boards. For the first time, I saw 'administrative research' before me" (Adorno, 1969: 342).

And although the head of the project Paul Lazarsfeld was aware of the distinction between this type of research and the more critical research typical in interwar Europe, he makes it understood to Adorno that there was little to no room for critical or reflective work in this project. Adorno more or less complied but started noticing stark differences between him and his colleagues, for example, in the way the word method was used. Method for the other project members was synonymous with technique, in contrast with Adorno's ideas in which method is closely associated with epistemology. And he was deeply surprised when he discovered how easily it was accepted that all science is measurement, including the study of culture. Beneath such differences lurked a deeper conflict over what constitutes knowledge.

Adorno recounts one particular instance where he was confronted with some empirical questions to which he predicted all the outcomes to one of his fellow project workers. The colleague in turn looked at Adorno as possessing some particular intuition, while Adorno felt that he had simply used his common sense. Later, it was suggested to him that he should be cautious in developing too many ideas as hypotheses, before they were tested, for these ideas might bias the objectivity of his finding. Adorno was dumbstruck, what he had considered to be knowledge was turned into a suggestion for a hypothesis. Or, as he puts it: "Skepticism toward the unproved can easily turn into a veto upon thought" (Adorno, 1969: 351). This experience resonates strongly with some of the arguments developed in the introductory chapter of this book, and the preceding chapter about the nature of the knowledge that these European scholars possessed.

To account for this difference, Adorno draws a distinction between the expert technician and the intellectual. It was in similar terms that a debate emerged in the United States over the future of the intellectual. Stuart Hughes, whose *Consciousness and Society* (1958) remains the classic intellectual history of Europe in the early decades of the twentieth century, ponders in the pages of the magazine 'Commentary' whether the intellectual is obsolete. He, like Adorno, distinguishes between intellectuals and technicians. Hughes, too, is critical of the fact that the social sciences are taken over by the technicians. But Hughes is also acutely aware the European ideal of the intellectual is historically quite unique: "by the 18th century there had come about that radical change that converted the characteristic European intellectual from a defender and rationalizer of existing institutions into their implacable critic" (Hughes, 1956: 315). He even quotes Schumpeter, who described intellectuals as 'nibbling away at the foundations of society', and shows great awareness that any society can only tolerate a small group of such intellectuals. Looking back, it is surely tempting to suggest that interwar Europe was plagued by an excess of intellectuals nibbling away at the foundations.

But, just as the European interwar period had been a unique period of opportunities for the public intellectual, so the large-scale change within the social science toward the technical and engineering attitude was a unique event. The scale tipped, as it were, from one extreme to the other. This change was to a great extent part of a conscious desire, on the part of scholars, to help improve society, instead of criticizing it. If anything, the wars and the crisis between the wars had shown that contemporary society had quite enough critics, or 'enemies' in Popper's language combative language. It is this change that is wonderfully captured by Carl Schorske, historian of Vienna, in a reflection on the change in the human sciences in the postwar years:

'My generation was drawn to economics', Robert Solow [the economist] told the participants at a conference in Pasadena in the voice of his generational culture, 'by the depression and to a lesser extent by the war; by the desire to fix things, to do good. Today economists are drawn more by the appeal of scientism'. (...) Paradoxically, the engagement of university social scientists in the reforming work of the New Deal—a logical extension of their previous academic roles as independent social analysts and critics—began their transformation into technical experts for whom mathematics and statistics were of the highest usefulness. The war, with its expanded demand for purely operational, applied scholarship in the service of relatively uncontested policy goals, likewise increased the imperative for scientific reliability.

(Schorske, 1997: 295–296)

It is one of the great ironies of the reception of Central-European scholarly work that both the positivism of the Vienna Circle and the totalitarian critiques of the Viennese students of civilization helped legitimize, this new type of social science. Positivism legitimized the objectivity of the methods of modern social science. The pursuit and spread of objective knowledge had had great attraction in the highly politicized interwar environment of Central Europe as an antidote to radical relativist claims and ideological uses of knowledge, but it was now used in an entirely different ideological context. With that new context came a new language. When Otto Neurath developed his visual statistics to spread knowledge or when Popper and Hayek reached out the general public they did so in a language that was shared between the scholar and the citizen (Dekker, 2014). The language of postwar social science, however, would be more and more self-contained. It was a language that was inward looking, technical and aimed at fellow academics and policy makers, not the public.

Such scientific pursuits, largely isolated from the public, needed to be legitimized, and it is here that the work of Popper and Hayek was so important. Their books written against totalitarianism of all kinds helped legitimize the free science of the West, against the planned science of the totalitarian states. Especially, Popper's *The Open Society and its Enemies* draws heavily on the ideals of criticism and rationalism characteristic of science to define what the open society entails.

Hayek, too, frequently made the link between freedom in science and freedom in society, also because his arguments for freedom were founded upon epistemological arguments. But Hayek's interest in the free pursuit of knowledge went further, during the 1940s, he was in close contact with Michael Polanyi, who had helped found the 'The Society for Freedom in Science'. The society was a response to planned science and in particular to J.D. Bernal's book *The Social Function of Science* (1939). Not unlike many economists, J.D. Bernal was impressed by Soviet efforts to plan and rationalize, in this case, the growth and accumulation of knowledge. The 'Society for Freedom in Science' resisted not just the centrally directed planning of science, but also demanded autonomy in the dispersion of funds and it was critical of controlled teamwork (McGucken, 1978).

This rhetoric of the free pursuit of science was important and successful in creating an ethos of independence and objectivity, of truth for truth's sake. But that was not the reality of the Cold-War science. Funds were increasingly controlled by government agencies and corporations such as the RAND-corporation. Or in Mirowski's words, that typically tend to overstate matters a bit: "This was the period of the belief in the possibility of technological planning (. . .) freedom of inquiry was tolerated because it served as explicit instantiation of the superiority of Western political and social organization over Soviet totalitarianism" (Mirowski, 2012: 65). But even the more measured historian of science, Bernstein argues: "like all their academic colleagues, independent of field and skill, economists were the legatees of a peculiar system of public educational finance that had, as its cardinal tributary, the work of the weaponeers" (Bernstein, 2001: 103). The agreement on national interests and the clear enemy that had to be defeated could mask the fact that the practice of science was closer the ideal of planned science than it was to that of the free, and individual, pursuit of knowledge.

2 Depoliticization and repoliticization: a political and an economic legacy

It is roughly agreed that it took until the 1970s for an Austrian revival to start in the United States. That complicates writing a history of the initial reception of the Viennese tradition. For when should we say that this initial American reception started? Was that in 1940 when Mises set foot on American soil? Or was that when Rothbard published *Man, Economy and State* (1962)? Or when Israel Kirzner started developing his views on Austrian theory, in an attempt to open a dialogue with mainstream economics in the 1960s and early 1970s? (Vaughn, 1994: 92–111). Or, is it rather at the first meeting of the Mont-Pèlerin Society, which even though held in Switzerland, brought together European and American scholars interested in reviving liberalism in 1947?

Finding the right answer to that question goes a long way toward answering the question what the legacy of the Austrians is. The answer is, in part, that what happened to the Austrian legacy was that it soon fragmented. This book has argued for the importance of the concept of civilization in Viennese economic and liberal thought, and a particular scholarly attitude, that of the student of society. That is, undeniably, not the legacy that emerged in the United States. The next chapter will sketch what an approach of the study of civilization might entail for modern economics. But here we are concerned with exploring how the Viennese tradition was continued in the United States.

This fragmentation can only be understood in the context of American postwar social science that we explored in the previous section. Neither the empiricism, the engineering attitude nor the emphasis on value–freedom, was conducive to the Viennese. As we have seen in the previous chapters, they had expressed strong criticism of the first two, and had felt the need to cross the fact-value divide in the deep crisis of the 1930s. The second aspect of the postwar context was the strong emphasis, at least within universities, on disciplinary boundaries. These boundaries became entrenched by increasingly standardized undergraduate and graduate courses that were redesigned during the early years after the war (Bernstein, 2001: 82–88). Studying broad themes such as civilization and the culture that enables markets to flourish fitted poorly within the postwar disciplines.

It was in the outgrowth of this context that an Austrian revival took place. As Karen Vaughn in her book *Austrian Economics in America* points out both Murray Rothbard and Israel Kirzner attempted to reintroduce Austrian insights into mainstream economics. That attempt was not very successful in the case of Rothbard, although he attracted a group of 'neo-Austrian' followers. Rothbard subsequently moved away from economics and become more focused on history and libertarianism as a political movement. Kirzner, on the other hand, had more of an influence on mainstream economics. Both authors, as Vaughn emphasizes, remain quite close to the prevailing orthodoxy of their time, particularly in the role that equilibrium plays in their contributions.

Despite the fact that their contributions are a combination of the neoclassical orthodoxy at the time and Austrian insights, both authors were of great importance in the subsequent self-conscious construction of an alternative Austrian paradigm, the then current Kuhnian term, to mainstream economics. But even that way of framing, as an alternative paradigm to neoclassical economics, made this new Austrian school as much a child of its time, as it was a continuation of the tradition that existed in Vienna. Framed as an alternative approach to study the economy, it was an academic and economic approach through and through. Therefore, issues that have concerned us in this book such as moral and social norms as well as ideological factors have been largely neglected. And while latently presented the role and responsibilities of the scholar has also received little attention within this Austrian school of economics until very recently.

The other legacy of the Viennese students of civilization is separated from this academic path. Its most important institution is the Mont-Pèlerin Society (MPS) that we already briefly encountered in Chapter 7. This society is set up by Hayek, with the help of other refugee liberals from Europe, most notably Wilhelm Röpke, with the aim of renewing liberal ideals and influencing public opinion in the long run. The society initially consists of economists, historians, political philosophers and public intellectuals, who, together formulate the aim of analysing the underlying moral and economic causes of the current crisis and to redefine the role of the state in society (Hennecke, 2000: 221–223).

The MPS consciously limits its membership and Hayek makes sure that all members have a clear liberal outlook. But it is within this society that the broad conversation about culture, morality, politics and economics, the conversation about Western civilization, was first continued by the Viennese after the war. Mises is reluctant to return to Europe, a lost continent in his eyes, for the first meeting but joins as do Karl Popper and Fritz Machlup (for a complete list of participants Plickert, 2008: 138). It was here that the European liberals, sidetracked by socialists and fascists, gathered and joined forces with a substantial number of Americans to reinvigorate the liberal project. By now, the history of the MPS has been well documented, including the fact that particularly the continental participants sought to keep the conversation broad and inclusive, both in membership as well as in analysis. That analysis, Hayek, Röpke and others continental liberals argued, should include the spiritual and moral direction of liberalism. Despite these efforts they were not able to steer the MPS in that direction in the long run, when it was increasingly dominated by economic issues and economists, after which many other students of society such as historians, legal scholars and political scientists no longer attended (Burgin, 2012: 123–151). It was in this sense that what happened in the MPS mirrored, with some delay, what had happened within the discipline of economics.

For a decade or so, however, the MPS provided a platform for scholarly discussion that transgressed disciplinary boundaries, and the fact-value divide. It sought to promote an intellectually informed liberalism that would be able to sustain itself, after liberalism had failed so horribly to counter the rise of fascism and socialism in the interwar period. It was not just an ideological society, and certainly no unified whole, but like the circles in Vienna, it brought scholars with different backgrounds, but similar interests and ideals, together to discuss and share ideas. It was through the MPS that the more political legacy, which we discussed in the introduction of this book was established.

The MPS created a legacy of Austrian thought that was far more political. A legacy that was further promoted by the works in political philosophy that Hayek published including *The Constitution of Liberty* and *Law, Legislation and Liberty*. But the purpose and meaning of that political work changed. It was no longer the lament of a civilization in decline, but an attempt to contribute to a new form of liberalism. The most vivid example of this process can undoubtedly be found in Hayek's work. When he moved to the United States, he worked primarily on *The Constitution of Liberty* which is dedicated to the 'unknown civilization that is growing in America'. And the second edition of 'The Road to Serfdom' includes an insightful preface that reveals how Hayek conceived of the changed meaning of his work. While *The Road to Serfdom* was originally written to warn about the dangers of socialism at home and against fascism, it was softer on the Soviet Union: "I had to restrain myself somewhat in my comments on the regime of our wartime ally" (Hayek, 1956/2007: 40). In the preface, written in the Cold War context of the 1950s, Hayek is crystal clear that socialism is the real enemy. But he also attempts to broaden the scope of his argument. He argues that the book can also be read as a warning against the encroaching welfare state and its conflicting aims, as well as the excessive use of coercive powers by the state to bring about change in.

In this new introduction, it also becomes clear that Hayek's goal has shifted from providing a warning, to making a contribution:

Only if we understand why and how certain kinds of economic controls tend to paralyze the driving forces of a free society, and which kinds of measures are particularly dangerous in this respect, can we hope that social experimentation will not lead us into situations none of us want. It is a contribution to this task that this book is intended.

(Hayek, 1956/2007: 44–45)

It is still very much Viennese in spirit, it is hesitant, reluctant, and skeptical; more about what we should not do, than what we should do, but it is forward looking. That same spirit pervades the *Constitution of Liberty* and constitutes the new context of Hayek's work. The reception of this work has been mostly critical, and the MPS is a frequent scapegoat for critics of neoliberalism (for an exception, see Shearmur, 1996). It is beyond the scope of this chapter to examine that legacy in any great detail, but the preceding chapters should have made amply clear that there is no simple relationship between the Viennese tradition and what today passes as neoliberalism or neoliberal policies.

The curious split between universities organized around disciplines and societies and think-tanks that aimed at interdisciplinarity as well as moral and social goals outside of academia is well captured by historian of science Philip Mirowski. He argues: "[For universities] disciplinarity became the arbiter of certified knowledge and the hallmark of serious intellectual endeavour, while for knowledge areas too novel to claim such legitimacy (. . .) special trans-disciplinary incubators were set up outside the ivy walls, to hasten development. Hence the rise of the Cold War university was paralleled by the rise of the Cold War think tank complex" (Mirowski, 2012: 68). But even such think-tanks were, in the long run, not free from disciplinary constraints as Burgin's history of the MPS has demonstrated.

3 Individual trajectories

Given the context of Cold War, academic life it was no mere coincidence that Hayek ended up not in the economics faculty of the University of Chicago, but in The Committee on Social Thought. A separate faculty set up at the university by John Nef and Frank Knight, among others, with the idea that shared issues underlie all forms of scholarship, including the arts. In fact, Hayek was happy with this position precisely because it was concerned with what he described as 'borderline problems in the social sciences', and in an interview, he later claimed that he was bored with the purely economic atmosphere at the LSE. In that same interview he speaks very positively about especially the initial period on this committee:

I announced a seminar on comparative scientific method, and the people who came included Sewall Wright, the great geneticist; Enrico Fermi, the physicist; and a crowd of people of that quality. It only happened once; we couldn't repeat this. But that first seminar I had in Chicago was one of the most interesting experiences I had.

(Hayek interviewed by Buchanan, 1979: 262)

Hayek was back in a cultured conversation with scholars from many fields. And not just scholars; the committee on social thought also invited individuals from the literary world. Hayek, shaped as he was, by Viennese intellectual life, never fitted easily in the postwar disciplines, but thrived in an atmosphere like the one in which he came of age.

At one point, there was the opportunity that he could restart in Vienna what had been lost during WWII. In the same interview with James Buchanan, Hayek explains that he could get money from the Ford Foundation, a lot of money, to start a new center in Vienna. Then Buchanan asks whether this was to reestablish the University of Vienna, to which Hayek responds quite accurately: "Well, to reestablish its tradition" (Hayek, 1979: 253). Of course reestablishing the University of Vienna would have been nearly a contradictio in terminis, for in many fields it had never really been established, and it certainly had not been the center of scholarly life in the interwar period. What Hayek consequently sought to do was to reestablish its tradition, and for this he needed to bring the people back: "to bring all the refugees who were still active back to Vienna – people like Schrödinger and Popper and – Oh, I had a marvelous list! I think we could have made an excellent center" (Hayek, 1979: 253). This is Hayek's nostalgia for a tradition, for the Viennese conversation, which always took place on the borderlines between disciplines and between science and society; a conversation that never took place in an ivory tower, but always occurred in the middle of the cultural life of the city. But this initiative remained a nostalgic dream and never materialized.

The character and breadth of the Viennese tradition often puzzled outsiders and it made moving to another intellectual climate, another country a difficult process.[1] When Schumpeter visited the United States in 1913, he was asked to deliver a lecture by Seligman, an economics professor at Columbia. Seligman's description of the lecture is a wonderful example of this confusion: "[He did not only speak of economics] but the relation of economics to psychology and sociology. He was – what is very unusual – both brilliant and profound; his choice of novel illustrations taken from a great variety of different fields, shows a surprising breadth of culture, which is unusual in a specialist" (Seligman quoted in McCraw, 2007: 81). But Schumpeter was not a specialist, and never became one; he was a student of civilization, schooled in broad cultured

---

[1] Reisch study of the migration of the Wiener Kreis contains many examples of such difficulties (Reisch, 2005).

conversations not with just Wieser or Böhm-Bawerk, but with Marxists, Max Weber, and artists from Vienna. This is also exemplified by Hayek's tribute to his mentor Wieser. Hayek chose not to compare him to a great economist of the past, but to Goethe, the great symbol of German culture, who had: "Wide-ranging interests encompassing all fields of culture and art, worldly wisdom and the worldly tact of the minister of Old Austria combined with an aloofness from daily trivia" (Hayek, 1926/ 1992: 125).

While Hayek remained associated with the important institutions of American academic life, Mises' position was more on the margin. Even though his former students, especially Machlup, tried to help him obtain a position at a prestigious American university; he failed to do so. His first years were spent on a Rockefeller fellowship supplemented by work for the business community in New York (Hülsmann, 2007: 789–836). Mises himself grew ever more stubborn and staunch in his defense of free markets, which also marginalized his position in the MPS. But even in his case, when he did obtain an association with the economics department of New York University, the first thing he did was set up a seminar that resembled, at least in set-up and in type of attendants, the one he had run in Vienna.

Two other prominent members of the Geistkreis and the Mises Kreis in Vienna Fritz Machlup and Gottfried Haberler fared much better in the American academic system. Haberler joined Schumpeter in 1936 to work at Harvard. But his work afterward soon lost much of its Austrian flavor. Machlup was hired by the newly founded University of Buffalo to move on The Johns Hopkins University in 1947, and he, in 1960 he was called upon to fill the position of liberal historian of thought Jacob Viner (Haberler, 1983: 11). Machlup stayed in close contact with many of his former Viennese colleagues throughout his career. His scholarly output is not only very prolific, but is also an exemplary instance of the breadth of the Viennese scholars. It deals with issues of methodology, the position of the social sciences as well as more technical work in finance and microeconomics. As many other Austrian émigré economists, not necessarily of the circles we discussed in this book, he remained concerned with international economic integration and development (one can also think of Alexander Gerschenkron and Paul Rosenstein-Rodan in this regard). His pioneering work on the importance of knowledge and information in the contemporary economy is another example of this breadth, and the (self-)reflexive character of Viennese work. Machlup's work is a constant reminder that economists deal in meaning, and that the choice of words has consequences. Wieser and Hayek were concerned about the meaning of liberalism, Hayek with the meaning of social justice, and Machlup's work too is full of concern with the meaning of economic concepts. His studies in economic semantics are detailed studies of the language games of economists and the many *meanings* of central economic concepts. His attempt is certainly not to pin down these meanings definitively:

> There are those who do so in a rather authoritarian fashion by declaring what [a given contested term means]. This, considering the existence of dozens of conflicting views stated by economists in good standing, betray a lack of humility on the part of the defining author.
>
> (Machlup, 1959: 110)

His work has received too little attention here, but it reflects the qualities that define the Viennese scholars. It is wide in scope, reflexive, and it reflects their belief, so aptly captured by George Steiner in the epigraph of this chapter, that the meaning of words matter. Moreover, it is Machlup who describes the economist as a 'student of knowledge production' in his pioneering study 'The Production and Distribution of Knowledge in the United States' (1962).

The migration had made the Viennese perhaps particularly aware of the importance of meaning in economics and politics. That is evident in Hayek's attempt to carve out his liberal position. Liberalism, as a political movement, rapidly changed throughout the twentieth century, and the word liberal had a very different meaning in the United States than in Europe. It is with these issues that Hayek wrestles in the postscript of the *Constitution of Liberty* entitled 'Why I Am Not a Conservative', and even in the earlier Individualism: True and False. In the former, he makes clear that he is not a conservative as that term is understood in the American sense, because his political philosophy is essentially forward looking. Even though he respects traditions and acknowledges the value of for instance religion, he is concerned with progress. But Hayek acknowledges that what he believes is true liberalism has died away in most places, and he finds himself in disagreement with both rationalistic liberalism and the English utilitarian liberalism. In that same issue, he expresses some discontent with the label 'libertarianism'. But that is the label now commonly associated with Austrian thought.

That association is understandable. Both Hayek and Mises put forward policies, while in the United States, that are very much in line with a government that is as minimal as possible. But this book has tried to demonstrate that the more constant element of the Viennese tradition has been a reluctant belief in progress. An outlook that thinks of freedom as a tradition, that has respect for institutions that have proven their worth but that is "at least willing to examine critically the existing and to change it wherever necessary" (Hayek, 1960: 411). What such an outlook might entail in the 'here' and the 'now' is the subject of Chapter 10.

What it means to be a student of civilization

On modern economics and the study of civilization

When we look for examples of man's control over culture we begin first to wonder, then to doubt.
—Leslie A. White, 1949

1 What it means to be a student of civilization

When I first started working on this project about five years ago, I envisioned it as a critical project about modernism in economics. My aim was to understand how economics became a professional and autonomous discipline, which in increasingly abstract ways represented the economy and which at the same time developed into a discipline in which the idea of 'Machbarkeit' in German or 'maakbaarheid' in Dutch became almost universally ingrained. This concept is perhaps best understood as a belief in social engineering, the idea that social change can be brought about through government policies, policies that would be designed by professional experts from the social sciences. Few traces of that initial project are left; sometimes, I think I failed to answer my initial question. At other moments, I am more hopeful and I think that I have in fact reached something of an answer, albeit a negative answer to that initial question. My study of modernism led me to places where modernism as a cultural movement flourished, Vienna being a prime example. Instead of finding out directly what this modern or modernist attitude entailed, I have come to study a group of Viennese scholars who I think have attempted to resist this modernist attitude.

The Viennese students of civilization deny that economics is an autonomous science, and argue that our study of markets is part of a wider study of civilization. They resist the idea that social engineering can achieve much, by stressing the importance of social, cultural and economic processes beyond our control, and they emphasize the impossibility of foreseeing the full consequences of our actions. They 'fail' to become professional economists, even though they do occasionally obtain university positions. They resist the pressure of specialization along (sub)disciplinary lines. Their intended audience is the interested layman as much as their professional colleagues or policy makers. Their representations of the economy and society are verbal and tied to human experience (more phenomenological than empirical in philosophical language). Their main goal is understanding rather than explanation and prediction or, stronger yet, design. The goals of their inquiry are never purely academic, but always social, cultural and economic as well. They remain skeptical about quantification, the idea that we know the economy primarily through a measurement of it. They refuse to accept that scientific knowledge is the only valid type of knowledge; they even suggest that there are very clear limitations to scientific knowledge. In short, they reject many of the characteristics I initially identified with modernism (although they certainly did not remain immune to these trends). Instead of providing an answer to what made economics modernist, I have come to study one of the (few) alternatives to modernist economics, or social science, in the twentieth century. In Chapter 9, we briefly explored the extent to which the American reception has shaped the legacy they left behind. This chapter aims to uncover what the tradition would have looked like if they would have continued along more or less the same lines. That is a big 'if', for if anything, the preceding chapters have shown the importance of the context, and how this context was far from stable even in Vienna. Nonetheless, if the goal is to examine alternatives to modernist economics, this is the question we should ask.

I have labelled that alternative perspective the study of civilization, done by students instead of scientists. So what does it mean to be a student of civilization? What are the characteristics of this study of civilization? What does he or she study, and what is the appropriate attitude for the student? To give an answer to this question I have developed a list of the five most important characteristics of the student or study of civilization that I have distilled from the previous chapters.

I   The scholar is always a student and never the master of his subject

Humility and modesty are perhaps the most characteristic and distinctive elements of the Viennese tradition. Against the idea that the social scientist is the master of society or even the modern prophet the Viennese posit a humble student, who is sometimes capable of understanding the world around him, but whose knowledge is always limited and whose capability to bring about social change is even more restricted. The primary reason they adopt this attitude is because they recognize the strength and importance of cultural, or rather civilizational processes. Cultural institutions such as law, language, markets, money, political institutions, traditions and morals have come about, they argue, as unintended consequences of human interaction, without any intervention by social scientists. The primary goal of the student of civilization is to understand how these institutions function and what role they have in fostering or hampering mutually beneficial human interaction. Since the student is aware of his own fallibility the study of his own limitations and the limitations of his own knowledge are an important part of his work (see also point 4).

Another way of putting this is to say that they have developed a third eye for the stuff-in-between: the institutions, relations, traditions and values which exist between individuals. The stuff-in-between that exists between markets and governments, our civil society, and the social forces that are at the heart of Wieser's analysis. Or, we could think of the knowledge that exists between the personal and the objective. It is their perception of this stuff in between that distinguishes the Viennese students of civilization from virtually all modern economists. And it is that stuff-in-between that distinguishes groups of people from one another, the stuff that gives human interaction its particular flavor, that which makes up culture. It is also this part of life that is so often neglected in rationalist social science, and the policies that follow from it. Menger wondered how money and credit emerged, Wieser why social change was such a slow process, Mises why the economy could not be planned, Hayek why traditions were so important: all questions about the stuff-in-between. Hayek develops this insight into a general idea according to which language, law and markets are the three most important achievements of civilization. It is therefore such a pity, almost frustrating, that Hayek and Mises sometimes resorted to a simple dichotomy between socialism and capitalism, at times ignoring all the stuff-in-between.

II There is a difference between knowledge from and knowledge about civilization

Perhaps the central insight we gained from studying the Viennese students of civilization is that it is helpful to make a distinction between knowledge about and knowledge from civilization. This distinction is central to their idea of the institutions of civilization as evolved (complex) structures and processors of knowledge. If we wish to learn about justice, it makes sense to study (successful) traditions and institutions in which this concept has evolved (the common law that Hayek so admired). And if we want to understand what an efficient process of exchange and distribution looks like we should study the institutions that evolved to serve this purpose, most importantly the market. If we want to learn about effective ways of communication we should study actually existing languages, for they have evolved for this purpose. So when Wieser discusses the misguided rationalism of his age, he discusses the attempts to replace the languages of the world with Esperanto (ignoring the knowledge contained in evolved languages), when Mises and Hayek discuss the rationalism of their age they discuss the attempts to plan the economy (ignoring the knowledge contained in existing business practices). This rationalism, they argue, ignores the knowledge from civilization, the knowledge embedded in institutions and the interaction and flexibility that these 'irrational' institutions allow. In that sense, Michael Polanyi's concept of 'tacit knowledge' is part of this knowledge embedded in institutions and practices (Polanyi, 1958).[1] From Polanyi, Hayek also adopts a difference between knowledge that and knowledge how, the knowledge from civilization and the knowledge about civilization (Caldwell, 2004: 307).

In Hayek's later work, he very explicitly argues that culture and cultural institutions have enabled human intelligence, and rationality. In Chapter 3, I have shown that the individual in the Viennese tradition was always conceptualized as in possession of limited knowledge, highly dependent on others and surrounded by uncertainty. The institutions of civilization help the individual (however imperfectly) to cope with these circumstances.

On the other hand, there is the knowledge about civilization, which is not fundamentally different from what we consider traditional social scientific knowledge. That should not obscure the fact that there are clear limits to what the student of civilization *can* know, he can never have complete information about the particulars at any given moment in time (knowledge that), but he can know certain processes, the way in which certain cultural institutions operate (knowledge how).[2] The Viennese

---

[1] The spirit of Polanyi's book is very much in line with what follows in this section: "I have traced the tacit personal interactions which make possible the flow of communications, the transmission of social lore from one generation to the other and the maintenance of an articulate consensus" (Polanyi, 1958: 212).

[2] A similar point, including the distinction between knowledge from and knowledge about, is made by McCloskey: "An economist looking at the business world is like a critic

students of civilization are famous for their claim that planning is impossible because the central collection of all relevant price information would be impossible. One could well extend this argument to claim that it would be impossible for a linguist to map out all the possible uses and functions of words. That information is dispersed throughout society and possessed by heterogeneous individuals. More importantly, both markets and languages are dynamic processes, so mapping itself would be rather beside the point. The information possessed by the student of civilization is thus always limited. Like the individual who is always in possession of a very limited amount of knowledge in the economic theory of the Viennese, so the knowledge of the student of civilization is always limited. The student is highly dependent on others, and in need of constant interaction to partly overcome these limitations.

III Markets are cultural institutions with cultural and moral effects

The Viennese students of civilization show that markets are cultural institutions; neither natural, nor designed. This means that markets have come about more or less organically through human interaction. It also means that markets will work better or worse in different cultures; in that sense, one could speak of more and less market-conducive cultures. The Viennese students of civilization especially stress the values foresight, prudence and temperance as conducive to the development of extensive markets. In terms of institutions, they claim that the protection of property rights is especially important, and that central planning hampers markets. Temperance is especially important for it leads to markets for what Menger calls higher order goods, in modern economics often called capital goods. These goods are not produced for consumption; they are means, which will help improve the production process of what are ultimately to become consumer goods. The Viennese students of civilization believe that the progress of civilization is tightly bound up with the adjustment of our horizon further into the future and the expansion of human knowledge which enable us to produce (ever) higher order goods.

Markets for the Viennese students are not only supported by culture, they also have cultural and moral effects. In Chapter 4, I have explored

looking at the art world (...) Human scientists and critics of human arts, in other words, write history, not prophecy. Economics teaches this, the limit on social engineering. It teaches that we can be wise and good but not profitably foresighted in detail, even if we are economists (McCloskey, 1994: 73).

how markets limit as well enable individual freedom. They limit individual freedom, because they make humans more dependent on one another and because they force us to produce that for which others are willing to pay. Markets enable freedom, because they increase the possibilities of the individual, and they enable individuals to specialize (within bounds) in the direction that he or she prefers. The disciplinary effects of markets are somewhat more complicated, but they bring out wonderfully how the Viennese students of civilization conceptualize freedom. The disciplinary forces of the market, such as competition, instill certain values in individuals, it civilizes them. But such forces will most likely be experienced as a burden by the individual. He might feel insecurity about his income, about the right choices to make, he might feel competitive pressures, or might find it very hard to restrain certain desires. This burden, this strain of civilization is, however, an inevitable part of the civilizing process.

IV There is a therapeutic or tragic element to the work of students of civilization

Another distinctive feature of the Viennese students of civilization is that there is a therapeutic element to their thought, therapeutic both about what it means to be a student of civilization and a therapeutic element about what it means to be human. Let us start with the latter, which is perhaps best illustrated by the characterization of economics as a dismal science. Economics for the Viennese is indeed a dismal science for it emphasizes unfortunate characteristics of human life: the unavoidable scarcity, the necessity of making (painful) choices, the fact that there are almost invariably trade-offs involved in our attempts to realize our goals. These facts are all recognized by mainstream economists, but they are hardly ever presented in a therapeutic way. For the Viennese it is very important to *show* their fellow citizens that such inconveniences are unavoidable, that they have to be accepted. That is also the message that follows from their concept 'the strain of civilization'. This strain consists of the responsibility individuals bear for their own choices, the acceptance of powerful social forces such as the force of competition, the necessary restraint of our instincts, and the submission to norms that we do not fully comprehend. In therapeutic terms, they advocate the acceptance of those facts of life one cannot change without enjoying the benefits of our civilization.

There is also a more hopeful therapeutic element to their thought, facts of life for which we should be grateful. Hayek especially stresses the marvel or wonder with which we should look at the market process

(Hayek, 1945: 527). If he had been religious, he could have claimed that we should 'praise' the market. This view is implicit in Viennese thought going back since the beginning in Menger's work, who already emphasizes the importance of organically grown institutions, and the limits of our rationality. The civilization that the Viennese study, the cultural institutions, norms and traditions more generally deserve our admiration, they argue. Law, language and markets to use this trio once more, are institutions that are very beneficial to humans and that have not been designed by us. Like we sometimes marvel at the wonders of nature (see Chapter 6), so the Viennese argue we should marvel at the wonders of civilization.

There are also elements of their work that are therapeutic for their fellow students of civilization (and for themselves as students). These pertain mainly to the 'social enthusiasm' of many students of civilization who hope to improve the world and cure various social ills. Like the therapeutic skeptics in medicine, the Viennese students of civilization want to make clear to their fellow students that they should be cautious and recognize that their sphere of influence is limited. This is an especially important realization, because not only his own inclinations might lead the student to bite off more than he can chew. The outside world, citizens, governments and businessmen, expect the student of civilization to deliver cures and solutions. The therapeutic value of their work lies in the fact that they make other students of civilization aware of these pressures, aware of their own urge to alter social outcomes (especially those that seem unjust), aware of the limits of their knowledge, and aware of the limits of their power to alter the world.

Another way of putting this is that they emphasize, and here there are clear links with the work of the sociologist Berger, the human condition. They emphasize the limits of human capabilities and the tragic elements in life, those things that we cannot change. That perspective has led some to conclude their work is pessimistic or even fatalistic. I believe, on the contrary, that it is more helpful to think of their work of therapeutic or tragic. My emphasis on fate in Chapter 7 is an attempt to bring these tragic elements out. In Chapters 6 and 7 I demonstrated how the Viennese students of civilization dealt with tragedy, how they occupied various positions on a spectrum that the Austrian novelist Adalbert Stifter once described: "[when faced with destruction and tragedy] the strong man submits to it humbly, the weakling rebels and complains, the common run of man is stupefied" (Stifter quoted in Magris, 1989: 148). In that sense, the work of the Viennese students of civilization is also character building, it is edifying.

V The study of civilization is a social process between various students and their culture

Claudio Magris further praised that same novelist Stifter because he: "[inquired] into the secret of moderation, of that acceptance of limits which enables the individual to subordinate his own vanity to a value above the merely personal, to open himself to sociability and to dialogue with others" (Magris, 1989: 129). It is not only in terms of moderation that there is a close relation between the work of Stifter and that of the Viennese students, but also in the importance of dialogue with others. In the Viennese circles the frequency and high level of intellectual conversation helped bring about great contributions to culture and scholarly work. As Stifter points out, for such conversations to be successful, there has to be a social spirit and willingness to subordinate oneself to the conversational norms and the shared aims of the conversation. In that sense, one might say that the humility stressed with regard to knowledge is reflected in the social practice of the conversation. That same humility is reflected in their view of freedom, in which the individual subordinates himself to cultural norms and traditions.

It is like the example of freedom speech I gave in the introduction: meaningful freedom of speech is achieved (perhaps paradoxically) when individuals are willing to observe (to submit to) conversational norms. Freedom of speech does not mean that every individual can say what he likes when he likes it; that would not generate meaningful conversations. It is this idea of freedom that is at the heart of Hayek's theory, not Berlin's idea of 'negative freedom' as is often implicitly assumed. The observance of such conversational norms was practiced in the Viennese conversations although, as such things go, not without the occasional transgression. It was undoubtedly partly because of this spirit of sociability and humility that the Viennese conversations achieved the level of creativity and origin- ality for which we now remember them.

The fact that the practice of scholarly work is a social process is not just reflected in the manner in which their work was conducted, but also in the goals that were pursued. The goals of the Viennese students were not just scholarly; they were not purely autonomous scientific goals. Their goals were social, cultural and economic, civilizational, if you pardon the neolo- gism. Others have sometimes labelled their work philosophical, because it is not restricted to the purely empirical, or political, because it is moral as well, but a better way to understand the work in the Viennese tradition is to realize that they were attempting to understand society, understand civilization, as well as to contribute to it. This becomes most clear when Hayek and Popper called their work their 'war effort'. But the earlier work of the Viennese students of civilization was just as much an attempt to steer their civilization in the right direction, even though they realized that their capability to do so was limited. Carl Menger already summed it up in a quote we encountered earlier:

> But never (...) may science dispense with testing for their suitability those institutions which have come about 'organically'. It must, when careful investigation so requires, change and better them (...). No era may renounce this 'calling'.
>
> (Menger, 1883/2009: 234)

This list sums up to most important characteristics of the Viennese students of civilization, but I hope that it also invites us to add individuals or groups of scholars to this tradition. In the more reflective Chapters 5 and 8, I have suggested several authors who might well fit into this tradition. Within economics, a couple of them stand out to me: Kenneth Boulding, Albert Hirschman and Frank Knight, and the recent work of Peter Boettke (who identifies himself with the modern Austrian school of economics). I hope it also invites us, as I attempted at various points, to find links with other disciplines. My knowledge of these other disciplines is rather limited but I suggested connections to the work of the anthropologist Malinowski, sociologists Norbert Elias and Peter Berger, political scientists and intellectual historians J.G.A. Pocock and Quentin Skinner, and somewhat more tentatively with cultural historian Johan Huizinga. These are only first suggestions, you are free to add your own suggestions.

Instead of attempting to formulate yet more lists, it is time for some additional reflections on the idea of civilization at the end of this book.

2 When civilization breaks down

A chapter in Hayek's *Road to Serfdom* is called the totalitarians in our midst. Some of the first words in the *Open Society and its Enemies* by Popper make clear that some of our gravest mistakes come from what "admittedly is a part of our intellectual heritage" (Popper, 1945: v). Or as literary critic George Steiner put it: "The blackness did not spring up in the Gobi desert or the rain forests of the Amazon. It rose from within, and from the core of European civilization" (Steiner, 1967: 14–15). These authors were attempting to come to grips with what was widely perceived as the breakdown of a civilization: the rise of Nazism, the Holocaust, and the total war. This breakdown had occurred in Europe, right at the heart of the civilization that the Viennese had studied. Even after the war the effects of this breakdown were severe; these authors felt that their civilization was infected. Language had been deformed through propaganda and intellectual errors; our idea of the law had been corrupted through a confusion of law and legislation, and our rationalist idea of markets was misguided. George Steiner even wondered whether silence was the only appropriate response for the novelist or poet when language was so deeply corrupted. When we study Hayek's postwar work, we soon notice how much he is concerned with correcting the use of language: his criticism of 'social justice', his distinction between law and legislation, the disentanglement of true and false individualism, his concern with the various uses of liberalism and freedom, etc. The illness was severe, and cures were not easily found. A deeper question also emerged: Was their own civilization partly to blame for the atrocities of WWII?

It is an issue that Elias, the most prominent writer on the subject of the civilizing process in the twentieth century, also confronted in his book *The Germans* (Elias, 1996). His study was partly prompted by the fact that several critics accused his theory of the civilizing process as linear and optimistic. These critics frequently pointed to WWII and the 1930s as a clear counterexample to such linear ideas about civilization. They apparently failed to notice that the work of Elias, as well as that of Hayek, Popper and Malinowski, was written in response to these developments. Their intellectual efforts were an attempt to show their fellow citizens what was at stake, but especially what the value was of the civilization they usually took for granted. It is central to Elias' work to show the origins and the importance of the manners and morals we now take for granted, and it was central to the work of Hayek and Mises to demonstrate the complexity and importance of market processes, which they felt were too easily taken for granted. These authors were well aware that there was a possibility of a breakdown of civilization or a decivilizing process. In fact, they wrote their works to warn their fellow citizens that grave dangers were lurking. As Elias put it: "Contemporaries did not then conceive of civilization as a condition which, if it is to be maintained or improved, requires a constant effort based on a degree of understanding of how it works" (Elias, 1996: 314).

However true that might be, it should not obscure the fact that such a decivilizing process was something to be understood, to be explained. Just after WWI, Mises and Schumpeter were attempting to come to grips with the outburst of violence, nationalist sentiments and romantic longing. In the same manner, Popper, Hayek, Elias and others were attempting to come to grips with the political movements of the 1930s and WWII. In Chapter 3, we saw that Mises and Schumpeter were struggling to understand and empathize with what they believed to be atavistic cultural sentiments. And although Mises attempted to go beyond merely thinking of these developments as atavistic remnants in a rationalizing society, he did not really manage to do so. What however came to fruition in the work of Hayek, Popper and Elias (and Freud although Hayek did not liked to acknowledge this) was an alternative understanding of these so-called atavistic sentiments. They argued that the civilizing process had come at a price; the restraint of instincts had put a heavy burden on individuals. The political movements of the interwar period exploited the dissatisfaction with this burden; they promised the relief of these restraints in combination with the same level of prosperity and freedom.

What Elias, in his book on the Germans attempts, and Popper and Hayek in their work of the 1940s attempt, is to understand how these once restrained sentiments were once more unleashed. They trace this development within Western or European civilization, and hence do not provide a triumphant picture of Western civilization. On the contrary, they chastise significant parts of that civilization, especially the misguided rationalism or scientism that emerged in the early nineteenth century. One can criticize their respective efforts to do so: Popper may rely too heavily on the rationalism that it critiques; Hayek may be criticized for a reliance on evolutionary theory while at the same time criticizing the direction of this evolution; Elias' explanation might rely too much on German exceptionalism, and he may be criticized for ultimately resorting to atavistic arguments. It is, however, simply unfair to claim that these authors thought of the civilizing process as a natural or linear process. They wanted to show their contemporaries that civilization is a cultural process for which we have a shared responsibility. The work of the students of civilization is not triumphalist or uncritical about our intellectual heritage, it is instead a reminder how fragile that civilization is and remains. The question that does spring from their analysis, and which they only partly answer, is whether the burden of civilization might at any point become too heavy.

Their work also raises interesting questions about our ability to distinguish civilizing from decivilizing processes. In the introduction to Elias' study on *The Germans* Eric Dunning and Stephen Mennell, for example, wonder to what extent the informalization processes in the 1960s and 70s are part of a civilizing or decivilizing process (Dunning and Mennell, 1996; Wouters, 1986). If one draws an analogy to economics, one could wonder what more and less civilized markets look like, and especially to what extent predatory as opposed to mutually beneficial interaction still takes place on markets. The analysis of the students of civilization also makes us wonder to what extent the most important elements of our civilization are sufficiently supported within society. These are open issues that contemporary students of civilization should take up.

3 The scholarly heritage and traditions

At various points in this book, we have reflected on scholarly practices and virtues, especially the awareness of his the limitations of the scholar. There is, however, one element of our scholarly practice that we have so far largely ignored: the relation of the students of civilization to their own intellectual heritage.

In the study of civilization by the Viennese, we find great respect for the knowledge embedded in institutions and traditions that have been passed down and cultivated generation after generation. But within economics (a tradition of thought to which I will refer most here) we have in the twentieth century instead largely neglected this insight. We have behaved like the rationalist who attempted to plan society from the ground up, like the avant-garde artists who wanted to reinvent painting, and the modernist architects who wanted to destroy cities to build them anew, of course rationally and according to plan. The work of Thomas Kuhn even lent some legitimation to the idea that every so many decades a scholarly field would be revolutionized and become incompatible with all that went on before. Such sentiments, however are contrasted by our experience of reading the classics. When we read Aristotle, Smith, Marx or in this case the Viennese, we still find many valuable things, including valuable things with which we disagree. More importantly we recognize that they are part of a more or less continuous intellectual tradition.

Although we know that a complete revolution of economic thought is not possible or desirable, we have seen many instances in which older thinkers were discarded because they were unscientific, or ideological. At other instances, we have felt the need to once again prove, using the latest methodology, things that were well-known to our predecessors. To give just one example: the recent stream of experiments designed to show that individuals are not fully rational, wholly self-interested and sometimes jealous, spiteful or altruistic. No doubt some of these experiments have helped us to understand the institutional setting under which human beings are jealous or altruistic, but many of these experiments merely reestablished old wisdom.[3] Especially outsiders repeatedly raised their eyebrows when they found out that economists were only now finding out (or proving?) that human beings were not perfectly rational. A more hopeful way of putting it, was that these economists were rediscovering a neglected part of their intellectual heritage. It is this heritage that I want to talk about some more.

Our relation to our intellectual heritage is not an issue that is frequently raised, or at least I have not come across it often. How should the student of the economy relate to the students that came before him? Do we stand on the shoulders of giants, or do we feel the need to seriously reconstruct our intellectual buildings? An interesting point to start this inquiry from is with the work of Gadamer. He confronts the issue head-on when he argues in favor of prejudice in scholarly work. Prejudice seems a straightforward reason for us to discard the work of earlier economists, especially political prejudice. Even one of the more subtle authors on the issue, Joseph Schumpeter, warns against the dangers of preconceptions which are "dangerous to the cumulative growth of our knowledge and the scientific character of our analytic endeavours" (Schumpeter, 1949: 347). In that sense, he is completely in line with what Gadamer sees as the most important legacy of the Enlightenment: "the prejudice against prejudice, which denies tradition its power" (Gadamer, 2004: 273). Gadamer on the other hand, argues that we have come to think mistakenly of prejudices as purely negative. According to him, prejudices are an essential part of everyday life *and* scholarly practice. We hold prejudices for authorities, says Adam Smith, and we hold prejudices against astrological hypotheses (with the possible exception of Jevons and his sun-spot theory of the business cycle). We also hold prejudices for tradition; we continue doing certain things because that has been the way to do it for a long time. We of course do not do so uncritically, as Gadamer acknowledges, the greatest value of the Enlightenment period has been precisely its emphasis on a critical attitude. That attitude, however, should not be taken to its extreme. The justification of many practices and morals lies not in their rational justification, but in tradition according to Gadamer (the Viennese students of civilization would be nodding at this point). This is not a passive process, traditions are not automatically transferred to new generations, they have to be 'affirmed, embraced, cultivated' (Gadamer, 2004: 282). These prejudices and beliefs that have been passed on to us are not just

---

[3]   It is somewhat ironic that Smith's work on our moral sentiments also gained renewed popularity during this period.

myths and distortions, they are what previous generations felt was worth preserving. These beliefs have been tested in the past, and therefore command our respect.[4]

These prejudices and traditions help us see, think, understand. Against the idea that the social scientist is a disinterested observer, who tries to detach himself from time, place and his own biographical situation, Gadamer places a social scientist who is interested, often passionately involved and located in space and time. Without such characteristics interpretation, understanding, and the necessary empathy would be impossible in the first place. To describe this set of prejudices and traditions, that which is commonly believed, Gadamer uses the term 'sensus communis'. Science, or rather the scholarly conversation, is a social endeavor in which we constantly accept or reject one another's prejudices, opinions and theories. The agreement in such conversations is often far larger than the disagreement, he argues, although we sometimes hardly notice this. Economists share the notions of 'the individual', the 'market', and so forth. The accepted views, theories and prejudices create a common ground, which makes communication possible in the first place as modern Austrian economist Don Lavoie has argued (Lavoie, 2011). That these prejudices, or concepts and theories, are passed down to us by tradition does not discredit them in any scientific conversation, it usually warrants extra attention for them. We would certainly not get very far if we were to start every conversation by precisely defining every term we use (even though we sometimes have to do this for certain contested terms). These shared concepts, this shared understanding of the world, is what Gadamer calls the *sensus communis*.

It is the common ground, which in conversations between peers is taken for granted. We soon notice how important these are in discussions if one engages in a conversation with those outside our field. There, the conversation does not take place as naturally as one hopes, but words, concepts and meanings are used and understood differently.[5] Gadamer's term, which was originally coined by Aristotle, does not just refer to a shared understanding, an overlapping consensus, but it also refers to a community: a group of people who share this same sense. And it is this shared understanding that often differentiates various social groups and fields.

---

[4]   The Viennese students of civilization would also have nodded when in the same context Gadamer makes a connection with freedom: "Does being situated within traditions really mean being subject to prejudices and limited in one's freedom? Is not, rather, all human existence, even the freest, limited and qualified in various ways? If this is true, the idea of an absolute reason is not a possibility for historical humanity" (Gadamer, 2004: 277).

[5]   For a more extended discussion of these issue, see Klamer (2007), especially Chapter 3.

Economists have a different 'sensus communis' than sociologists, who have a different 'sensus communis' than political scientists. Understanding economics means understanding and learning this shared sense, and passing on this shared understanding. This particular sense is the bulk of our academic education; as such, it is very close to what I labeled as the sensitivities in the Chapter 8.

To locate the origins of our current 'sensus communis' is one of the tasks of the history of a particular discipline. Through the practice of the history of our discipline, we understand where our current beliefs, prejudices and theories come from. In that sense, the history of a discipline is a way to critically reflect on our current sensus communis, the knowledge that we currently take for granted. During periods of economic of financial crises, we will for example, reconsider our image of the economy as an automatically stabilizing system, and look for alternative conceptualizations of the economy. If we wish to understand why we think about the market as we do, and how this could be done alternatively, again the history of a discipline is indispensable. It is for this purpose that we need history, and why our own intellectual history should be an integral part of the social sciences. As Lavoie puts it: "History of thought can no longer be seen as an extra specialty for those with a peculiar curiosity about ideas of dead men, but must be seen as an integral part of any scientific discipline" (Lavoie, 2011: 112). I would add that separating between the history of a subject and the subject itself is wrongheaded. This book, even though it discusses scholars of the past, is concerned with economic thought and the study of our civilization, rather than with 'merely' the history of that study.

The 'sensus communis' does not only help us communicate, it also helps us to form judgments that are so central in scholarly practice. It helps us to make judgments when choosing between various books to read, theories to study, arguments to evaluate, concepts to be developed further and questions to ask. In other words, it helps us to *act* scholarly. For Gadamer there is no fundamental difference between acting in everyday life and acting as a scholar, both rely on experience, practice, skills and judgment. We learn by doing, but more than anything else we learn by studying how others do it. To do so our own tradition is important, for it is from our own scholarly traditions that we can learn these skills. The study of our own traditions, the practice and judgments of others, teaches us to make our own judgments – judgments that, as Gadamer argues, 'presuppose education and maturity' (Gadamer, 1975: 312). Our everyday scholarly judgments require weighing various aspects that are not necessarily easily commensurable: desirability, effectiveness, feasibility, accordance with earlier beliefs, etc.

A sense of judgment is also what we appreciate in others. Among historians of economics, Schumpeter's *History of Economic Analysis* (1954) is as popular for his judgments about scholarly contributions as for its historical accuracy. And Jacob Viner, who noted this quality of Schumpeter's work in his original review of the work, himself was also known for both his knowledge and his sense of judgment. Viner, by the way, was called 'the greatest historian of economic thought that ever lived' by Mark Blaug, another judgment (Blaug, 1962: 256). Authority in science undoubtedly depends as much on theoretical contributions as it does on this sense of judgment. Authorities gain this credibility, for we have learned to trust their judgment. Such judgments allow us to claim that somebody is a great scholar. And no, I do not think that such a claim is an unfounded value statement.

The reader might by now guess that I am uncomfortable with the prejudice against 'unfounded' knowledge. The knowledge *from* civilization is unfounded in a scientific sense, but very valuable in our everyday life. The knowledge embedded in successful institutions might be scientifically unsound but is of great importance to human interaction. In the same sense, our judgments have value. The reason that we can make such informed judgments, or value statements if you like, is because we have developed a conception of goodness in various practices. Mark Blaug has an idea of what a good historian of economic thought is, and therefore he can claim that Viner is the greatest that ever lived. Similarly, we evaluate the actions of other based on such standards. We can claim about a student that he is a good student, because he has acquired mastery of the required subjects, or because he has shown the right type of attitude. MacIntyre claims that such evaluations, such judgments have for a long time been central to the moral discourse. These judgments could be formed because it was roughly clear what functions or goals institutions or objects served. This means that contrary to folk wisdom one can sometimes proceed from certain 'is' statements to 'ought' statements (MacIntyre, 1984: 57–58). Or, more precisely we can sometimes move from statements about somebody's practices and attitude, to statements about the value of a particular contribution or person. If a student shows the right attitude and has acquired a good understanding of the required concepts, we can call him a good student. I believe that these types of evaluative judgments are part and parcel of what scholars do. They have implicitly or explicitly recognized the purpose of various scholarly activities, and can hence judge whether the activity is performed well. Such standards are not absolute, or objective, they emerge in scholarly interaction.

Just like the Viennese students of civilization showed the importance of moral traditions and historically grown institutions in society, I think it is good for us to recognize the importance of our own intellectual tradition. It is perhaps time for what Gadamer called 'a rehabilitation of authority and tradition'. This is not to say that we should get rid of our critical faculties, but to once again appreciate the role of both authority and tradition within social thought. When Popper called for piecemeal engineering in society many agreed with its antirevolutionary spirit. Hayek made this spirit an explicit concern in what he labeled the counter-revolution in science. In social thought, on the contrary, we have continued to act like revolutionaries. In essence, this antirevolutionary mindset is similar to the modesty so central in the Viennese tradition; we should practice modesty with respect to the existing body of knowledge as well to the historically grown institutions. Humility should make us reluctant to believe too easily that our 'rationality' is greater than that of the past. To practice this humility is a skill, and should not be taken to some extreme. Too much respect for tradition is just as bad as the hubris that Hayek condemned. It is just that the balance in the past century has tended more toward this hubris, than to the side of humility.

The strait between the Scylla of hubris and the Charybdis of deference might be narrow. As some scholars have observed it is the essential tension within Hayek's work. His call for respect of our traditions and historically grown institutions was combined with a vehement criticism of the current state of affairs, and the development of social thought since the nineteenth century in general. One may accuse him of being inconsistent, of pleading for modesty and radical reform at the same time. That is certainly the most convenient response (it would probably even be partly right). But if we like to challenge ourselves, it is more insightful to recognize the tension inherent in our relation and Hayek's relation to traditions. We build on them, we cultivate them, but at the same time we sometimes feel that our traditions are no longer suited to the current circumstances, or worse yet, that our traditions are being corrupted by contemporary developments. If we at least recognize that both feelings, the need for reform and the need for a return, are expressions of our relationship to that tradition that would be a big step in the right direction. When we apply the modesty of the Viennese students of civilization to our own heritage it leads to a respect for the social scientific knowledge that has grown historically, and a cultivation of that tradition. That respect should be combined with an attempt to gradually improve these traditions, to keep them relevant. To conclude, once more, with Menger, we may 'not renounce that calling'.

Bibliography

Adorno, Theodor W. 1969. "Scientific Experiences of a European Scholar in America." In *The Intellectual Migration: Europe and America, 1930–1960*, ed. Donald. Fleming and Bernard Bailyn, pp. 338–370. Cambridge, MA: Harvard University Press.

Akerlof, George A. and Rachel E. Kranton. 2010. *Identity Economics: How Our Identities Shape Our Work, Wages and Well-Being*. Princeton: Princeton University Press.

Allen, Robert L. 1994. *Opening Doors the Life and Work of Joseph Schumpeter, Volume 1: Europe*. New Jersey: Transaction Publishers.

Amadae, S. M. 2003. *Rationalizing Capitalist Democracy: The Cold War Origins of Rational Choice Liberalism*. Chicago: University of Chicago Press.

Arendt, Hannah. 1968. *Men in Dark Times*. San Diego: Harcourt Brace Janovich.

Aristotle. 2009. *Nichomachean Ethics*, ed. David Ross and Lesley Brown. Oxford: Oxford University Press.

Bailes, Christopher. 2012. *"Ludwig Wittgenstein and Hermann Broch: The Need for Fiction and Logic in Moral Philosophy"*. Washington University Open Scholarship.

Berger, Peter L. 1963. *Invitation to Sociology: A Humanistic Perspective*. New York: Anchor Books.

Berger, Peter L. and Hansfried Kellner. 1982. *Sociology Reinterpreted*. Harmondsworth: Penguin Books.

Berman, Sheri. 1997. "Civil Society and the Collapse of the Weimar Republic." *World Politics* 49 (3): 401–429.

Bernal, J. D. 1939. *The Social Function of Science*. London: Routledge & Sons.

Bernstein, Michael A. 2001. *A Perilous Progress: Economists and Public Purpose in Twentieth-Century America*. Princeton: Princeton University Press.

Birner, Jack. 1999. "The Surprising Place of Cognitive Psychology in the Work of F.A. Hayek." *History of Economic Ideas* 7 (1–2): 43–84.

Blaug, Mark. 1962. *Economic Theory in Retrospect*. London: Heinemann.

———. 1992. *The Methodology of Economics*. Cambridge: Cambridge University Press.

Boettke, Peter J. 1994. *The Elgar Companion to Austrian Economics*. Cheltenham: Edward Elgar.

———. 2010. *Handbook on Contemporary Austrian Economics*. Cheltenham: Edward Elgar.

2012. *Living Economics: Yesterday, Today, and Tomorrow.* Oakland: The Independent Institute.

Bohm, Franz, Walter Eucken, and Hans Grossmann-Doerth. 1936/1989. "The Ordo Manifesto of 1936." In *Germany's Social Market Economy*, ed. Alan Peacock and Hans Wilgerodt, 15–26. London: Trade Policy Research Centre.

Boltanski, Lu and Laurent Thévenot. 2006. *On Justification: Economies of Worth.* Princeton: Princeton University Press.

Boulding, Kenneth E. 1963. "Towards a Pure Theory of Threat Systems." *The American Economic Review* 53 (2): 424–434.

1969. "Economics as a Moral Science." *The American Economic Review* 59 (1): 1–12.

Broch, Hermann. 1946a. "Geschichtsgesetz Und Willensfreiheit." In *Massenpsychologie: Schriften Aus Dem Nachlass*, 237–312. Zürich: Rhein-Verlag.

1946b. *The Death of Virgil.* London: George Routledge & Sons.

2002. "Hugo von Hofmannstahl and His Time: Art and Its Non-Style at the End of the Nineteenth Century." In *Geist and Zeitgeist: The Spiritual in an Unspiritual Age*, ed. John Hargraves, 141–210. New York: Counterpoint.

Buck, Peter. 1985. "Adjusting to Military Life: The Social Sciences Go to War, 1941–1950." In *Military Enterprise and Technological Change: Perspectives on the American Experience*, ed. Merritt Roe Smith, 203–52. Cambridge, MA: MIT Press.

Burgin, Angus. 2012. *The Great Persuasion: Reinventing Free Markets Since the Depression.* Cambridge: Harvard University Press.

Böhm-Bawerk, Eugen von. 1891. *The Positive Theory of Capital.* London: Macmillan and Company.

1914/1924. "Macht Oder Ökonomisch Gesetz." In *Gesammelte Schriften von Eugen von Böhm Bawerk*, ed. Franz X. Weiss, 230–300. Wien: Hölder-Pichler-Tempsky.

Caldwell, Bruce. 1988. "Hayek's Transformation." *History of Political Economy* 20 (4): 513–541.

1997. "Introduction." In *The Collected Works of F.A. Hayek: Volume X.* Chicago: University of Chicago Press.

2004. *Hayek's Challenge.* Chicago: University of Chicago Press.

Cassidy, John. 2000. "The Hayek Century." *Hoover's Digest* (3). www.hoover.org/publications/hoover-digest/article/6405.

2010. "Interview with John Cochrane (After the Blow-up Series)." *The New Yorker* (January 13). www.newyorker.com/online/blogs/johncassidy/2010/01/interview-with-john-cochrane.html.

Clarke, Maurice D. 1888. "Therapeutic Nihilism." *Boston Medical and Surgical Journal* 119 (9): 199–201.

Coase, Ronald H. 1934. "The Nature of the Firm." *Economica* 4 (16): 386–405.

Coen, Deborah R. 2007. *Vienna in the Age of Uncertainty: Science, Liberalism, and Private Life.* Chicago: University of Chicago Press.

Collins, Randall. 1998. *The Sociology of Philosophies: A Global Theory of Intellectual Change.* Harvard: Harvard University Press.

2004. *Interaction Ritual Chains.* Princeton: Princeton University Press.

Congdon, Lee. 1991. *Exile and Social Thought: Hungarian Intellectuals in Germany and Austria 1919–1934.* Princeton: Princeton University Press.

Cowen, Tyler. 2007. *Discover Your Inner Economist.* New York: Dutton.

2013. "One Further Thought on the Reinhart and Rogoff Fracas." *Marginal Revolution*. http://marginalrevolution.com/marginalrevolution/2013/04/one-further-thought-on-the-reinhart-and-rogoff-fracas.html.

Crankshaw, Edward. 1938. *Vienna: The Image of a Culture in Decline*. London: Macmillan.

Cravens, Hamilton. 2012. "Column Right, March! Nationalism, Scientific Positivism, and the Conservative Turn of the American Social Sciences in the Cold War Era." In *Cold War Social Science: Knowledge Production, Liberal Democracy, and Human Nature*, ed. Mark Solovey and Hamilton Cravens, 117–35. New York: Palgrave Macmillan.

Craver, Earlene. 1986. "The Emigration of the Austrian Economists." *History of Political Economy* 18 (1): 1–32.

Craver, Eearlen and Axel Leijonhufvud. 1987. "Economics in America: the Continental Influence." *History of Political Economy*, 19 (2): 173–182.

Cushing, James T. 1994. *Quantum Mechanics: Historical Contingency and the Copenhagen Hegemony*. Chicago: University of Chicago Press.

Dahms, Hans-Joachim. 1995. The Migration of the Vienna Circle. In *Vertreibung der Vernunft: The Cultural Exodus from Austria*, ed. Friedrich Stadler and Peter Weibel, 57–79. Wien: Springer-Verlag.

Davis, John B. 2011. *Individuals and Identity in Economics*. Cambridge: Cambridge University Press.

Dekker, Erwin (2014). "The Intellectual Networks of Otto Neurath: Between the Coffeehouse and Academia." In *European Encounters: Intellectual Exchange and the Rethinking of Europe 1914–1945*.

Dietl, Joseph. 1845. "Praktische Wahrnehmungen Nach Den Ergebnissen Im Wiedner-Bezirkskrankenhause." *Zeitschrift Der K.u.k. Gesellschaft Der Aerzte Zu Wien* 1 (2): 9–26.

1849. *Der Aderlass in Der Lungentzündung. Klinisch Und Physiologisch Erötert.* Wien: Kaulfuss Witwe, Prandel & Comp.

Drucker, Peter F. 1939. *The End of Economic Man: A Study of the New Totalitarianism*. London: William Heinemann.

Dunning, Eric and Stephen Mennell. 1996. "Preface." In *The Germans: Power Struggles and the Development of Habitus in the Nineteenth and Twentieth Centuries*, vii–xvi. Cambridge: Polity Press.

Ebenstein, Alan. 2003. *Hayek's Journey: The Mind of Friedrich Hayek*. New York: Palgrave Macmillan.

Ebner, Alexander. 2005. "Hayek on Entrepreneurship: Competition, Market Process and Cultural Evolution." In *Entrepreneurship, Money and Coordination*, ed. Jürgen G. Backhaus, 131–149. Cheltenham: Edward Elgar.

Ekelund, Robert B. and Robert F. Hébert. 1983. *A History of Economic Theory and Method*. Auckland: McGraw-Hill.

Elias, Norbert. 1939/2000. *The Civilizing Process: Sociogenetic and Psychogenetic Investigations*. Malden: Blackwell Publishing.

1996. *The Germans: Power Struggles and the Development of Habitus in the Nineteenth and Twentieth Centuries*. Oxford: Polity Press.

Engel-Janosi, Friedrich. 1974. *... Aber ein Stolzer Bettler: Erinnerungen aus einer Verlorenen Generation*. Graz: Styria.

Fleck, Christian. 1996. Emigration of Social Scientists' Schools from Austria. In *Forced Migration and Scientific Change*, eds. Mitchell G. Ash & Alfons Söllner, 198–223. Cambridge, MA: Cambridge University Press.

Foss, Nicolai Juul. 1995. "More on 'Hayek's Transformation'." *History of Political Economy* 27 (2): 345–364.

Francis, Mark and Barrie Stacy. 1985. "Freud and the Enlightenment." In *The Viennese Enlightenment*, ed. Mark Francis, pp. 88–128. Kent: Croom Helm.

Frank, Robert H. 2008. *The Economic Naturalist*. London: Virgin Books.

Franz, Georg. 1955. *Liberalismus: Die Deutschliberale Bewegung in der Habsburgischen Monarchie*. München: G.D.W. Callwey.

Freud, Sigmund. 1930. *Civilization and Its Discontents*. London: Hogarth Press.

Fuchs, Albert. 1949. *Geistige Strömungen in Österreich 1867–1918*. Wien: Globus Verlag.

Fukuyama, Francis. 1989. "The End of History?" *National Interest* (16): 3–18.

Gadamer, Hans-Georg. 1975. "Philosophy & Social Criticism." *Philosophy & Social Criticism* 2: 307.

2004. *Truth and Method*. London: Continuum.

Gray, John. 1984. *Hayek on Liberty*. New York: Basil Blackwell.

2000. *Two Faces of Liberalism*. New York: Polity Press.

Grillparzer, Franz. 1962. *King Ottocar: His Rise and Fall*. Ed. Arthur Burkhard. Yarmouth Port: The Register Press.

Groenewegen, Peter D. 2001. *Physicians and Political Economy: Six Studies of the Work of Doctor-Economists*. London: Routledge.

Gruen, William. 1939. "What Is Logical Empiricism." *Partisan Review* 6 (5): 64–77.

Haag, John. 1976. "Othmar Spann and the Quest for a 'True State'." *Austrian History Yearbook* 12: 227–250.

Haberler, Gottfried von. 1983. "Fritz Machlup: In Memoriam." *Cato Journal* 3: 11–14.

Hacohen, Malachi H. 2000. *Karl Popper, the Formative Years, 1902–1945: Politics and Philosophy in Interwar Vienna*. Cambridge: Cambridge University Press.

Hahn, Hans, Otto Neurath, and Rudolf Carnap. 1929/1979. "Wissenschaftliche Weltauffassung: Der Wiener Kreis." In *Otto Neurath: Wissenschaftliche Weltauffassung, Sozialismus Und Logischer Empirismus*, ed. Rainer Hegelsmann, 79–101. Frankfurt am Main: Suhrkamp Verlag.

Hahn, Robert W. 1989. "Economic Prescriptions for Environmental Problems: How the Patient Followed the Doctor's Orders." *Journal of Economic Perspectives* 3 (2): 95–114.

Hamann, Brigitte (ed). 1979. *Majestät, Ich Warne Sie … : Geheime Und Private Schriften*. Wien: Amalthea.

Hayek, Friedrich A. von. 1926/1992. "Friedrich von Wieser (1851–1926)." In *The Collected Works of F.A. Hayek: Volume IV, The Fortunes of Liberalism*, 108–125. London: Routledge.

1933. "The Trend of Economic Thinking." *Economica* (40): 121–137.

1937. "Economics and Knowledge." *Economica* 4 (13): 33–54.

1939. *Freedom and the Economic System*. Chicago: University of Chicago Press.

1944/1992. "Historians and the Future of Europe." In *The Collected Works of F.A. Hayek: Volume IV, The Fortunes of Liberalism*, ed. Peter G. Klein, 201–215. London: Routledge.

1944. *The Road to Serfdom*. Chicago: The University of Chicago Press.

1945. "The Use of Knowledge in Society." *The American Economic Review* 35 (4): 519–530.

1947/1967. "Opening Address to a Conference at Mont Pèlerin." In *Studies in Philosophy, Politics and Economics*, 148–159. Chicago: University of Chicago Press.

1948. "Individualism: True and False." *In Individualism & Economic Order*. Chicago: University of Chicago Press.

1949. "The Intellectuals and Socialism." *The University of Chicago Law Review* 16 (3): 417–433.

1952. *The Counter-Revolution of Science: Studies on the Abuse of Reason*. Glencoe: Free Press.

1956/2007. "Foreword to the 1956 American Paperback Edition." In *The Road to Serfdom: The Definitive Edition*, ed. Bruce Caldwell, 39–52. Chicago: University of Chicago Press.

1960. *The Constitution of Liberty*. Chicago: The University of Chicago Press.

1962. "The Moral Element in Enterprise." *The Freeman* 8 (July): 44–51.

1962. "The Pretence of Knowledge." *The Swedish Journal of Economics* 77 (4): 433–442.

1979. "Interviews with Hayek." http://mises.org/books/hayek_oral_history.pdf.

1981. "Foreword." In *Socialism*, ed. Ludwig von Mises, xix–xxiv. Indianapolis: Liberty Fund.

1982. *Law, Legislation and Liberty, Volume 3: The Political Order of a Free People*. Chicago: The University of Chicago Press.

1988. *The Collected Works of Friedrich August Hayek Vol I, The Fatal Conceit: The Errors of Socialism*, ed. W.W. Bartley III. Vol. I. London: Routledge.

1994. *Hayek on Hayek*. London: Routledge.

Heilbroner, Robert L. 1953. *The Worldly Philosophers: The Lives, Times, and Ideas of the Great Economic Thinkers*. New York: Simon & Schuster.

Heims, S. J. 1991. "Fritz London and the Community of Quantum Physicists." In *World Views and Scientific Discipline Formation*, ed. William R. Woordward. Vol. 134. Dordrecht: Kluwer.

Heizmann, Jürgen. 2003. "A Farewell to Art: Poetic Reflection in Broch's Der Tod Des Vergil." In *Hermann Broch, Visionary in Exile: The 2001 Yale Symposium*, ed. Paul Michael Lützeler, 187–200. Rochester: Camden House.

Helling, Ingeborg Katharina. 1984. "A. Schutz and F. Kaufmann: Sociology Between Science and Interpretation." *Human Studies* 7: 141–161.

Hennecke, Hans Jörg. 2000. *Friedrich August von Hayek: Die Tradition Der Freiheit*. Düsseldorf: Verlag Wirtschaft und Finanzen.

Hermann, Friedrich Wilhelm. 1832. *Staatswirtschaftliche Untersuchungen*. München: Anton Weberschen Buchhandlung.

Heyne, Paul T. 1973. *The Economic Way of Thinking*. Chicago: Science Research Associates.

Heyt, Friso D. 1999. "Popper's Vienna. A Contribution to the History of the Ideas of Critical Rationalism." *Innovation: The European Journal of Social Science Research* 12 (4): 525–541.

Hicks, John. 1939. *Value and Capital: An Inquiry into Some Fundamental Principles of Economic Theory*. Oxford, UK: Clarendon Press.

1984. "The Formation of an Economist." In *The Economics of John Hicks*, ed. Dieter Helm, 281–290. New York: Basil Blackwell.

Hirschman, Albert O. 1977. *The Passions and the Interests: Political Arguments for Capitalism Before Its Triumph*. Princeton: Princeton University Press.

1982. "Rival Interpretations of Market Society: Civilizing, Destructive, or Feeble?" *Journal of Economic Literature* 20 (4): 1463–1484.

Homans, Jennifer. 2012. "Tony Judt: A Final Victory." *New York Review of Books* (March).

Horwitz, Steven. 2005. "Review Essay Friedrich Hayek, Austrian Economist." *Journal of the History of Economic Thought* 27 (1): 71–85.

Howson, Susan. 2006. "Hayek's Journey: The Mind of Friedrich Hayek Review." *History of Political Economy* 38 (3): 555–556.

Hughes, Stuart H. 1956. "Is the Intellectual Obsolete?" *Commentary* 22 (4): 313.

1958. *Consciousness and Society: the Reorientation of European Social Thought, 1890–1930*. New York: Knopf.

Huizinga, Johan. 1938. *Homo Ludens: Proeve Eener Bepaling Van Het Spel-element Der Cultuur*. Haarlem: H.D. Tjeenk Willink & Zoon.

1949. *Homo Ludens-A Study of the Play - Element in Culture*. London: Routledge & Kegan Paul.

Hülsmann, Jörg Guido. 2007. *Mises: The Last Knight of Liberalism*. Auburn: Mises Institute.

Huntington, Samuel P. 1998. *The Clash of Civilizations and the Remaking of World Order*. London: Simon & Schuster.

Hutchison, Terence W. 1964. *Positive Economics and Policy Objectives*. Chicago: University of Chicago Press.

Ingrao, Bruno and Giorgio Israel. 1990. *The Invisible Hand*. Cambridge: MIT Press.

Jabloner, Clemens. 1998. "Kelsen and His Circle: The Viennese Years." *European Journal of International Law* 9 (2): 368–385.

Janik, Allan. 1981. "Therapeutic Nihilism: How Not to Write About Otto Weininger." In *Structure and Gestalt*, ed. Barry Smith, 263–292. Amsterdam: John Benjamins.

1985. *Essays on Wittgenstein and Weininger*. Amsterdam: Rodopi.

Janik, Allan and Stephen Toulmin. 1973. *Wittgenstein's Vienna*. New York: Simon & Schuster.

Johnston, William M. 1972. *The Austrian Mind: An Intellectual and Social History, 1848–1938*. Berkeley: University of California Press.

Judson, Pieter M. 1996. *Exclusive Revolutionaries: Liberal Politics, Social Experience, and National Identity in the Austrian Empire 1848–1914*. Ann Arbor: University of Michigan Press.

Judt, Tony. 2010. *Ill Fares the Land*. New York: Penguin Press.

Kaufmann, Felix. 1992. *Wiener Lieder zu Philosophie und Ökonomie*. Stuttgart: Gustav Fischer Verlag.

Keynes, John Maynard. 1924. "Alfred Marshall 1842–1924." *The Economic Journal* 34 (135): 311–372.

1930/1963. *Essays in Persuasion*. London: W.W. Norton & Company.

1936. *The General Theory of Employment, Interest and Money*. London: Macmillan and Co.

Kirzner, Israel M. 1987. "The Austrian School of Economics." In *The New Palgrave Dictionary of Economics*, ed. J. Eatwell, M. Milgate and Peter Newman. London: Macmillan.

Klamer, Arjo. 2007. *Speaking of Economics: How to Get in the Conversation*. London: Routledge.

Klausinger, Hansjörg. 2005. Die Austroliberalen und die Kampagne in "Neuen Wiener Tagblatt", 1931–1934. In *Wirtschaftspolitische Beiträge in kritischer Zeit (1931–1934)*, 11–36. Marburg: Metropolis Verlag.

2006. "In the Wilderness": Emigration and the Decline of the Austrian School. *History of Political Economy*, 38(4), 617–664.

2013. *Academic Anti-Semitism and the Austrian School: Vienna, 1918–1945* (No. 155) (pp. 1–25).

2014. *Hans Mayer, Last Knight of the Austrian School, Vienna Branch*. Paper presented at HOPE, Duke University. http://hope.econ.duke.edu/sites/default/files/Klausinger_CHOPE1.pdf

Knight, Frank H. 1923. "The Ethics of Competition." *The Quarterly Journal of Economics* 37 (4): 579–624.

Konrád, György. 1984. *Antipolitics*. New York: Harcourt Brace Janovich.

Koppl, Roger, Steve Horwitz, and Pierre Desrochers. 2010. *What Is so Austrian About Austrian Economics*. Bingley: Emerald Group.

Kurrild-Klitgaard, Peter. 2003. "The Viennese Connection: Alfred Schutz and the Austrian School." *The Quarterly Journal of Austrian Economics* 6 (2): 35–67.

Lavoie, Don. 1985. *Rivalry and Central Planning: The Socialist Calculation Debate Reconsidered*. Cambridge: Cambridge University Press.

2011. "The Interpretive Dimension of Economics." *The Review of Austrian Economics* 24 (2): 91–128.

Lachmann, Ludwig M. 1982. "The Salvage of Ideas: Problems of the Revival of Austrian Economic Thought." *Journal of Institutional and Theoretical Economics* 138: 629–45.

Lederer, Emil. 1940. *State of the Masses: The Threat of the Classless Society*. New York: W.W. Norton & Company.

Leonard, Robert J. 1998. "The History of Science Society, Ethics and the Excluded Middle : Karl Menger and Social Science in Interwar Vienna." *Isis* 89 (1): 1–26.

2010. *Von Neumann, Morgenstern, and the Creation of Game Theory: From Chess to Social Science, 1900–1960*. Cambridge: Cambridge University Press.

2011. "The Collapse of Interwar Vienna: Oskar Morgenstern's Community, 1925–50." *History of Political Economy* 43 (1) (February 28): 83–130.

Leser, Norbert. 1981. *Das Geistige Leben Wiens in Der Zwischenkriegszeit*. Wien: Österreichischer Bundesverlag.

Lesky, Erna. 1976. *The Vienna Medical School of the 19th Century*. Baltimore: Johns Hopkins University Press.

Liebersohn, Harry. 1990. *Fate and Utopia in German Sociology, 1870–1923*. Cambridge: MIT Press.

Lipking, Lawrence. 1981. *The Life of the Poet: Beginning and Ending of Poetic Careers*. Chicago: The University of Chicago Press.

Littlechild, Stephen. 1990. *Austrian Economics: Volume 1–3*. Cheltenham: Edward Elgar.

MacIntyre, Alasdair C. 1984. *After Virtue: A Study in Moral Theory*. Notre Dame: University of Notre Dame Press.

Machlup, Fritz. 1932/2005a. "Kontingentverträge?". In *Wirtschaftpublizistische Beiträge in kritischer Zeit (1931–1934)* ed. H. Klausinger, 69–72. Marburg: Metropolis Verlag.

1932/2005b. "Währungspolitische Quacksalbereien". In *Wirtschaftpublizistische Beiträge in kritischer Zeit (1931–1934)* ed. H. Klausinger, 72–74. Marburg: Metropolis Verlag.

1932/2005c. "Industrieförderung?". In *Wirtschaftpublizistische Beiträge in kritischer Zeit (1931–1934)* ed. H. Klausinger, 116–117. Marburg: Metropolis Verlag.

1933/2005b. "Ärzte der Wirtschaft". In *Wirtschaftpublizistische Beiträge in kritischer Zeit (1931–1934)* ed. H. Klausinger, 202–206. Marburg: Metropolis Verlag.

1959. "Statics and Dynamics: Kaleidoscopic Words." *Southern Economic Journal* 26 (2): 91–110.

1962. *The Production and Distribution of Knowledge in the United States*. Princeton: Princeton University Press.

Madison, G Brent. 1990. "How Individualistic Is Methodological Individualism." *Critical Review* 4 (1–2): 41–60.

Magris, Claudio. 1989. *Danube*. New York: Farrar, Straus and Giroux.

Malinowski, Bronislaw. 1941. "Man's Culture and Man's Behaviour." *Sigma Xi Quarterly* 29 (3–4): 182–196.

1947. *Freedom and Civilization*. London: George Allen & Unwin.

McCloskey, Deirdre N. 1994. *Knowledge and Persuasion in Economics*. Cambridge: Cambridge University Press.

2006. *The Bourgeois Virtues: Ethics for an Age of Commerce*. Chicago: The University of Chicago Press.

McCraw, Thomas K. 2007. *Prophet of Innovation : Joseph Schumpeter and Creative Destruction*. Cambridge: Belknap Press of Harvard University Press.

McGill, V. J. 1936. "An Evaluation of Logical Positivism." *Science & Society* 1 (1): 45–80.

McGucken, William. 1978. "On Freedom and Planning in Science: The Society for Freedom in Science, 1940-46." *Minerva* 16 (1): 42–72.

Medema, Steven G. 2009. *The Hesitant Hand: Taming Self-Interest in the History of Economic Ideas*. Princeton: Princeton University Press.

Menger, Anton. 1886. *Das Recht Auf Den Vollen Arbeitsertrag in Geschichtlicher Darstellung*. Stuttgart: J.G. Cotta.

Menger, Carl. 1871/1950. *Principles of Economics*. Glencoe: The Free Press.

1883/2009. *Investigations into the Method of the Social Sciences*. Auburn: Mises Institute.

1891/1935. *The Collected Works of Carl Menger Vol. 3: Kleinere Schriften zur Methode und Geschichte der Volkswirtschaftslehre*. London: The London School of Economics and Political Science.

Menger, Karl. 1994. *Reminiscences of the Vienna Circle and the Mathematical Colloquium*, eds. Louise Golland, Brian McGuiness, and Abe Sklar. Dordrecht: Kluwer Academic.

Menger, Max. 1866. *Die Auf Selbsthilfe Gestützten Genossenschaften Im Handwerker- Und Arbeiterstande : Vorträge Gehalten Im Fortbildungs-Verein Für Buchdrucker in Wien*. Wien: Fortbildungs-Verein für Buchdrucker in Wien.

1873. *Die Wahlreform in Österreich*. Vienna: Verlag von K. Rosner.

Mennell, Stephen and Johan Goudsblom. 1997. "Civilizing Processes-Myth or Reality? A Comment on Duerr's Critique of Elias." *Comparative Studies in Society and History* 39 (4): 729–733.

Mirowski, Philip. 2002. *Machine Dreams: Economics Becomes a Cyborg Science.* Cambridge, UK: Cambridge University Press.

2009. "Postface: Defining Neoliberalism." In *The Road from Mont-Pèlerin: The Making of the Neoliberal Thought Collective,* ed. Philip Mirowski and Dieter Plehwe, pp. 417–455. Cambridge: Harvard University Press.

2012. A History Best Served Cold. In *Uncertain Empire: American History and the Idea of the Cold War,* ed. Joel Isaac and Duncan Bell, pp. 61–74. Oxford: Oxford University Press.

Mirowski, Philip, and Dieter Plehwe. 2009. *The Road from Mont Pèlerin: The Making of the Neoliberal Thought Collective.* Cambridge: Harvard University Press.

Mises, Ludwig von. 1919/1983. *Nation, State and Economy: Contributions to the Politics and History of Our Time.* New York: New York University Press.

1922/1951. *Socialism: An Economic and Sociological Analysis.* New Haven: Yale University Press.

1926/1977. *A Critique of Interventionism.* New York: Arlington House.

1931. "Die Psychologischen Wurzeln des Widerstandes gegen die Nationaloekonomische Theorie." Eds. Ludwig von Mises and Arthur Spiethoff. *Schriften Des Vereins Für Sozialpolitik* 183 (1): 275–295.

1932. "Review of 'Die Letzten Jahrzehnte Einer Großmacht' by Rudolph Sieghart." *Economica* 38: 477–78.

1942/1978. *Ludwig Von Mises, Notes and Recollections.* South Holland: Libertarian Press.

1949/2007. *Human Action: A Treatise on Economics.* Indianapolis: Liberty Fund.

1944. *Omnipotent Government: The Rise of the Total State and Total War.* Yale: Yale University Press.

2002. *Selected Writings of Ludwig von Mises: Between Two World Wars.* Ed. Richard M Ebeling. Indianapolis: Liberty Fund.

Morgenstern, Oskar. 1928. *Wirtschaftsprognose: Eine Untersuchung Ihrer Voraussetzungen Und Möglichkeiten.* Wien: Julius Fischer Verlag.

Mulder, Henk L. 1968. "Wissenschaftliche Weltauffassung - Der Wiener Kreis." *Journal of the History of Philosophy* 6 (4): 386–390.

Müller, Karl H. 1998. "The Ideal Worlds of the Austrian Political Economists." In *Vertreibung Der Vernunft: The Cultural Exodus from Austria,* ed. Friedrich Stadler and Peter Weibel, 146–159. Wien: Springer.

Musil, Robert. 1930. *Der Mann Ohne Eigenschaften.* Berlin: Rowohlt.

Neider, Heinrich. 1973. "Memories of Otto Neurath." In *Empiricism and Sociology,* ed. Marie Neurath and Robert S. Cohen, 45–49. Dordrecht: D. Reidel Publishing Company.

Nelson, Julie A. 2006. *Economics for Humans.* Chicago: The University of Chicago Press.

Neurath, Otto. 1916/2004. "Economics in Kind, Calculation in Kind and Their Relation to War Economics." In *Economic Writings: Selections 1904–1945,* ed. Thomas E. Uebel and Robert S. Cohen, 299–311. Dordrecht: Springer.

1917/2004. "The Economic Order of the Future and the Economic Sciences." In *Economic Writings: Selections 1904–1945,* ed. Thomas E. Uebel and Robert S. Cohen, 241–261. Dordrecht: Springer.

1919/2004. "War Economy." In *Economic Writings: Selections 1904–1945*, ed. Thomas E. Uebel and Robert S. Cohen, 153–199. Dordrecht: Springer.

Nietzsche, Friedrich. 1887/2006. *On the Genealogy of Morality*. Ed. Keith Ansell-Pearson. Cambridge: Cambridge University Press.

Novick, Peter. 1988. *That Noble Dream: The "Objectivity Question" and the American Historical Profession*. Cambridge, UK: Cambridge University Press.

Nozick, Robert. 1974. *Anarchy, State and Utopia*. New York: Basic Books.

O'Hear, A. (2009). Popperian Individualism Today. In *Rethinking Popper* eds. Z. Parusnikova and Robert S. Cohen, 205–214. Dordrecht: Springer.

Oakeshott, Michael. 1962. *Rationalism in Politics and Other Essays*. London: Methuen.

Ostrom, Elinor. 1990. *Governing the Commons: The Evolution of Institutions for Collective Action*. Cambridge: Cambridge University Press.

Plehwe, Dieter. 2009. "Introduction." In *The Road from Mont-Pèlerin: The Making of the Neoliberal Thought Collective*, 1–42. Cambridge: Harvard University Press.

Plener, Ernst von. 1911. *Erinnerungen - Bd. 1. Jugend, Paris und London bis 1873*. Stuttgart: Deutsche Verlags-Anstalt.

Pocock, J. G. A. 2009. *Political Thought and History: Essays on Theory and Method*. Cambridge: Cambridge University Press.

Polanyi, Karl. 1945. *Origins of Our Time: The Great Transformation*. Ed. Victor Gollancz. London.

Polanyi, Michael. 1940. *The Contempt of Freedom: The Russian Experiment and After*. London: Watts & Co.

1958. *Personal Knowledge: Towards a Post-Critical Philosophy*. London: Routledge & Kegan Paul.

Popper, Karl R. 1945. *The Open Society and Its Enemies, Volume 1: The Spell of Plato*. London: Routledge.

1950/2003. "Preface to the Second Edition." In *The Open Society and Its Enemies. Volume One: The Spell of Plato*, xi–xiii. London: Routledge.

(1950/2008). The Open Society after Five Years: Prefaces to the American Edition. In *After the Open Society: Selected Social and Political Writings*, eds. J. Shearmur & P. Norris Turner, 169–181. London: Routledge.

1963/2008. The Open Society and the Democratic State. In *After the Open Society: Selected Social and Political Writings*, eds. J. Shearmur & P. Norris Turner, 231–248. London: Routledge.

1976. *Unended Quest: An Intellectual Autobiography*. Glasgow: William Collins Sons & Co.

1994. *The Myth of the Framework: In Defence of Science and Rationality*. London: Routledge.

Porter, Theodore M. 2012. "Positioning the Social Sciences in Cold War America." In *Cold War Social Science: Knowledge Production, Liberal Democracy, and Human Nature*, ed. Mark Solovey and Hamilton Cravens, x – xvi. New York: Palgrave Macmillan.

Rawls, John. 1971. *A Theory of Justice*. Cambridge: Belknap Press.

1996. *Political Liberalism*. New York: Columbia University Press.

Reisch, George A. 2005. *How the Cold War Transformed Philosophy of Science: To the Icy Slopes of Logic*. Cambridge: Cambridge University Press.

Robbins, Lionel R. 1932. *An Essay on the Nature and Significance of Economic Science.* Macmillan and Co.

Roll, Eric. 1973. *A History of Economic Thought.* London: Faber.

Rorty, Richard. 1979. *Philosophy and the Mirror of Nature.* Princeton: Princeton University Press.

Roth, Alvin E. 2002. "The Economist as Engineer: Game Theory, Experimentation, and Computation as Tools for Design Economics." *Econometrica* 70 (4): 1341–1378.

Roth, Joseph. 1996. *The Radetzky March.* New York: Everyman's Library.

Sandel, Michael J. 2012. *What Money Can't Buy: The Moral Limits of Markets.* New York: Farrar, Straus and Giroux.

Schäffle, Albert Eberhard Friedrich. 1861. *Die Nationalökonomie oder allgemeine Wirtschaftslehre.* Leipzig: Verlag von Otto Spamer.

Schlant, Ernestine. 1971. "Hermann Broch Als Politischer Utopist Zwischen 'Geschichtsgesetz Und Willensfreiheit." *Literatur Und Kritik* 6: 207–213.

Schorske, Carl E. 1980. *Fin-de-siècle Vienna: Politics and Culture.* New York: Alfred Knopf.

———. 1997. "The New Rigorism in the Human Sciences, 1940–1960." *Daedalus* 126 (1): 289–309.

Schulak, Eugen M. and Herbert Unterköfler. 2011. *Austrian School of Economics: A History of Its Ideas, Ambassadors, and Institutions.* Auburn: Ludwig von Mises Institute.

Schumpeter, Joseph A. 1912. *Theorie Der Wirtschaftlichen Entwicklung.* Berlin: Duncker & Humblot.

———. 1919/1950. "The Crisis of the Tax-State." In *International Economic Papers: Translations Prepared for the International Economic Association.* Vol. 6. London: Macmillan.

———. 1919/1951. *Imperialism and Social Classes.* Ed. Paul M Sweezy. Oxford: Blackwell.

———. 1943/1976. *Capitalism, Socialism, and Democracy.* London: George Allen & Unwin.

———. 1946/1976. "Preface to the Second Edition" In *Capitalism, Socialism and Democracy,* 411–414. London: George Allen & Unwin.

———. 1949. "Science and Ideology." *The American Economic Review* 39 (2): 346–359.

———. 1954. *History of Economic Analysis.* Oxford: Oxford University Press.

Sedlacek, Tomas. 2011. *Economics of Good and Evil: The Quest for Economic Meaning from Gilgamesh to Wall Street.* Oxford: Oxford University Press.

Shearmur, Jeremy. 1996. *Hayek and After: Hayekian Liberalism as a Research Programme.* London: Routledge.

Sieghart, Rudolf. 1932. *Die Letzten Jahrzehnte Einer Grossmacht: Menschen, Völker, Probleme Des Habsburger-Reichs.* Berlin: Ullstein.

Small, Albion W. 1924. "Some Contributions to the History of Sociology. Section XVII. The Attempt (1860–80) to Reconstruct Economic Theory on a Sociological Basis." *American Journal of Sociology* 30 (1): 49–86.

Smith, Adam. 1975. *The Wealth of Nations: The Prosperity Classic.* Oxford: Oxford University Press.

Smith, Barry. 1990. "On the Austrianness of Austrian Economics." *Critical Review* 4 (1–2): 212–238.

Smithies, Arthur. 1951. "Memorial: Joseph Alois Schumpeter, 1883–1950." In *Schumpeter, Social Scientist*, ed. Seymour E Harris, 11–23. Cambridge: Harvard University Press.

Sombart, Werner. 1908. *Sozialismus Und Soziale Bewegung*. Jena: Gustav Fischer Verlag.

Spiegel, Henry W. 1983. *The Growth of Economic Thought*. Revised and *Expanded Edition*. Durham: Duke University Press.

Spiel, Hilde. 1987. *Vienna's Golden Autumn*. London: Weidenfeld and Nicolson.

Stadler, Friedrich. 1994. "Heinrich Gomperz Und Karl Popper im Kontext des Logischen Empirismus." In *Heinrich Gomperz, Karl Popper und die Österreichische Philosophie*. Amsterdam: Rodopi.

2003. "What Is the Vienna Circle?: Some Methodological and Historiographical Answers." In *The Vienna Circle and Logical Empiricism: Re-evaluation and Future Perspectives*, XI–XXIII. Dordrecht: Kluwer Academic.

Starr, Paul. 1976. "The Politics of Therapeutic Nihilism." *The Hastings Center Report* 6 (5): 24–30.

Steiner, George. 1967. *Language and Silence: Essays 1958–1966*. London: Faber and Faber.

Sternhell, Zeev, and Jacob L. Talmon. 1996. *The Intellectual Revolt Against Liberal Democracy, 1870–1945: International Conference in Memory of Jacob L. Talmon*. Jerusalem: Israel Academy of Sciences and Humanities.

Storr, Virgil. 2013. *Understanding the Culture of Markets*. Abingdon: Routledge.

Streissler, Erich and Monika Streissler. 1994. *Carl Menger's Lecture to Crown Prince Rudolf of Austria*. Cheltenham: Edward Elgar.

Strigl, Richard. 1932/2005. "Rückkehr zu gesunder Währungspolitik!". In *Wirtschaftspublizistische Beiträge in kritischer Zeit (1931–1934)*, ed. H. Klausinger, 100–112. Marburg: Metropolis Verlag.

Szeps, Berta. 1938. *My Life and History*. London: Cassell.

Thomas, Richard F. 2004. *Virgil and the Augustan Reception*. Cambridge: Cambridge University Press.

Timms, Edward. 1986. *Karl Kraus, Apocalyptic Satirist : Culture and Catastrophe in Habsburg Vienna*. New Haven: Yale University Press.

1993. "Die Wiener Kreise: Schöpferische Interaktionen in Der Wiener Moderne." In *Die Wiener Jahrhundertwende: Einflüsse, Umwelt, Wirkungen*, ed. Jürgen Nautz and Richard Vahrenkamp, 128–143. Wien: Böhlau Verlag.

2009. "Cultural Parameters Between the Wars: A Reassessment of the Vienna Circles." In Interwar Vienna, ed. *Deborah Holmes and Lisa Silverman*, 21–30. Rochester: Camden House.

Uchitelle, Louis. 1999. "A Challenge to Scientific Economics: An Older School Looks at a Broad, More Intuitive Picture While Modernists See Just the Numbers and Facts." *The New York Times*.

Vaughn, Karen I. 1994. *Austrian Economics in America*. Cambridge: Cambridge University Press.

Wasserman, Janek. 2014. *Black Vienna: The Radical Right in the Red City, 1918–1938*. Ithaca: Cornell University Press.

Watkins, John. 1997. "Karl Popper: A Memoir." *The American Scholar* 66(2): 205–19.

Weber, Alfred. 1998. "Civilization and Culture - A Synthesis." In *Classical Readings in Culture and Civilization*. London: Routledge.

Weigand, Hermann J. 1947. "Broch's Death of Vergil: Program Notes." *PMLA* 62 (2): 525–554.

Weintraub, Roy E. 2002. *How Economics Became a Mathematical Science*. Durham: Duke University Press.

White, Leslie A. 1949. *The Science of Culture: A Study of Man and Civilization*. New York: Farrar, Straus and Company.

Wiesemann, C. 1991. *Josef Dietl Und Der Therapeutische Nihilismus. Zum Historischen Und Politischen Hintergrund Einer Medizinischen These*. Frankfurt am Mainz: Peter Lang.

Wieser, Friedrich von. 1907a. "Unsere Gesellschaftliche und Politische Entwicklung Seit 1848, Teil I." *Neue Freie Presse*, 8th of February.

1907b. "Unsere Gesellschaftliche und Politische Entwicklung Seit 1848, Teil II." *Neue Freie Presse*, 9th of February.

1907c. "Unsere Gesellschaftliche und Politische Entwicklung Seit 1848, Teil III." *Neue Freie Presse*, 12th of February.

1910. *Recht und Macht: Sechs Vorträge*. Leipzig: Verlag von Duncker & Humblot.

Wistrich, Robert S. 1996. "Intellectuals and Mass Politics in Fin-de-siècle Vienna." In *The Intellectual Revolt Against Liberal Democracy 1870–1945*, eds. Zeev Sternhell and Jacob L. Talmon, 70–86. Jerusalem: The Israel Academy of Sciences and Humanities.

Wouters, Cas. 1986. "Formalization and Informalization: Changing Tension Balances in Civilizing Processes." *Theory Culture Society* 3 (2): 1–18.

Yagi, Kiichiro. 1991. "Max Menger's Liberal Position." *The Kyoto University Economic Review* 61(1–14): 1–14.

Zuidhof, P.W. 2011. *Imagining Markets : The Discursive Politics of Neoliberalism*. University of Amsterdam, unpublished dissertation.

Zweig, Stefan. 1943. *The World of Yesterday*. New York: The Viking Press.

Index

Gerald M. Koot, *English Historical Economics, 1870–1926: The Rise of Economic History and Mercantilism* (1988)

Kim Kyun, *Equilibrium Business Cycle Theory in Historical Perspective* (1988)

William J. Barber, *From New Era to New Deal: Herbert Hoover, the Economists, and American Economic Policy, 1921–1933* (1985)

Takashi Negishi, *Economic Theories in a Non-Walrasian Tradition* (1985)